The End of
Shareholder Value

**Other Titles by Allan A. Kennedy
(with Terrence E. Deal):**

The New Corporate Cultures
Corporate Cultures

The End of Shareholder Value

The Real Effects of the Shareholder Value Phenomenon and the Crisis it is Bringing to Business

Allan A. Kennedy

ORION BUSINESS
BOOKS

Copyright © 2000 by Allan A. Kennedy

All rights reserved.

The right of Allan Kennedy to be identified as the author of this work
has been asserted by her in accordance with the Copyright, Designs and Patents
Act 1988.

First published in Great Britain in 2000 by
Orion Business
An imprint of The Orion Publishing Group Ltd
Orion House, 5 Upper St Martin's Lane, London WC2H 9EA

Published by arrangement with Perseus Publishing, USA.

A CIP catalogue record for this book is available from the British Library.

ISBN 1-84203-049-3

Printed and bound in Great Britain by MPG Books, Bodmin, Cornwall

Contents

Acknowledgments

As part of the research behind this book, I conducted hundreds of interviews. I am grateful, therefore, to many people whose candor and insight helped shape my ideas.

In addition to those I interviewed, a number of dedicated people helped me with specific research to complete the book. Chief among them was the indomitable Mary Palmer, a reference librarian at the Kirstein Business Branch of the Boston Public Library, who spent countless evenings and weekends searching out the often obscure references and facts I felt were essential to my argument. Her tenacity, skill, and relentless good humor helped make this book possible. Chris Kane assisted immeasurably with the analysis of financial reports included in Chapters 4 and 5. The research into evolving employee practices discussed in Chapter 5 was ably supported by Dan Picard and the staff of Picard International, Aninda Mattoo, and Karen McEvoy. Karen, in fact, carried most of the burden of the survey of third-party agents reported in this chapter.

Nick Philipson, the executive editor of business books at Perseus and other staff members aided me throughout the process of writing the book. My agent, Rhonda Winchell of the Author's Agency, even signed on to e-mail for the first time ever to be more accessible at odd hours of the day and night and offered a number of useful suggestions that have influenced the book.

Along the way, a number of friends and colleagues were kind enough to read all or part of the manuscript and offer suggestions for how it might be improved. These included Terry Deal, Michael Kennedy, Alison Kennedy, Susan Krieger, David Sanders, Dennis Powers, Jonathon McDonnell-Murphy, Doug Nelson, Alice Colwell, and Ken Kalb. The book is much better for their comments. My wife, Alison, and other close family friends and relatives put up with the long hours, demands for silence, and generally cranky mood that seems to be part of the process of writing a book. Without their help and support, the book would not have been written. They are not to be blamed for the result, however: Any errors of judgment or fact are my responsibility alone.

Allan A. Kennedy
October 1999

Introduction to the UK Edition

This book chronicles the rise and impending demise of the idea that the purpose of business is the maximization of shareholder value. My intention in writing it was to alert managers everywhere – but especially in the United States, where shareholder value thinking reigns supreme – to the dangers inherent in a single-minded focus on this objective. In the United Kingdom and Europe, the shareholder value movement is gaining strength but has not yet swept aside all other notions about corporate purpose. My hope for European readers, then, is that this book will both help them avoid the excesses so apparent on the U.S. business scene yet allow them to recognize the strong points of shareholder value thinking. In this Introduction to the UK edition of the book, let me briefly summarize what the shareholder value movement was all about, its strengths and weaknesses, and the lessons European managers can learn from the experience of corporations in the United States.

What is Shareholder Value and Where Did it Come From?

Shareholder value had its origins in the observations of a number of academic accountants who saw that they could better predict stock market price levels by discounting future cash-flow streams associated with a business rather than analyzing accounting measures of performance like earnings per share. The idea might have stayed in the academic world had it not been spotted by a new and very aggressive breed of American investment banker in the late 1970s and early 1980s. These bankers used the insight of the academics to launch raids on companies whose stocks appeared to be undervalued in the stock market. When their raids succeeded, they proceeded to restructure the firms that came under their control to release their hidden reserves of value, then sold the reinvigorated companies to new owners – having made exceedingly handsome profits in the meantime.

The very real threat from these raiders caused business people across the board to begin to pay attention to the idea of shareholder value. Starting in the United States, where the raiders were first active, companies in the 1980s began to realign executive compensation schemes to place an increasing emphasis on stock options, tying senior managers' future pay directly to their success in raising companies' stock prices. Driven by these incentives, managers began to mimic the raiders by restructuring their operations to get rid of underperforming parts; cutting costs to improve across-the-board performance; closing older plants; moving production to new, lower-cost venues usually in other areas of the world; and outsourcing any activities that outside vendors could accomplish at a lower cost. The results of these actions, especially in the late 1990s, were significant increases in corporate performance and profitability, an unprecedented rise in stock market values, and booming executive pay levels as managers cashed in what had become extremely valuable options at the peak of the bull market in equities.

What Went Wrong?

Along the way to these higher levels of performance and executive pay, a subtle change in thinking emerged. Initially, the shareholder value approach (and the analytic tools that accompanied it) had been a useful resource for managers looking to do their jobs better and improve the performance of the companies under their care. As more and more managers were paid with stock options and as the U.S. equity markets soared in the 1990s, this means to a sensible end became an end in itself. Top executives in many companies saw that they could achieve remarkable personal wealth by making sure they pushed their companies' stock prices to new heights. By the end of the 1990s, shareholder value thinking had turned into a farce. It had become short-termism, coupled with an extant view that getting as much as you can as quickly as you can is an acceptable *modus operandi* in the world of commerce. If you have any doubt that this is what happened, just look at the rationale behind many of the dot.com startups rushed into the stock market in the closing years of the twentieth century.

Suddenly managers everywhere were making decisions solely on the basis of whether the outcome would spur their stock prices ever higher. If more cost cuts were called for, so be it, whatever the long-term consequences. If internal costs were slow to come out, turn to your suppliers and demand dramatic reductions in their costs as a price of continuing to do business with you. If cutbacks in research and development were necessary to make the numbers, then cut back R&D. If those steps failed to produce the desired outcome in the stock market, take the money that might have been invested in building the business for the future and use it to buy back stock on the market. And if all that still did not drive up the stock price, cook up another blockbuster deal to get Wall Street's attention.

In the race to maximize shareholder value, the interests of other legitimate stakeholders were trampled. Loyal longtime employees were laid off or forced into early retirement. The ranks and economics of suppliers were decimated by repeated demands for lower prices and increased services. Government incentive programs were exploited to the fullest to fund the next shift of a plant from one part of the world to another, lower-cost locale. Even the interests of customers were neglected as companies pruned long-standing product lines to leave only the most profitable items and used aggressive price tactics to extract every last coin from the consumer's pocket.

Of course these mistreated stakeholders reacted, and the vehemence of their reaction is threatening future corporate welfare more with every day. In the United States, a tight labor market brought on by the unprecedented economic expansion helped workers in their rapid move toward a market-based employment system in which people look out for themselves and their own careers and use every means available to charge employers top money for their talents. Suppliers who survived the onslaughts of the late 1980s and early 1990s consolidated so quickly that in many industries they now hold the upper hand over the companies they sell to. Customers showed their disdain for how they were being treated by taking back the loyalty they had once invested in brands and buying from the cheapest outlets, increasingly over the Internet. Even governments, historically slow to act, have begun to level the playing field for themselves so that corporate opportunism will eventually find few outlets.

With futures mortgaged in pursuit of higher stock prices now and angry stakeholders demanding a bigger and bigger piece of the corporate pie, the prognosis for corporate success is quite glum. That, unfortunately, is the legacy on the U.S. business scene after less than two decades of obsession with maximizing shareholder value.

What Can Be Learned from the Shareholder Value Era?

The shareholder value movement would never have gained such primacy in the minds of corporate managers, board members, and investors if it had not brought with it something valuable. What it brought was a heightened sense of managerial accountability for performance. Before the shareholder value movement moved to center stage in the mid-1980s, many companies were run by their managers as near personal fiefdoms; they answered to no one regarding results. Some companies moved from crisis to crisis with no concern about their languishing stock market prices. Other companies preferred to rest on their laurels, continuing obsolete strategies and producing mediocre financial results while watching their market shares decline steadily because of inroads from more aggressive competitors, often overseas firms. Still other firms tried to do what was right to improve the performance of their companies but shackled themselves with misplaced loyalties to old products and uncompetitive factories and approaches to the marketplace. In the relatively benign corporate governance environment leading up to the 1980s, the managers responsible for these often-lackluster results were left in place long after their sell-by dates had passed, carrying on the tradition of mediocrity they had inherited from their forebears.

The rising tide of shareholder value thinking put an end to all this. Companies that persisted in underperforming suddenly became targets for unwanted takeovers. As more and more managers and board members recognized the threat, managers in companies that failed to improve the bottom line were removed by their suddenly interested boards. Moreover, as executive compensation became more heavily influenced by stock options and senior managers realized they had a lot to gain by taking steps to boost performance and encourage the stock market to look more favourably on their shares, scores of managers began to run their enterprises more effectively on their own initiative. Shareholder value thinking, therefore – along with technology and a relatively favourable economic and fiscal environment – can take a substantial share of the credit for the undoubted gains in productivity and performance seen in the 1990s.

The Opportunity for UK and Other European Managers and Investors

The shareholder value movement that swept across the U.S. business landscape in the late 1980s and 1990s has been much slower to gain full acceptance in Europe. There are a number of reasons why this is true, some substantial, other circumstantial. For example, workers' rights to participate in the inner workings of top management are enshrined in law in Germany, making it much harder for German companies to pursue the maximization of welfare for one stakeholder, the shareholder, at the expense of others. Similarly, across much of Continental Europe long-term equity holdings of banks and insurance companies insulate managers from the kinds of short-term pressures their counterparts across the Atlantic feel they face. Even in the United Kingdom, whose system of commerce is most similar to that of the United States, differences in both philosophy and practice have held back the forces of change that shareholder value thinking unleashed in America. For example, the reliance on a nonexecutive chairman to head UK companies, in sharp contrast to the situation in the United States, has built a degree of distance into corporate governance and virtually guaranteed that the kind of stock-option-induced incentives at work in the United States are generally not present. Whatever the specific reasons, Europe is blessed by not yet having jumped on the shareholder value bandwagon.

Despite the presence of these institutional barriers to the adoption of shareholder value thinking in Europe, the movement has nonetheless had an impact on how business is conducted. In the mid-1980s, Lloyds Bank (now Lloyds TSB) became one of the first major European companies to begin looking at its business portfolio from a shareholder value perspective. Many would credit its emergence as one of the leading financial institutions in Europe to the ongoing results of this scrutiny. The newly merged Asdea Brown Boveri (ABB) under the leadership of Percy Barnevik was driven to excel by an intense focus on creating shareholder value, among other things. Many other companies in the UK and on the Continent followed the lead of these trendsetters to achieve sizable performance gains.

Having seen the value in shareholder value thinking from these and other examples, neither the UK nor the rest of Europe rushed to make it the be-all and end-all of business that it became in the United States. The debate about its importance continues to this day. For example, Gerhard Schröder, the chancellor of Germany, was roundly criticized at the end of 1999 for encouraging a bailout for the ailing Philipp Holzmann AG and for speaking out against the mooted takeover of the German telecommunications company Mannesmann by its British competitor Vodafone AirTouch (a merger that was finally agreed in early February 2000); his public rejection of the "Anglo-Saxon business model" drew considerable support from both the public and business circles, however. Still other pundits on the European business scene continue to push the argument that for European companies to regain their competitive edge against U.S. companies on a global basis, they will have to move to a more shareholder-centric view of the world. That there is concern about competitiveness and a lack of consensus on whether the shareholder value route is the way to go is tremendously good news for Europe as a whole and EUropean companies in particular.

In the book that follows, I describe how the adoption of shareholder value thinking to the exclusion of everything else has likely affected the prospects of U.S. companies. Despite the records being attained on the stock market, this future does not look bright. Many U.S. companies should long ago have begun rethinking what they are all about; they will probably do so when the current stock market bubble finally breaks.

In the UK and the rest of Europe, there is still time for companies and managers to extract the best from shareholder value – especially the notion that performance really counts and managers ought to be held accountable for it – while avoiding the downside so many of their U.S. counterparts now face. It is my sincere hope that this book will help steer people to the right course as they keep up this fundamental debate about what they are in business to accomplish.

Allan A. Kennedy
February 2000

The End of
Shareholder Value

PART ONE

The Changing
Purpose of Business

In a period of just under 200 years, corporations have grown from anomalies in the social and economic life of the world to perhaps the major institutions in modern society. They have risen to such prominence because of their ability to adapt to changing circumstances in the world. Along the way they have even refashioned their most fundamental beliefs about why they exist in the first place. Part 1 chronicles this evolution of purpose in the corporations that are so important in all our lives.

Chapter 1 explores the origins of some of the oldest and still largest of the world's corporations. With only a few exceptions, these companies, the household names of the corporate landscape, were founded as family enterprises by entrepreneurs in the late nineteenth or early twentieth centuries. Although these companies have adjusted to changing circumstances over time, many retain the family flavor of their earliest days. Chapter 2 moves on to the companies founded just before and just after the Second World War. The entrepreneurs of these companies were technocrats eager to bring new ideas or inventions to society. They built companies based on meritocratic principles and led the movement toward the professional system of management that is the norm for all corporations today—including the former family firms that were quick to recognize its merits and adopt its precepts.

Chapter 3 then looks at the new-economy companies founded in the last thirty years of the twentieth century. As financial markets became larger and more sophisticated, the people who founded successful companies became wealthy as a result of their entrepreneurship. Other aspiring entrepreneurs took note and in the latter stages of the twentieth century jumped into the corporate fray with the sole purpose of cashing in on their initiative. As a new rationale for business came to the fore, the rationale that business existed for the sole purpose of maximizing shareholder value, managers of existing companies found they, too, could share in the bounty by rewarding themselves with stock options. As a result, in the last two decades of the twentieth century the shareholder value revolution swept across the whole corporate environment, as company after company embraced shareholder value and its exclusive focus on a higher stock price now as the driving rationale for their existence. Chapter 3 ends, therefore, on the rush by entrepreneurs to launch and float Internet companies to cash in on the exuberant stock market of the 1990s. A revolution in thinking about corporate purpose occurred with little thought as to its consequences for society at large. Describing this revolution is the intent of the first part of this book.

CHAPTER 1

Business in the Nineteenth Century: Families and Financiers

Society at large dictates the size and shape of the institutions that dominate most people's day-to-day lives. This is true of families and governments, which have varied in their makeup in keeping with the times. It is also true of business. The companies that are now household names were for the most part founded in the mid- to late nineteenth or early twentieth century. As each successive generation passes, new names are added to the pantheon of business success stories. But with only a few exceptions, the old names continue to thrive as well. Because of these companies' size and longevity, most people think of them as "big business." Few remember (or ever knew) that most of these great enterprises started as small, entrepreneurial ventures run by individuals struggling just to survive. Fewer still look to the origins of these companies for lessons to be learned about the world we live in today.

Small businesses survive and prosper when the economic situation around them is conducive to growth and prosperity. In the history of modern business, there have been three such eras from which most major companies now in existence derive. The first of these encompassed the latter stages of the nineteenth century, when the inventions and discoveries of the scientific revolution fueled the initiative of individuals who hoped to exploit the new technologies and the increasing wealth of the rapidly urbanizing workforce. Most of the large companies we know as pillars of industry were founded in these heady days. The second such era of company formation and survival occurred in the aftermath of World War II, as returning soldiers seeking to reclaim their lives fueled the postwar economic expansion. Coming after the war and the great economic depression that preceded it, the flowering of so

3

many enterprises in the 1940s and 1950s filled a gap between their industrial revolution forebears and the businesses of the high-tech revolution still to come. After a period of relative consolidation in the late 1960s and inflation-ridden 1970s, the advent of microprocessor technology fueled the third large period of business gestation, culminating at the turn of the twentieth century with the proliferation of Internet firms and promises.

Each era of business formation owes its existence to the larger economic circumstances of the time, as well as the skills and perseverance of the founding entrepreneurs. Yet each of these three major eras generated its own type of company quite different from those of the other two periods. In this and the two succeeding chapters, I analyze the characters of companies that epitomize the eras in which they were founded; in so doing I highlight how business has changed and will change again as society evolves.

This chapter concerns itself with the dinosaurs of modern business, household names such as Procter & Gamble, Heinz, Unilever, AT&T, General Motors (GM), Sears, Gillette, and Dow Chemical. Lots of firms were created around the dawn of the twentieth century. Almost all of them began as family enterprises intended to improve the way of life for the families of the founding entrepreneurs. Although the pursuit of wealth as an end unto itself was not unknown one hundred years ago, a careful examination of the histories of firms founded in those days suggests that wealth (at least huge accumulations of wealth) was a by-product of the success of the firms, not the reason they were started in the first place.

Of course, of all the firms founded around the turn of the twentieth century, only a handful have survived to become the names we recognize today. Three factors distinguished those firms that did last. First, they were almost always led by extraordinary individuals who simply would not give up no matter what adversity they faced. Second, they were almost always founded on the basis of some form of innovation—either an application of technology or an innovation in how to bring products to market. Finally, they needed money to pass beyond the stage of cozy family enterprise to become large and thriving institutions. An early involvement with shrewd investors who guided the companies through their adolescent years seems in retrospect almost as important as the people and ideas who established the firms.

Procter & Gamble: The Creation of a Family Enterprise

In a review of the businesses that were created during the latter stages of the industrial revolution and subsequently came to dominate economic life around the globe, there is perhaps no better place to start than with Procter & Gamble (P&G). James Gamble arrived in Cincinnati in 1819, the son of a Methodist minister from what is now Northern Ireland who emigrated with his family to escape the depressed economic conditions back home. Originally destined for Illinois, the Gamble family was so impressed by the bustle and vibrancy of Cincinnati that they decided to make it their home. Because there was no pressing demand at the time for ministers, Gamble's father opened a greenhouse as a means of supporting his family. For a time, James himself worked with his father in the business before apprenticing himself to a well-established soap manufacturer, William Bell. He spent eight years under Bell before setting out on his own with a young friend, Hiram Knowlton, in a candle- and soap-manufacturing concern. By the age of thirty, Gamble felt himself well-off enough to marry the daughter of a locally prominent candle maker, Alexander Norris.

At around the time Gamble was setting up shop with Knowlton, William Procter arrived in Cincinnati from London. A robbery of his shop there had left the young entrepreneur $8,000 ($135,000) in debt,[1] and Procter had immigrated to America to make his fortune, repay his creditors, and rebuild his life. Unfortunately, his wife, Martha, took ill with cholera on the boat trip down the Ohio River and died just as the boat landed in Cincinnati. A discouraged Procter worked briefly for a bank before spotting the same opportunity that had appealed to Gamble. Ever the entrepreneur, he went into business on his own as a candle maker and a few years later was prosperous enough to get married again—to James Gamble's sister-in-law, Olivia.

Both soap and candle making depended on the availability of animal fats, their essential ingredient. Cincinnati was a regional center of the hog-slaughtering industry, so these raw materials were in abundance. Moreover, the river port had grown so quickly that when Procter and Gamble independently set up their shops, soap and candles were being imported to serve the ever-increasing needs of the local population. Substituting local products for these imports presented both enterprising young men with the market opportunity they would use to launch their careers. Whereas Gamble concentrated on soap and Procter on candles, they soon found themselves in friendly competition for the raw materials necessary to make their products.

---

[1]Using a data series on consumer price movements year by year contained in table 121 of the *Handbook of Labor Statistics—1973* (published by the Bureau of Labor Statistics of the U.S. Department of Labor), I have inflated all pre–1990 figures from the history of companies into my best estimate of 2000 prices (assuming an inflation rate of 3.5 percent for 1999). These inflated figures are shown in parentheses following the original dollar amounts to help modern readers get a better feeling for the relative size of businesses that operated in earlier eras. Where foreign currencies were involved, I used conversion rates available at: http://www.globalfindata.com.

At the suggestion of their father-in-law, Gamble eventually dissolved his partnership with Knowlton and entered into a new partnership with Procter in 1837. The new business, Procter & Gamble's Manufactory, is the direct precursor of the business now known worldwide as P&G.

Within months after establishing their partnership, the brothers-in-law expressed their faith in the potential of the business by investing $1,000 ($15,000) in a plot of land on the outskirts of Cincinnati. In very short order, they began to pioneer techniques for advertising, branding, research and development (R&D), production, and virtually every other aspect of the fledgling business. For example, it was the custom to mark each box shipped downriver from the factory to market with some symbol that indicated the company, so the mostly illiterate dockhands could recognize whose product was in which box. Procter and Gamble chose a moon and stars to represent their company. Their continuing use of this symbol as a way to identify their products made it one of the earliest recognizable business trademarks. By 1848, just ten years after they had gone into business together, they were reporting annual profits of $26,000 ($450,000). Procter had long since paid back his debt to London backers.

In this mid-nineteenth-century, family-oriented style of business, the original Procter and Gamble were soon joined by Procter's two sons, William Alexander and George Procter, and by Gamble's son, James Norris Gamble, who delayed entry into the family business long enough to gain a college education in chemistry at the University of Maryland. There was more than enough to keep these offspring busy. By 1859, sales of P&G surpassed $1 million ($18 million) for the first time. Twenty years later, a workman went to lunch and forgot to turn off the crutchers used to grind the ingredients for P&G's new white soap, Ivory, and ended up aerating the mixture so much that the final product floated. Since a lot of soap in those days was used in industrial settings to allow workers ending their shifts to clean up at communal tubs, this unplanned innovation proved to be a significant marketing advantage for the new soap. When Harley Procter, another of William's sons, convinced his partners to budget $11,000 (almost $200,000) and commissioned a chemist to analyze the contents of Ivory versus competing brands in 1882, leading to the slogan "99 and 44/100% pure," the future of the company as a branded consumer products powerhouse was secure.

Unilever: Edible Oils

Family-centered businesses were not the exclusive purview of entrepreneurs based in America during the nineteenth century. Indeed, the family roots of Unilever, one of P&G's largest direct competitors on the global business stage, extend deeper into the past. Unilever as the entity we know today was formed by the merger in 1929 of the British company Lever Brothers with the Dutch company Margarine Unie. Both companies had long and storied family histories.

The Lever Brothers story began around the time Procter and Gamble were arriving in America, when James Lever was apprenticed as a lad of fourteen to a grocer in the town of Bolton, England. After several years of apprenticeship, young Lever was sent by his employer to oversee the operations of a new branch store in the city of Manchester. With the experience he gained in this store, he felt bold enough by 1842 to return to Bolton and open his own grocery in partnership with a fellow apprentice. He continued in this business for the next twenty-two years before exiting retail and entering the more lucrative wholesale grocery business. His son, William Lever, joined him in this operation in 1867 at the age of sixteen.

Even for the son of the owner, life in the wholesale grocery business in the middle of the nineteenth century was very hands-on. In his early days working for his father, William Lever is reported to have had duties such as sweeping up in the evening, taking down the shutters in the morning, and cutting and individually wrapping bars of soap, which arrived at the wholesaler in the form of 3-pound slabs. There was also a lot to learn about the details of the business, such as developing a keen nose to make sure that bulk supplies of flour and other commodities had not gone bad. Lever was a fast learner, however, and within three years had transferred from the main shop to the traveling staff of the business, that is, to field sales and service. He did so well in this job that two years later his father made him a partner in the business with an annual salary of £800 (approximately $60,000)—not bad for a man of twenty-one.

The two principal commodities that young Lever found himself buying and reselling to retail grocers were butter and soap—luxuries the increasingly affluent working classes were eager to consume. Since the demand for butter in the UK far exceeded local supplies, wholesalers such as Lever ventured far afield in search of the product. Two of the major sources of supply in those days were the Netherlands and Ireland, but it was Lever who began changing the market perception of these products by advertising in all the local newspapers that covered his trading region about the exceptional qualities of the Irish butter he procured. Although Lever was not alone in this practice, he and others like him were instigators in the branding of products that was to become so familiar to us all.

In the case of soap, Lever had an even better idea. Why not manufacture the soap himself instead of paying the inflated price of the existing soap manufacturers? In 1885 he acted on this idea by convincing his father and other relatives to invest £27,000 (approximately $2.5 million) in the purchase of a small soap-manufacturing facility. In less than ten years, the manufacturing and marketing operations of Lever Brothers had grown so large that the company was taken public, with an initial market capitalization of £1.5 million (about $150 million). Lever's partners in this new company, in keeping with the times, were his father, his brother, and the man he had hired to oversee the operation of his soap factories. Although the recent valuations of Internet-related start-ups put even sums like $150 million to shame, Lever's venture into the soap business could hardly be called a failure.

While Lever was building up his soap business in the UK, two families across the English Channel were making their fortunes in the butter, and subsequently margarine, markets (margarine being a lower-cost and readily available substitute for the increasingly scarce butter). The first of these was the three Jurgens brothers, Willem, Jan, and Leonard, who settled in the small Dutch town of Oss in 1801. When Willem and Leonard married into the Van Valkenburg family, the largest grocery-trading family in the region, they positioned themselves in the business in a big way. But it wasn't until Willem's two sons, Anton and Johannes, entered the business in 1854 that the Jurgens name became widely known outside of their immediate area. Anton and Johannes opened the markets in the UK and Germany to the family's rapidly growing trade. By 1906 the Jurgens family business had become so large that it was transferred into a public company capitalized at 7.5 million guilders (around $270 million).

As the Jurgens expanded their butter trade with countries around the Netherlands, their main competitor was another Dutch family living in the village of Oss from 1858 onward, the Van den Berghs. The patriarch of this family, Simon, was soon succeeded in the business by his sons, Jacob, Henry, Arnold, Isaac, and Sam, who quickly expanded their butter business into the margarine trade and extended their distribution throughout eastern Europe (although their principal export market remained England). The firm's English operations were so important that when it finally did go public, the holding company it launched to hold the family interests was British, Van den Bergh's Margarine Ltd. The profits of this company in 1894, the year before it went public, were £103,000 (approximately $10 million).

Lever Brothers, the Jurgens interests, and the Van den Bergh company vied with one another for the ever-expanding market for basic consumer products. Their most direct competition was in procuring the animal fats that were the essential raw materials for soaps as well as margarine. Given the similarities in manufacturing processes, all three companies at times crossed the line and competed with finished products—the Dutch going into soaps and Lever experimenting with margarine. Starting in the first decade of the twentieth century, the companies, especially the two Dutch concerns, tried to offset the negative effects of this direct competition by arranging profit-sharing schemes one to another. These schemes were never very satisfactory, however, and with all of the firms suffering under the impact of the recession in Europe after World War I, discussions were started with a view to putting the firms together—first the two Dutch concerns under the name of Margarine Unie in the Netherlands and Margarine Union in the UK, followed soon thereafter by a merger with Lever Brothers, creating Unilever. The principal negotiators of these precedent-setting arrangements were Anton Jurgens, Paul Rijkens acting for the Van den Bergh interests, and John McDowell acting on behalf of the Lever family. The new company came into existence in the summer of 1929, right before the onset of the Great Depression. Although professional managers were mainly responsible for carrying the firm forward, the principles of the business continued as they had been laid down by the long progression of family proprietors who came before.

That so many companies established in the late nineteenth century became household names in the twentieth century is not just an irrelevant piece of historical trivia. These firms (the ones described above and hundreds more) were shaped by the circumstances that surrounded their founding. They were designed as family firms, and long-standing traditions of treating employees as "family members" became part of their very raison d'être. These companies were also characterized by strong ethical underpinnings—the kind a firm would naturally acquire if it were a family firm and the family cared about its reputation for fair dealing, which most of the founders did. These businesses remain the products of their family origins, even as they have come to dominate economic life in the twentieth century.

Gillette: The Invention of Disposability

King Camp Gillette was a born salesman, a tinkerer who followed in the footsteps of a father who held several patents and dreamed about how society could be better. Gillette supported his family working as the crack salesman of bottle caps for the Crown Cork and Seal Company. His dreaming sustained his vision of himself.

One morning in 1895 in his bathroom in Brookline, Massachusetts, he pictured how shaving could be made better. In his own words recorded decades later, "As I stood there with my razor in my hand, my eyes resting on it lightly as a bird settling down on its nest, the Gillette razor was born. I saw it all in a moment. . . . I could see the way the blade could be held in the holder; then came the idea of sharpening the two opposite edges on the thin piece of steel that was uniform in thickness throughout, thus doubling its services; and following in sequence came the clamping plates for the blade and a handle equally disposed between the two edges of the blade." Thus the idea for the safety razor was born. It took Gillette six years of tinkering before he finally had a working model good enough to be awarded the patent that was to become the source of his fortune. A breakthrough it was, however. No more sharpening blades against a strop. No more taking the razor out to a knife sharpener to regain its edge. The safety razor and its successors were to revolutionize the way the world shaved in the years ahead. Gillette and his financial backers were to become rich indeed on the back of his invention.

Although the safety razor is without a doubt King C. Gillette's most lasting contribution to humankind, his interests extended well beyond inventing useful products and getting rich. In 1894, the year before he had his breakthrough idea for shaving, Gillette published *The Human Drift,* which described his concept for a utopian community to be built under a glass dome on the shores of Lake Erie near Niagara Falls. He followed up this initial effort with a thirty-four-page pamphlet in 1897 urging the establishment of a corporation to pursue his idealistic notions. In 1908, the year he was heavily involved in the launch of the Gillette Safety Razor Company, Gillette took time out of his busy schedule to write another book, *World Corporation.* This book argued for a new body that would oversee and eventually supplant all governments on the planet. As late as 1924, when Gillette was already a wealthy and respected businessman, he once again took up his pen to write *The People's Corporation,* offering up his latest utopian vision for how the world should evolve to serve the needs of the many. Gillette's ideas as expressed in these many writings may not have been sound or sensible enough to gather much attention, but they surely register as a mark of a man of diverse interests and concerns. He was not alone in the heady days of late-nineteenth and early-twentieth-century entrepreneurship.

Sears Roebuck: Bringing the Market to the Consumer

Richard Warren Sears was a farmer's son who in 1879, at the age of sixteen, found himself the sole provider for his mother and sisters when his father died unexpectedly. To fulfill his family responsibilities, Sears took a job as a railroad station agent in North Redwood, Minnesota. Aside from a steady income, the part-time job gave him lots of time and preferential freight rates to pursue other moneymaking opportunities. And pursue them he did.

At that time in America, farmers in isolated communities spread across the prairies were enjoying increasing incomes as the rapidly urbanizing population sought their produce. They had few organized opportunities to spend their money, however, because of the absence of a developed retail industry serving their home communities. As the station agent on the railroad in a typical small rural community, Sears moved quickly to fill the gap. He built a thriving business bringing into the community wood, coal, and other products farmers needed and shipping out farm produce. When a shipment of watches appeared on his loading dock with no customer ready to pay for them, Sears made a deal with the manufacturer to take the watches off his hands and sell them on down the line. This proved to be so lucrative that in 1887 Sears upped stakes and moved his fledgling trading business to Chicago, the hub of the transportation network for the American farm belt. There he set up a firm to sell watches to farmers by taking out ads in the emerging farm journals and, over time, developing flyers exclusive to his own company. Before long he branched out from watches to jewelry, silverware, and any other items he could get his hands on at a favorable price. The business was such a success that he soon hired a watch repairman to work with him. The man's name was Alvah Roebuck.

The business boomed, and in 1889 Sears sold it to another Chicago-area businessman with the intent of retiring to Iowa. Retirement apparently didn't suit him, so later in 1889 Sears set up a new company with Roebuck as his partner. Three years later the business was incorporated as Sears, Roebuck and Company. By 1893 the range of products it offered included firearms, sewing machines, bicycles, pianos, organs, men's and boys' clothing, some athletic gear, and of course watches—all goods his farm-based customers could not get unless they ordered them from his catalogue.

The company was such a success that two years later Roebuck, tired of the long hours and hard work the business entailed, asked Sears to buy him out. The selling price for his one-third interest in the company was $25,000 (roughly $500,000). Sears turned around and within months sold a one-half share in the business to two other Chicago-area businessmen for $75,000 ($1.5 million). The partnership was not a happy one. Sears was difficult to get along with despite his brilliance in selling. In 1901 Julius Rosenwald bought out the other Chicago investor in the business, Aaron Nussbaum, for $1.25 million (roughly $25 million). This remarkable increase in the valuation of the company's shares reflected the steadily growing revenue of the business. In 1895, the year Rosenwald and Nussbaum first made their investment, Sears Roebuck had sales of approximately $750,000 ($15 million); by 1901, when Nussbaum cashed in, sales were $10 million ($200+ million). The invention of a new method of sales, mail-order catalogues, was proving its worth in the early days of the twentieth century.

If Richard Sears was the inventor of the concept and the super salesman who made it work in its early years, Julius Rosenwald was the merchandising and management genius who made it grow into the leading retailer in the United States. His philosophy, as reported in a historical annex to the company's 1940 annual report, was simple:

1. Sell for less by buying for less.
2. Sell for less by cutting the cost of sales.
3. Make less profit on each individual item and increase your aggregate profit by selling more items.

To each of these basic rules of mass merchandising, Rosenwald added, *"But maintain the quality."* Rosenwald also had strong ideas about how a company should be run. He inscribed these in a coda to his statement of merchandising philosophy: "Treat people fairly and honestly and generously and their response will be fair and honest and generous." Successful entrepreneurs and capitalists, men like Sears and Rosenwald succeeded as well in building lasting institutions.

Dow Chemical: An Explosion of Chemicals

Herbert Henry Dow was straight out of college with a degree in chemical engineering when he struck out on his own. A friend of Dow's, A. W. Smith, later quoted Dow as saying while he was still in school, "I'd rather work for myself for $3,000 ($50,000) a year than to work for someone else and make $10,000 ($170,000)"—a true sign of a young man with bold expectations.

Herbert Dow's father, Joseph, was a master mechanic and inventor who had moved from his home in New England to the Midwest early in his career. His son showed similar creative tendencies. As a boy, he had invented an incubator and built a small but thriving business selling first the incubator and later incubator kits for self-assembly. Hatching eggs was far from his only interest, however. An uncle of his once remarked that "it would take six men to keep up with all of your [Dow's] ideas." Dow immediately responded that the six men wouldn't be enough.

Inventiveness was not the only characteristic of the youthful Dow. He was stubborn as well. His first chemical venture, the Canton Chemical Company, founded in partnership with three investors from Cleveland, was dissolved a little more than a year after it was set up because of continuing losses. Undaunted, Dow returned to Cleveland, where he convinced a new backer to invest $500 (around $10,000) in a new chemical plant to be built in Michigan, the Midland Chemical Works. Like its predecessor, the new plant was designed to extract bromine—a valuable ingredient in the production of patent medicines and the development of film—from water; this time, though, he started with saltwater rather than groundwater and used electricity instead of mechanical means. Within a year Dow succeeded in producing bromine—though not in commercial quantities, because of the limited scale of the plant. Dow persuaded his initial investor in Cleveland to admit another two investors to the partnership and returned to Midland with several thousand dollars (around $40,000–$50,000 by best estimates) to continue work on the plant. This amount of money proved inadequate as well, and by the end of 1892 the partnership was dissolved. In collaboration with his original investor in the company, Dow persuaded yet another group of Cleveland investors to underwrite a new corporation capitalized at $100,000 but endowed with only $20,000 ($400,000) in cash—half equity from the investors and half a loan from a bank. Dow was named treasurer of the new corporation and received $100 (around $2,000) a month in salary for acting as general manager. The new and more substantial investors in the venture were not altogether happy that Dow was in full control of the plant. In early 1894 they replaced Dow as general manager, appointing the brother of one of the investors to the post.

With less and less to do with the operation of the bromine plant, Dow began to invest his energy in developing a process to extract chlorine from the wastewater of the plant, a product very much in demand in the rapidly growing paper industry. He even got the go-ahead from the board of the bromine company to set up a small plant adjacent to the existing operation in Midland. The first day the addition came on-line, it blew up (perhaps a precursor of problems that were to dog the company many years later). The managers of the now moneymaking bromine plant were furious. They hired a new chemist to work in the plant and further restricted Dow's operational duties (although he remained a substantial shareholder in the company).

Dow went back to his original investor, asking him to finance a third chemical operation. With initial capital of $16,667 (just over $300,000) available for investment, Dow launched another partnership. After working out most of the kinks in the chlorine extraction process, Dow requested more money to build a large-scale production plant. The original investors in this third venture, along with a group of new investors, agreed to set up a new company, the Dow Chemical Company, in May 1897. Along with a substantial shareholding in the company, Dow received an increased salary of $500 ($10,000) a month. The company allotted $83,333.33 ($1.5 million) to build the plant. The new plant was plagued by a series of explosions in the chlorine cells used to extract the valuable chemical from the water. While this was going on, Dow managed to regain control of the Midland Chemical Company, his previous venture, by buying out the existing shareholders for $40,000 (around $800,000). After solving the technical problems at the chlorine plant and turning it into a highly profitable venture, Dow persuaded the now happy investors to buy out his interests in the Midland Chemical Company and merge them with Dow Chemical. In 1900 the thirty-four-year-old Dow was a one-quarter owner of a major and profitable chemical company. One wonders how many entrepreneurs today would have had Dow's persistence.

Invention, a will to succeed, and strong family and community ties all seemed to be essential in launching the turn-of-the-century companies that so dominated life in the twentieth century. As illustrated by the Dow story, finance played a key role as well. It was the unique combination of financiers, usually self-made individuals investing their own funds, and strong-minded entrepreneurs that launched big business as we know it today. Because there was such a personal touch in their creation, both from a financial point of view as well as a managerial/entrepreneurial perspective, these companies came to have distinctive and easily identified cultures. Let's look briefly at the financial aspects before moving on.

AT&T: Money with Strings for Every Venture

No matter how good his ideas were, Herbert Dow would never have got his chemical enterprise off the ground if he had not had the ongoing and substantial support of his Cleveland backers. Dow's experience in attracting essentially private investors for his ventures was mirrored by that of many entrepreneurs of the late nineteenth and early twentieth centuries. Although the stock market did exist in those days (and had been around for a long time), it was the province of speculators and trust builders. The invention of the now ubiquitous mutual fund industry lay twenty years away. Moreover, other forms of capital to support fledgling entrepreneurs, such as venture capital funds, were still far in the future.

Dow was lucky in the degree of support he was able to garner from the Cleveland business community—luck that paid off in spades when his company became a great success. Indeed, finding the right financial backers was a key factor for success in turn-of-the-century business ventures. Those with the right backers built great companies and profited from the experience. Others were less fortunate.

Alexander Graham Bell filed for a patent on his invention of the telephone in February 1876. His work on the invention had been funded by a partnership that involved his father-in-law to be, Gardiner Hubbard, and his close friend, George Sanders. After further experimentation to improve the nascent telephone equipment he was using, the partnership was superseded in July 1877 by an unincorporated association, the Bell Telephone Company. Bell; his assistant, Thomas A. Watson; and members of the Hubbard and Sanders families were the initial shareholders in this new venture. But Hubbard and Sanders were already at the limits of the money they could afford (or were willing) to invest in the new technology. Hubbard offered the entire telephony patent to the then thriving Western Union Company around this time for $100,000 (around $1.6 million). Fortunately for Bell and his early backers, Western Union turned down the proposal.

The need for money was further aggravated by Hubbard's decision to lease telephone services to potential customers rather than sell it. To make up the financial shortfall, in early 1878 the original shareholders in Bell Telephone recruited investors from the conservative but shrewd Boston business community, including Charles S. Bradley, Alexander Cochrane, William F. Saltonstall, and Richard S. Fay. These new investors assumed control of the corporation and installed William H. Forbes as its president in place of Hubbard. With this change in leadership, Bell himself resigned from the board and the following year resigned from the company itself. Between 1879 and 1883 he and his wife, Mabel, sold their stock in the company his invention had created—as did most of the other early investors. Although Bell and all the initial backers were made comfortable for the rest of their lives by the proceeds of their stock sales, none gained the fabulous wealth that accrued to their successors in this most important of companies. And none had any say whatsoever in how the company was run.

H. J. Heinz: In a Pickle over Money

Bell and his partners were not the only nineteenth-century entrepreneurs who suffered from money problems. Some learned a bitter lesson early, allowing them to capitalize on their successes and build great fortunes later. An interesting case in point is Henry J. Heinz. Born in 1844 just across the river from Pittsburgh, Heinz was the son of Germans who had immigrated to the area a few years earlier. He was a precocious boy, albeit one tied closely to his conservative German family of three brothers and four sisters, mostly because of the strong influence of his mother. His father, John Heinz, built a kiln and opened a brick-making business shortly after his first son was born. In the manner of the times, the family had a garden to produce vegetables for their own use. By the age of eight, Henry had carved out part of the garden for his own use and was selling produce to neighbors up and down the road. At fifteen, he became his father's assistant in the brick business, continuing the garden venture on the side. By the time Heinz was seventeen, his garden business was producing revenues of $2,400 ($50,000), a substantial sum at any age but a near fortune for so young a man.

At twenty one, Heinz used his savings to buy a half interest in his father's company. He immediately set out to grow the operation by installing heating so that brick-making could continue during the long winter months. But four years later, the pull of the produce business was too great. Heinz set up shop with L. C. Noble to grow and bottle food for sale (because of the absence of refrigeration at that time, everything other than fresh produce was preserved and bottled for use in the nongrowing seasons).

The new business, Heinz, Noble & Company, prospered mightily. It expanded its product line from horseradish to sauerkraut, pickles, vinegar, and a variety of other condiments and extended its marketing reach from Pittsburgh into most of the major surrounding cities. Until the great recession, which started in 1873 as a result of speculation in railroad stocks on Wall Street, the firm even prospered. The recession, however, wiped it out. In trying to stave off the inevitable, Heinz resorted to borrowing money from friends. Even this was not enough; in late 1875 Heinz, Noble & Company filed for bankruptcy. At the time it had assets of $110,000 and liabilities of $160,000 ($1.6 million and $2.3 million). And Heinz's troubles were not over. An immediate dispute arose as to whether the partners had secretly moved goods from their warehouse to get them out of the hands of creditors. Heinz vigorously denied the charge and years later was vindicated in court. He resolved to pay off all the unpaid debts and for years carried around a notebook recording the amounts he still owed various people.

Under the terms of the bankruptcy, Heinz was prohibited from entering into any business partnerships until the bankruptcy was resolved. The family rallied round, however. In the middle of February 1876, just seven weeks after the original company had moved into receivership, his brother, John; cousin Frederick; mother; and wife (who got her hands on some money by selling property) set up a new company, the F. & J. Heinz Company, and hired Henry to manage it. If he could extricate himself from bankruptcy, he would be able to become a major shareholder in the new company because of his wife's ownership of 50 percent of the shares. The company, capitalized at $3,000 (approximately $40,000), immediately began to prosper. By 1879 it reported profits of $31,000 (more than $0.5 million) for the year. Heinz was not able to discharge his obligations fully until 1885, at which point he resumed his rightful role in the company. His experience with the bankruptcy had taught him an invaluable lesson: It was years before he allowed anyone else a substantial stake in the company.

General Motors: Wheeling and Dealing into Oblivion

Even a significant businessman like William C. Durant had difficulties in controlling the finances of his great entity, General Motors, albeit difficulties on a scale unheard of by small fry such as Henry Heinz. At the dawn of the twentieth century, Will Durant, a self-made man, was the leading wagon and carriage maker in the United States. Fascinated with the new technology of the automobile, and no doubt motivated to protect his interests in wagons and carriages, he reorganized the failing Buick Motor Company in 1904 and turned it into the leading car manufacturer in the United States. In 1908, at around the time Henry Ford was introducing the Model T that would be the runaway best-seller for the next twenty years, Durant created General Motors by bringing together his Buick operations with those of Oldsmobile, Oakland (now the Pontiac car brand), and Cadillac. Between 1908 and 1910, Durant brought twenty-five other automotive companies into GM, sowing the seed for the largest company in the world.

In assembling GM, Durant was operating from a position of great strength based on his turnaround of Buick. In 1907, the year before Durant established GM, Buick had earned $1.7 million on sales of $7.5 million (profits of $30 million on sales of about $140 million). Two years after founding GM, Durant lost control of the company because of the success of Ford's new car and his continued interest in buying other companies. A group of financiers headed by James J. Storrow of Boston and Albert Strauss of New York took over GM in return for arranging a loan for the company of $15 million (just shy of $300 million). Durant remained a major shareholder, however. The bankers ran the company so successfully with the help of two other pioneering names in the industry, Charles Nash and Walter Chrysler, that in 1915 they were able to declare a dividend of $50 ($846) per share, the largest ever for a public company up to that time. The total dividend payout came to $8 million ($135 million).

With bankers and financiers in charge of the company for such a long and prosperous period, it should be little surprise that GM developed a system of management that relied heavily on tight financial controls to pull together the disparate activities of the company. Financial control and decentralization have been a hallmark of GM's management system ever since.

Excluded from direct management of his creation, Durant secretly bought even more shares in GM and worked with another automotive pioneer, Louis Chevrolet, to bring out a direct, low-priced competitor to Ford's Model T. Durant hoped that by merging Chevrolet with GM he would regain control of the company. And he would have, except for the appearance on the scene of the Du Pont family and company, which in 1917 bought just over 25 percent of GM. Durant was indeed reinstalled as president, with Pierre S. Du Pont as chairman. He continued to invest in companies that would fill out the GM family, such as the Fisher Body Company. But the post–World War I slump hit the car industry hard. In response to the crisis, Ford dropped his prices dramatically, and in a bid to support the price of

GM's stock, Durant pledged his own holdings as security against further buying into the heavily depressed stock market. When his financial maneuverings came to light in late 1920, he was forced to resign from the company for the final time. He had built a powerhouse, but he would not be around to see it grow to preeminence.

The adventures late-nineteenth-century entrepreneurs had with financiers colored the nature of the companies they left behind. Despite the continued and heavy backing of Cleveland investors, Dow's company for many years had to scrape along, minding its pennies to make ends meet. Such thrift has marked the company to this day. By contrast, General Motors inherited a philosophy of decentralization from its wheeler-dealer founder and tight financial controls from the bankers who took over from him when he was forced out. It has remained one of the most decentralized large companies in the world, bound into a coherent whole by the power and importance of its financial systems. After Henry Heinz's extended agony in bankruptcy, the H. J. Heinz Company (renamed after Henry officially rejoined) remained an extremely closely held, family-oriented firm for decades. Heinz descendants still hold a major share of company stock. No matter when they emerged, companies never escape their seminal influences. As eras change, the type and style of companies founded change as well. In the next chapter, I examine the characteristics of the World War II boom in business formation to see just how different these companies were from their predecessors.

CHAPTER 2

The Technocratic Revolution

The great companies of the twentieth century were for the most part founded as family enterprises in the late 1800s and early 1900s. The companies that began to hog newspaper headlines in the last half of the twentieth century were a new breed of company altogether. They represented the technocrat's appearance on center stage in the business world.

The technocrats who founded the midcentury companies were inventors and entrepreneurs like their forebears. Many, the high-tech entrepreneurs, found launching pads in one of the handful of universities (or their affiliated institutes) at the forefront in pursuing the promise of science and engineering to improve modern life. Others, like the creators of the discount retailers, got their start in small-town America serving an unmet need of the local community. Although the companies these entrepreneurs founded often involved family members in their early days, they were not family companies in the sense that their nineteenth-century predecessors had been. Family members, most often wives, served only as adjuncts in the struggling days of start-up. In fact, most of this new breed of entrepreneur so frowned on any hint of nepotism in their fledgling companies that they emphasized professional management and an internal meritocracy.

Most of these companies had few role models as they began to grow. Not surprisingly, therefore, they tended to look to their forebears for models of how companies should be run. Many developed "family" cultures—with the "family" defined as all those who worked loyally for the firm for many years, not those with blood ties to the founders. A number of the founding entrepreneurs of these companies were also social visionaries after their own fashion. They saw in their companies a means to make a difference in the world and only coincidentally to make a good living and perhaps get wealthy in the process. In this, too, they mirrored the habits of their predecessors. But they would never be mistaken up close for their earlier models: The nonhierarchical style of these technocrats would be more than enough to distinguish them from their more formal and conservative forebears. Despite such cosmetic differences, these next-generation companies, too, were to have a large impact on the world around them.

Polaroid: The Glare of Invention

If the nineteenth century, through many of the businesses it spawned, was the age of the inventor, the mid-twentieth century was the age of the engineer with a burning desire to make products that people would use. One of the first of this new kind of entrepreneur, and also one of the foremost inventors of his era, was Edwin Land of Polaroid. Born into a comfortable, middle-class family in Norwich, Connecticut, in 1909, Land was a special child. As a teenager he conducted experiments in his family's basement to test scientific theories he had read about in textbooks. When he entered Harvard in 1926, he was consumed with the idea of carving out an area of science he could call his own. One of his earliest interests in this respect was the phenomenon of polarized light. He was so obsessed with it that he decided not to return to Harvard for his sophomore year, preferring to spend the time in a dingy New York City apartment attempting to make a device to polarize light, something others had been trying for decades to create. In 1929 Land finally succeeded.

With his new invention in hand (and a new wife by his side), Land returned to Harvard. Urged on by his father, he was intent on finishing his degree. It was not to be. He met and became friendly with a young physics instructor, George Wheelwright III. In 1932, at Wheelwright's suggestion, he left Harvard one semester short of his degree requirements to go into partnership with Wheelwright, hoping to find applications for their increasing knowledge of polarization and related phenomena. They called their new venture together the Land-Wheelwright Laboratories and immediately set to work in a converted dairy barn on the outskirts of Boston. Land's goal was to make a sheet of translucent material that would polarize the light passing through it. In November 1934 the struggling business achieved its first breakthrough—an order from Eastman Kodak, the photography giant, for a Polascreen Filter to remove glare from black-and-white photos taken in bright sunshine. The order was for $10,000 ($128,000). Land was in good control of the science, but he and Wheelwright had to be able to make the product in quantity. From the December 24, 1934, through January 11, 1935, Land, Wheelwright, and two employees worked nonstop to finish a machine that could make the material they needed to fill the Kodak order. When they finally went home, the machine was working—not well, not without continual attention, but working. The partnership was off and running.

Flush with the success of meeting Kodak's needs, the young entrepreneurs started looking around for other products they could make with their polarized filters. Land was most interested in manufacturing a nonglare headlight system, but ten-plus years of negotiating with the entrenched automakers left them without a real product to sell the auto industry. In fact, in these early years the only product that enjoyed any real commercial success was Polaroid sunglasses, which they made on contract for the American Optical Company. These sunglasses were technically better at eliminating glare than any of the sunglasses then on the market, and Land and his colleagues could produce them for $3.00 a pair, substantially less than the cost of the inferior brands.

The sunglass business sustained the company for several years while its reputation for scientific innovation increased, but commercial success still eluded it. It received enough attention during these years, however, to be incorporated as the Polaroid Company, with Land as president and chief scientist and with new backing from Wall Street financiers like Averell Harriman, Lewis Strauss, and Jimmy Warburg—all major names in New York's investment banking industry. The Wall Street financiers put $375,000 ($4.5 million) into the maturing but still risky company. In 1939 its sales were less than $100,000 ($1.2 million), although the company was able to show a modest profit on its activities. By 1940 sales had dropped to $72,000 ($880,000), and the firm recorded a loss of about $100,000 ($1.2 million). The heating up of the U.S. economy in response to the impending threat of the war was the only thing that saved the company from going under.

For the next four years, the company's main concern was to deliver a variety of high-tech optical devices for the U.S. armed forces. With Land's genius for invention (especially invention under pressure), Polaroid did this with extraordinary success. In 1942, for example, the company recorded sales, almost all to the U.S. government, of $1 million ($11 million). By the end of the war in 1945, the company had 1,250 people on its payroll. Within months following the surrender of the Japanese, this workforce had plummeted to fewer than 500 people. Company history records that it was on a trip to Sante Fe, New Mexico, on war-related business, that Land had the idea that would revolutionize the company—a complete, dry-film camera and system to produce instant photographic prints. Minutes after the declaration of the end of the war, Land diverted his best engineers and technicians from defense contracts to the new system of photography he had envisaged.

But turning a concept into a working product for consumers was not easy. It took Land and his associates until early 1947 before they could demonstrate a prototype, which they did at the winter meeting of the Optical

Society of America in New York in the midst of a driving snowstorm. The prototype so amazed those who witnessed it that it was front-page news for the next several weeks. After all of this publicity, though, it took Polaroid another year and a half to turn out its new product for sale to consumers. The Polaroid Land Camera, Model 95, went on sale the day after Thanksgiving 1948 at Jordan Marsh Department Store in downtown Boston. The company had managed to make only fifty-six complete camera sets for that first day. They sold out within minutes, and the excitement over the new technology almost caused a good-natured riot among the customers eager to get their hands on the camera. Sixteen years after it came into being, Polaroid was on its way to becoming a multibillion-dollar company.

Hewlett-Packard: The Engineer's Way

Polaroid wasn't the only company given a boost by wartime production contracts. Three thousand miles away from where Edwin Land and George Wheelwright were setting up operations in Massachusetts, Bill Hewlett and Dave Packard were getting to know each other as engineering undergraduates at Stanford University. They met as freshmen in 1930, but their friendship developed slowly as they took more and more courses together and found out that they shared a love of outdoor life. After graduating from Stanford in 1934, Packard took a job with the venerable General Electric Company in Schenectady, New York, while his friend Hewlett continued in graduate school at Stanford. Their plans to start a company together were temporarily put on hold. When Hewlett extended his graduate work by spending a year at MIT in Boston, the friendship and collaboration were reestablished. During a visit Packard made to Palo Alto in 1937, the two roughed out their first crude business plan, initially calling their venture the Engineering Service Company, a name lost to history: They did not activate their partnership until 1938 and did not even formalize it until early 1939, by which time they had decided to call it the Hewlett-Packard Company (HP).

Hewlett and Packard kept busy doing odd jobs for friends in the local technical community south of San Francisco. One such job involved building a controller for commercial air-conditioning units being sold to hotels in the Bay area. Within a year, however, they realized their future lay in making products for sale. They designed an audio oscillator and put it on the market with encouraging results—especially when the Walt Disney Company ordered eight units to use on its new film *Fantasia*. Their operation—out of a garage in Palo Alto—was still modest; in their first full year the new business had sales of $5,369 (around $65,000). In a record they were to keep intact throughout the history of the company, they turned a profit of $1,563 (almost $20,000) on these modest sales. It was enough for them to begin hiring, move their operations to a more spacious facility, and work to expand the business. Characteristic of HP and many of the companies founded in this era, their egalitarian ideals led them to establish profit sharing with employees as soon as they began to expand, a tradition they continue to this day.

Although Hewlett and Packard's business was doing well at a very modest level, it could not avoid being swept up in the war production effort. Hewlett, a reservist, was drafted into the U.S. Signal Corps, and the company was asked to make products needed in support of the war effort. By the end of the war, when Hewlett returned from the service, the firm had 200 people engaged in its small manufacturing operation and listed over one hundred products for sale. By the 1950s its product line had matured to the point where sales began to boom. In 1957 Hewlett and Packard sold 10 percent of their shares in the company to the public, launching one of the first real high-flying technology stocks. They hit the $30 million ($180 million) sales level in 1958, one year after going public.

Hewlett and Packard shared with Ed Land a fierce determination to make products that would harness technological developments for the good of the public. They also shared other traits. Although the three were very different in personality, their approach to management of their new companies was similar: hands-on and informal. They also were, in different ways, committed social engineers and staunch advocates of meritocracy as the modus vivendi in the companies they founded and ran. As early as 1957, Hewlett and Packard held an off-site meeting for their senior managers in which they first formally articulated "the HP way," identifying profits, customer service, growth, employee interests, and good citizenship as the central features of their management philosophy. They didn't just say the words; that's how they ran the company as well. Many of the nineteenth-century companies espoused similar values, but these values were imposed from on high by owner-entrepreneurs who often were remote figures, much given in their later years to retiring amid fame and fortune to country mansions surrounded by family members and other interested parties. The new breed of entrepreneurs, all of whom built substantial fortunes from their business activities, were working manager-leaders of their enterprises, eager to inculcate their values and ideals in employees and colleagues around them. They succeeded to an extraordinary extent. These engineer-inventors were not alone in their pursuit of new ideas to improve the world.

Wal-Mart: A Passion for Selling

World War II may have saved the bacon for some inventors and entrepreneurs; its end, however, paved the way for one of the greatest social upheavals of modern times. When the war ended, millions of men returned home with experience under their belts, confidence in their own ability to get things done, and a burning desire to make up for lost time. Back home these former soldiers met the first generation of women whose formative experiences had been in the nation's factories and workplaces, where they had ably taken the place of the men who had been shipped overseas. These men and women married and set out to build lives of their own.

The war that had thrown people from different parts of the country and different cultures together in the front lines made postwar couples more mobile than any previous generation. They longed for their own place in the world, and in part to satisfy this longing they began moving to suburbs in unheard of numbers. Of course, a new house in the suburbs required new furnishings and appliances. So they bought furnishings and appliances at rates that hadn't been seen in decades, leading to an economic boom of unprecedented proportions. With the prosperity brought on by this consumer-fueled economic boom, this new generation found itself with more time on its hands. Some of this leisure time Americans spent eating out—not in the posh and formal restaurants once reserved for the privileged in society who could afford them but in the rapidly expanding chains of fast-food establishments that began to grow up to serve the new suburban communities. Naturally, some saw the opportunity that the increase in spending and changing life-style offered to those willing to go after it. A new generation of retail entrepreneurs arose, retailers who would change the face of retailing forever, quite as their predecessors at the turn of the century did with their expanded mail-order houses and convenient department stores.

Sam Walton's namesake grandfather had been a shopkeeper in a number of small towns in the Midwest in the mid-nineteenth century. Walton's father, Tom, the son of a second marriage, did not follow in his father's footsteps and ended up instead in the farm mortgage business, which, during the hard-pressed years of the depression, more often than not meant he was involved in repossessing farms from bankrupt farmers. The work may have been disheartening, but at least it provided the family with steady earnings, a rarity in those times. The family had just enough income that their children, most notably Sam, could afford to go to college.

While at the University of Missouri, Sam Walton augmented his income by selling newspapers and organizing others to do so for him; he held down other part-time jobs as well. At its peak, his newspaper venture earned him $4,000 (around $50,000). It is perhaps not surprising, therefore, that Walton took a job in retail with J. C. Penney after his graduation in 1940. Although he did not stay in the job long, his experience with Penney had a big impact on Walton. He learned to refer to his colleagues in the business as "associates." He learned the importance of keeping a finger on the pulse of retail trade by visiting one's own and competitive stores—an early version of retail management by walking around. He learned about giving local store managers a small stake in the profits from their stores as a way of having them buy into ownership in the stores' success. All these lessons he tucked away for future reference as he joined the millions of others of his age in military service. After the war it was natural that Walton would look again to retailing to earn his living and get ahead in the world.

Just before the war, Walton had married the daughter of a wealthy rancher and businessman from Oklahoma. It was his father-in-law who in 1946 advanced him the $20,000 ($180,000) to purchase his first store in the small town of Newport, Missouri, a Ben Franklin five-and-dime (similar to Woolworth's) carrying an array of merchandise at low prices. The store had a turnover of $72,000 (around $700,000) the year before Walton took it over. Confronted with this modest turnover and the traditionally low margins in retail, Walton had very little choice but to change the rules. Rather than maintaining informal agreements to fix prices with other merchants in the area, Walton began to offer discounts on selected items as a way to build volume. Rather than relying on established distributors to ship him goods to sell at the normal markup of 25 percent, he sought out manufacturers directly so that he could get goods at a markup of 5–10 percent. With these practices and careful attention to every detail in the business, within two and a half years he had doubled the volume going through his first store and had repaid in full the original loan from his father-in-law. Another two and a half years later he had increased turnover in the store to $250,000 (almost $1.7 million). Then his lease on the store ran out, and his landlord refused to renew it. Instead he gave Walton $50,000 ($330,000) for the business—a fair enough value but hardly what Walton had in mind.

Undeterred, and once again backed by his father-in-law, Walton purchased a Ben Franklin franchise in Bentonville, Arkansas. Two years later, he purchased a second store in Fayetteville. His confidence growing, he did not make this a Ben Franklin franchise, which freed him to sell any goods he could find. He recruited a manager for this second store in part by giving him a share in the profits it earned. Having read about a trend emerging in the country, he opened it as a self-service store and soon converted the original store in Bentonville to the same, lower-cost format. With both stores doing well, he talked his brother into borrowing some money with him to invest in a store in one of the pioneer shopping malls, on the outskirts of Kansas City. For a time, he was so enamored with the idea of shopping malls that he slowed down his expansion in the retail sector to explore plunging into the business of developing malls. After losing some money, he soon returned to his first love, retail. By 1962 he had sixteen stores operating mostly in small-town, Midwest America. Only a couple of these were the larger-scale versions for which Walton would become famous. One, a 20,000-square-foot store in St. Robert, Kansas, had a turnover of $2 million (almost $11 million) in 1962 alone.

Just around this time, the idea of the discount store was beginning to take hold. Price had always been a key factor for most retailers. Indeed, most of the retail revolutions that had occurred up to this point had in one way or another found some way to achieve a cost advantage and pass this advantage on to consumers in the form of lower prices. Discounters took the concept one step further. They ran no-frills stores loaded to the gills with merchandise bought at the lowest possible prices and passed on to consumers at the lowest possible markups. Volume was the name of the discount game, and Walton had already got a taste of the advantages of this approach in his store in St. Robert. He was determined not to be left behind in this burgeoning retail movement.

Walton had another advantage he was fully intent on capitalizing on: He planned to concentrate on retail outlets in towns so small that a good-sized retailer usually faced little or no local competition. Walton had proven that in the booming retail market following World War II there was plenty of demand in these small towns. He would focus his move into discounting in the same place. On July 2, 1962, Walton opened his first discount store, which he called Wal-Mart Discount City, in Rogers, Arkansas, just down the road from Bentonville. This store sold irons for $11.88 versus a manufacturer's suggested retail price of $17.95, Polaroid cameras for $74.37 versus the $100 suggested from Polaroid's home office, and Wilson baseball gloves for $5.97 versus $10.90. Consumers loved it. In its first year in business, the store had a turnover of $700,000 ($4 million), almost double the average of Walton's other stores. The revolution that would lead within thirty years to the largest retail chain in the world in terms of sales was under way.

McDonald's: Food for the Masses

In the mid-1950s, when Sam Walton was expanding his chain of variety stores around the Midwest, another and equally legendary midwesterner, Ray Kroc, was in the process of striking a deal with two California entrepreneurs that would launch the world's biggest retail chain in terms of number of outlets. Kroc did not invent the fast-food business. He did not invent franchising. Until he built his first McDonald's outlet on the outskirts of Chicago, he had never even run a restaurant. What he did do was improve so much on existing practices in all these areas that his creation, McDonald's Corporation, became during his tenure as CEO the leading consumer brand in the world.

Like Sam Walton, Kroc was first and foremost a salesman. Kroc got his first sales job in 1922, peddling paper cups for the Lily Cup Company. He supplemented his earnings by playing piano for a local radio station at night. Except for a stint in the mid-1920s selling real estate in Florida, until the mid-1950s—when he switched careers into the fast-food industry—Kroc spent virtually all of his time selling to the restaurant trade.

Most of his customers in his early days were the lunch counters located in pharmacies across the country. He became Lily's leading cup salesman when he convinced the large drugstore chain Walgreen's to begin selling takeout food in addition to the sit-down meals it specialized in. His exposure to the lunch-counter market and the milkshakes that were part of its stock-in-trade led to his first entrepreneurial venture in 1939. He began selling "multimixers" to soda fountains to speed their production of milkshakes during the busiest part of the day. Kroc's original company, Malt-A-Mixer Company (later renamed the Prince Castle Sales Division), capitalized on the increasing tendency of the American public to eat takeout food. By the late 1940s, Kroc was selling in excess of 9,000 multimixers a year and taking home a salary of $40,000 (close to $300,000)—a satisfying amount for a modestly successful, middle-aged entrepreneur.

While Kroc was busy building his multimixer business, two brothers in California were taking the first steps that would create the fast-food industry. Richard and Maurice McDonald (known universally as Dick and Mac) moved to California in the early 1930s. After knocking around doing odd jobs in Hollywood for a few years, they set out to build themselves a more stable source of income by capitalizing on the emergence of one of the many trends California was to become famous for over the years. In 1937 they opened a small drive-in restaurant just east of Pasadena.

Drive-in restaurants, started in the early 1930s in California, were booming because of the popularity and availability of the automobile, which was suddenly turning a largely urban population into a mobile consumer force. A drive-in consisted of a parking lot surrounding a small restaurant, often with limited inside seating (the McDonald brothers had none in their facility) and with service provided by carhops, who took the orders at the parked cars, picked up the orders at the restaurant, and delivered them to the customers in the parking lot. Most drive-ins of that day became hangouts for teenagers and young adults. The available space in the restaurant and parking lot set practical limits on how well any particular outlet would do.

The McDonald brothers' initial restaurant was successful enough that three years later, in 1940, they closed their original shop and opened a larger drive-in in San Bernardino, 50 miles east of Los Angeles. This restaurant produced annual sales of $200,000 ($2 million) and allowed the brothers to split around $50,000 ($500,000) in profits. They had it made, except for two factors: the difficulty of running a drive-in restaurant and competition from copycat outlets. With increasing competition for customers as well as for cooks and carhops to provide the restaurant service, the McDonald brothers felt they had to do something to improve their situation at their only restaurant facility. In 1948 they closed down the restaurant for three months, decided to concentrate exclusively on hamburgers—which had in any case accounted for 80 percent of their food sales—installed specially designed equipment in the kitchen to allow the hamburgers and accompanying milkshakes to be prepared on a production line, and installed windows where customers could come up and order their own food, eliminating the need for carhops. Everything was predicated on a quick turnaround for customers at the window. The modern fast-food enterprise had been invented. After a slow start while customers got used to the concept, sales took off. By the mid-1950s, the McDonald brothers were selling $350,000 ($2.2 million) worth of 15-cent hamburgers and splitting $100,000 ($600,000) a year in profits.

The McDonald brothers were so successful that their model for a fast-food restaurant was soon copied by a number of others in the California market. Some of these copycats even paid the McDonalds a franchise fee for the privilege—set by the highly informal brothers at $1,000 for a set of restaurant plans and a sincere wish of good luck. Sophistication in franchising was not one of the brothers' strong suits.

Ray Kroc became aware of the brothers' operation when he sold them the tenth multimixer for use in their small outlet. When he heard that all his mixers were in use during the heaviest parts of the day, he made the trip out to California to see for himself. What he found was a queue of people extending around the block waiting to buy their hamburgers with fries and milkshakes—a queue the brothers were moving forward at the rate of one customer every fifteen seconds or so. He was sold on the idea at once and shortly thereafter approached the McDonalds with the proposal that he franchise their operation nationally. The deal he worked out with them was that he would charge new franchise owners $950 for a franchise and extract 1.9 percent of their revenue as an ongoing franchise fee (0.5 percent of which would be paid on to the McDonalds for the right to use their name and copy their fast-food production system—a right they later sold).

To an early McDonald's franchisee, the deal they could strike with Kroc was a gold mine. Because of the simplicity of the McDonald's system, a new restaurant could be put up for around $75,000 (less than $500,000). Such a store could be expected to produce annual revenue of $200,000 ($1.2 million) and return an annual profit of almost $40,000 ($250,000)—a level of return that meant the initial investment in the restaurant could be paid back in just under two years. Not only that, but some of the new McDonald's outlets did even better. An early franchise in Waukegan, 50 miles north of Chicago, grossed $250,000 ($1.5 million) in its first year of operation and turned in a profit of $50,000 ($320,000) for its owner.

Ever the salesman, Kroc sold eighteen franchises in California his first year in the fast-food business. He also convinced a couple dozen members of his local golf club to open up franchises in the Chicago area. Successful selling was not the only key to Kroc's success in exploiting the McDonald's concept: He struck good deals with suppliers on behalf of his franchisees. He concentrated his early franchise sales in small towns rather than taking on the higher level of competition he would likely face in urban centers. He insisted on selling franchises one unit at a time, thus giving him decisive control over the quality of the brand as it was rolled out. He focused on recruiting owner-managers as franchisees instead of the financial investors who were so prevalent in other early franchise operations. Most important, he was committed to making the franchise work for the franchisee—something few others in the business cared about at that time. His reward was a multibillion-dollar global enterprise featuring the most famous brand name in the world. In setting up this empire, he made thousands of others, his franchisees, rich beyond their wildest dreams. Kroc himself died a wealthy man, many times wealthier than the laid-back McDonald brothers who invented the idea of a fast-food operation.

The launching and development of major retail operations like Wal-Mart and McDonald's in some respects represented a watershed in the evolution of big business in America. Unlike inventors who had established companies to commercialize a promising technology, retailers like Walton and Kroc were in the business to make a buck by delivering value to their customers. There is probably no business in the world that features such rapid and highly visible evidence of success (or failure) as retailing. Both Walton and Kroc were significant innovators, as innovative in their own fashion as many of the inventors who launched companies at the same time. They were also capitalizing on changes occurring in the broader economic environment. But whereas the inventors could take pride in innovation itself, the only meaningful return to retailers like Walton and Kroc was a robust bottom line. Others equally focused on bottom-line results were soon to follow.

Digital Equipment Corporation: Technology Travels

In 1957, two years after Kroc struck his landmark deal with the McDonald brothers, Ken Olsen, a thirty-one-year-old engineer at Lincoln Laboratories, an offshoot of MIT, got $70,000 ($427,000) of backing from the world's first real venture capital firm, American Research and Development (ARD), to launch an electronics business he was to call the Digital Equipment Corporation. For its $70,000 investment, ARD got to own 70 percent of the new company; Olsen was to retain only 12 percent of the initial stock in the company, a holding that was to be worth hundreds of millions of dollars in the years ahead. His start-up partner, Harlan (Andy) Anderson, initially took an 8 percent stake in the company; some years later Olsen forced him out of the company so that he could exercise unbridled control over the business.

The business plan for the new venture was to make commercial versions of a number of test circuits Olsen had designed when he worked for Lincoln Labs. Olsen's real intention was to design a new type of computer, but his venture backers initially advised against it in fear of the competitive muscle of IBM, whose $1 billion in revenue dominated the industry. In its first year in business, the company sold $94,000 ($550,000) worth of logic modules for testing computer memories and turned a small profit. It was not until 1959, however, that the company returned to Olsen's original vision of building a low-cost computer to compete with the mainframe computers then being sold by IBM.

Their first computer was called the PDP-1 and went for $120,000—a fraction of the cost of the much larger mainframe computers on the market. The computer was based on circuit designs Olsen and his associates in the business venture had developed while working for Lincoln Labs, used with the full blessing of officials at Lincoln Labs and MIT. Although quite a modest computer by today's standards (possessing, for example, only 4 kilobytes of memory), it was the technological marvel of its time. Moreover, it was inexpensive enough that engineers and scientists eager to get access to computing capability could afford to buy one. (I learned to program a computer on one of the earlier models of the PDP-1, which was installed at the Atomic Energy of Canada research facility in Chalk River, Ontario.) In the first couple of years after the PDP-1 was introduced, it sold in modest numbers, mainly to research organizations around the United States and Canada. In 1962 the product really took off when ITT ordered fifteen of the computers to use for controlling message switching in its telephone business. That year Digital reported sales of $6.5 million ($37 million) and turned in a profit of $807,000 ($4.6 million). The era of the high-flying, high-margin, high-tech company had arrived. That the technology may have originated someplace else was irrelevant. There were piles of money to be made by turning the technology into commercial products.

Intel: Making Money out of Sand

Olsen was a leader in the new world of high-tech business in more ways than one. His interest in control and financial rewards for his efforts was to strike a chord with many others in the technology business. The same year Olsen and his partner approached ARD for venture funding, Bob Noyce and Gordon Moore led a defection from Shockley Labs, a company set up to commercialize the transistor, invented by William Shockley when he worked at Bell Laboratories. The stated reason for the defection was the irascibility of Shockley; underlying it all was the pure and simple desire to make money. The company they set up was called Fairchild Semiconductor, and it would soon become the leading manufacturer of semiconductors in the world. The deal they struck with Sherman Fairchild to fund the company was even worse than the one Olsen struck with ARD: In return for initial funding, Fairchild retained the right to buy out any of the eight founding partners for $300,000 if the company was successful—an option he soon exercised.

Burned by the experience at Fairchild, Noyce and Moore were intent on avoiding the same mistake in 1968 when they bolted from Fairchild to set up their own company. Their venture capital deal with Arthur Rock for the founding of Intel involved fifteen separate investors, so the original entrepreneurs were virtually assured freedom to pursue their own interests in the company.

The business the new company set out to develop was the manufacturing of memory chips for the computer industry. The business in which Intel eventually prospered was making integrated circuits to power the computer revolution embodied in the personal computer. But the start-up's initial focus, as it was with Olsen's company, was to exploit technology its founders had developed while working at their previous firms. It is perhaps not surprising that Andy Grove, the man Noyce and Moore hired as director of operations in their start-up and who went on to lead the company to its subsequent preeminence, titled his autobiography *Only the Paranoid Survive*. As a former employee of both companies put it, "Intel was founded to steal the silicon gate process from Fairchild." A pundit may well have added, "And to make the founders filthy rich in the process."

Over the years, Intel came to dominate the semiconductor industry in a way no company had before or has since. It did this by maintaining a sterling record of continual and market-sensitive innovation. Nevertheless, understanding the origins of the company is essential to understanding its place in the history of corporations. Intel more than most companies of its era was founded on greed. As a leader in its industry and a model for others, it set the tone for the high-tech revolution that was to follow. The age of starting a business to get rich was upon us.

CHAPTER 3

Business as a Hobby;
Money as the Goal

The last three decades of the twentieth century were remarkable in modern economic history for the sheer amount of wealth created around the world. Critics of this era might correctly argue that the wealth was not well distributed, with most of it accumulating in the hands of an incredibly privileged few. However justified this post hoc criticism, the reality was that this era of prosperity fueled an almost unprecedented increase in the number of prominent new companies—companies that themselves became the vehicles for the wealth expansion under way.

The 1970s began inauspiciously, but there were signs even then that things were only going to get better. High government spending in the United States to finance the Vietnam War as well as a massive expansion in social welfare programs led to a mushrooming government deficit. The Organization of Petroleum Exporting Countries (OPEC) announced its oil price increases first in the early 1970s and then again at the end of the decade, a sequence that triggered worldwide inflation and left companies scrambling to keep their heads above water. It would have been easy to overlook the announcement in 1971 that a small California start-up company, Intel, had invented the first microprocessor, a device that was to revolutionize the way most of the world did work. It would have been just as easy to overlook the publication of a book by Alfred Rappaport, *Information for Decision Making,* that was to revolutionize the way people came to think about business. The microprocessor brought computers to virtually everyone's desktop; Rappaport brought to the mind of virtually every businessperson the idea that business existed only to increase shareholder wealth. The two together were to prove to be a very potent combination.

Microsoft: Computer Geeks to the Fore

The very first microprocessor Intel invented in 1971, the 4004, was not a very useful device. It had all of the logic required to run a computer on one silicon chip, but the chip was slow and had limited capacity. Intel kept working at it, however, and in 1974 introduced the next-generation model, the Intel 8008, which laid the groundwork for the personal computer revolution.

The first entrepreneur to use the 8008 as the basis of a computer was Ed Roberts, who made the chip the heart of his MITS Altair computer for hobbyists. Because it was the first of a new breed, the development of this machine was reported in the January 1975 issue of *Popular Electronics*. Two who soon read this report with real excitement were Paul Allen and Bill Gates, high school friends from Seattle who happened to be in Boston at the time—Allen as a programmer for Honeywell and Gates as a sophomore at Harvard. Having previously done commercial programming work in Seattle (despite their youth), Allen and Gates saw the potential the new Altair opened up. To realize that potential, the new computer would need software. Gates and Allen used a Digital Equipment Corporation PDP-10 computer in the Harvard Computation Center to simulate the operations of the new Intel 8008 chip. With this simulator, they developed a compiler program for the chip to enable it to run programs written in BASIC, the most popular high-level computer language around at that time. With their program in hand, Gates dropped out of Harvard and with Allen flew out to Albuquerque, where Roberts and MITS were located. As reported in Robert X. Cringely's *Accidental Empires,* the nineteen-year-old Gates was concerned that "the revolution could happen without us." The company they set up in their hometown of Seattle as the vehicle for selling this new software to Roberts was called Microsoft.

Microsoft's relationship with Roberts and MITS did not exactly thrive. The two young entrepreneurs began developing versions of their BASIC software for the variety of other microcomputers that were being developed at the same time. When Roberts claimed he owned all the rights to MITS BASIC and its offshoots, the two young programmers fought him and won. Their goal was to build a real business. As Gates is reported to have said at the time, "Money is made by setting de facto standards."

With microcomputers springing up all over the place in those early days of the industry, Gates and Allen built themselves a nice little business selling BASIC and a variety of other computer languages to the fledgling personal computer manufacturers. By 1980, when IBM turned up on their doorstep in Seattle, their company had almost fifty employees. IBM had decided that the personal computer revolution was potentially too big for it, the leader in the computer industry, to ignore. It set out to enter the market with a PC, a machine to be built almost exclusively with parts and components supplied from outside the IBM system. On the software side, IBM needed the languages Microsoft had to offer; even more, it needed an operating system for its new machine.

Up until that time, the leader in personal computer operating systems was a company called Digital Research (not to be confused with the minicomputer pioneer Digital Equipment). Its founder and CEO, Gary Kildall, and everyone else at Digital Research at the time assumed the firm had a de facto agreement with Microsoft: Digital Research would do operating systems; Microsoft would do languages. Someone should have checked with Gates.

IBM initially went to Digital Research in its search for an operating system. The company refused to sign the cumbersome nondisclosure agreement IBM required all vendors to enter into before it would deal with them. Gates had no such reservations. When he heard IBM was still in the market for an operating system given its rebuff at Digital Research, he offered to supply them one. He didn't mention that the system he had in mind was one he was going to buy for $50,000 ($120,000–$125,000) from another small Seattle start-up company. IBM signed on with Gates, giving him the right to sell his operating system to any other IBM-compatible product on the market. Gates's door to becoming the richest man in the world was open wide. Gates may have started out as a computer geek interested only in proving his programming expertise to his peers, but he clearly understood that the purpose of business was to make money.

Nike: Running for the Green

In the early 1960s, when Gates was still a toddler in Seattle, a young man from Washington State just south of Seattle, Phil Knight, was presenting a paper on a small business idea to his classmates at the Stanford Business School. His idea was to import custom-made running shoes from Japan and sell them along the West Coast at a price lower than that set by the German market leader in performance running shoes, Adidas.

Knight had been a good, but not record-setting, middle-distance runner at the University of Oregon under its fabled track coach, Bill Bowerman. On graduating from Stanford in 1962, Knight decided to take a year off. With funding from his father, he headed west to explore the Pacific region. On his way through Hawaii, he supplemented his funds by working for a time selling securities for Bernie Cornfeld's Investors Diversified Services. In those days Cornfeld was famous for his opening line to investors, "Do you sincerely want to be rich?" Soon he would become infamous for presiding over one of the biggest bankruptcies and investment frauds ever. Knight soon quit his job and moved on to Japan. The idea of importing low-cost Japanese running shoes had not left him. While he was in Japan, he made a cold call on a Japanese shoe manufacturer, Onitsuka, where he introduced himself as a distribution company interested in importing running shoes to the United States. Knight was so convincing that he left with an agreement allowing him to become a distributor for the Japanese company, and he placed an order for a sample of the shoes he would have available to sell.

When Knight finally arrived back home in spring 1963, he moved into his parents' house and took a job with the accounting firm of Coopers & Lybrand. When his initial order of shoes from Onitsuka failed to show up, he wrote the company, which replied that Onitsuka already had a distributor in the United States but would be happy to send him shoes as well if he restricted his activities to the western states. Knight readily agreed, "for the time being." Then he focused his energy on learning his new job as an auditor. His initial sample order of five pairs of shoes finally arrived in late November 1963. He sent two pairs to his old coach, Bowerman, in the hope of gaining an initial order.

Bowerman was by then famous in the not-so-prominent world of track and field. His collegiate team had first won the national intercollegiate championship in 1962, a considerable feat for a small and relatively unknown school on the West Coast. Bowerman was also an inveterate tinkerer. He routinely made special shoes for his own star runners, shoes fully 2 ounces lighter than the leading model by Adidas. They were cheaper as well—a fact not lost on Bowerman, who resented the high prices the German company charged. But since each pair took him about four hours to make by hand, only his very best athletes qualified to wear them.

When Bowerman received the sample shoes from his former student, he was intrigued. Here were shoes at least as good as the German models and available at a fraction of their price. He called up Knight and suggested a partnership. He would endorse the shoes and recommend them to athletes in return for a share of ownership in the new company. He would also contribute to the new company his own ideas for how to make the shoes even better. Knight was delighted, and the partnership was struck with a handshake. The Japanese shoes they would be distributing were known by the brand name Tigers. Encouraged, Knight sent off an order to Japan for 300 pairs of shoes. Instead of shoes, Knight got back another letter from Onitsuka wondering whether it should even be doing business with this new company. Emboldened, Knight wrote back, telling Onitsuka that America's most famous track coach had signed on with his company, that the company was the only one that really understood the world of competitive running, and that its sales would be handled by runners on a face-to-face basis with other athletes. His Japanese supplier gave in and began shipping him shoes.

Having had modest success with his first couple of small shipments, Knight returned to Japan in fall 1964 and negotiated a contract with his Japanese supplier that allowed him to take between 5,000 and 8,000 pairs of shoes from them over the next year. Even with assistance from his father in financing the first firm order for 1,000 pairs of shoes, Knight was strapped for cash, and with more and more shoes arriving every day, he needed all the help he could get in moving them. He found that help in Jeff Johnson, another Oregon running alumnus, who agreed to sell the new Tiger shoes on commission in his after-hours as a social worker in Los Angeles. In September 1965 Johnson left his day job to work for Knight full time. The total sales of the new company in 1965 were $20,000 (just over $100,000), on which the new company turned a modest profit of $3,240 (around $17,000). It was off and running.

Selling the shoes consisted mainly of going to local and regional track meets, talking to the athletes and giving sample shoes to the best of them, and taking orders as the reputation of the new shoes grew. Soon Johnson opened a small retail operation in Los Angeles to supplement his promotional work at meets (and get his shoe inventory out of his apartment, where runners had come at all hours of the day and night to fulfill their desire for shoes). A tinkerer like Bowerman in his spare time, Johnson also modified some of the initial Tiger models by adding padding to create the first full-length cushioned midsole, ideal for use by marathoners. He also started printing up T-shirts boldly emblazoned with the Tiger name, for the free advertising this would give them when their athletes were on training runs or at meets. So impressed was Knight with Johnson's success that he soon hired a high school track coach to take over the Los Angeles store and shipped Johnson east to replicate the operation on the East Coast. He also hired another runner in Oregon and opened a small store nearer to home. By 1969 this fledgling company of running enthusiasts had sales of $400,000 (almost $1.8 million); in 1970 they passed $1 million ($4.2 million).

This growth was not without its problems, however. First, their supplier in Japan more often than not would ship them shoes in the wrong sizes, wrong colors, and wrong amounts for what their rapidly expanding business in the United States required. Moreover, growing at almost 100 percent a year, the small company had trouble financing its growth. Although profits were fine, they had to pay Onitsuka for orders months before they received revenue for moving the shoes along. Finally, a new manager at Onitsuka was threatening to enforce its original division of the United States into a series of distribution territories and limit Knight's company to the West Coast. In the early 1970s, Knight decided to protect himself. He set out to have a new line of shoes manufactured that would be christened Nike. When the new shoes hit the market, the already fragile relationship with Onitsuka unraveled. With a new Japanese partner, Nissho Iwai, a major Japanese trading company, to finance the expansion, Knight and his colleagues set out on their own. The Nike Corporation was off to the races.

Oracle: Vaporware Hits It Big

In the final third of the twentieth century, the geography of new business start-ups shifted away from places like Arkansas toward a stretch of land just north of the Stanford University campus in California: Silicon Valley. The area had for years been the home of some technology businesses, most notably Hewlett-Packard. Maybe it was something about the air in California. Maybe it was just that people who went there for school never wanted to leave the place, creating a large pool of local technical talent. Whatever the reason, high-tech ventures there thrived.

These new ventures were different in character, culture, and focus from the business start-ups that had preceded them. Perhaps Sandy Kurtzig, the founder and CEO of ASK Computer (a firm she grew to several hundred million in revenue before selling it off to Computer Associates for close to $500 million), put it best: "In the late 1930s the first pioneers had settled in the Valley. They were engineers like William Hewlett and David Packard who turned to business in order to invent and build the research instruments they couldn't find on the shelves of existing manufacturers. Now they were being joined by a new breed of young men—and they were all men—engineer-entrepreneurs as intent on profit as on product." This ethic was still alive and well thirty years later, when the failed Internet entrepreneur Michael Wolff described an important component of any business discussion he had in Silicon Valley: "how we, the people at the table, could make as much money as fast as possible—even if that meant doing what we knew to be wrong or futile." The business of business start-ups had changed, and not necessarily for the better.

As good an example as any of the new California business ethic can be found in the history of the Oracle Corporation, the world's second largest independent software company at the end of the twentieth century. Oracle was founded by Larry Ellison. After dropping out of college, he learned to program a computer as a way to make a living. In 1966 he moved to California intent on making his fortune. For the next ten years, he lived a revolving-door life as a programmer, moving from one job to another in rapid succession. At one of these jobs, working for the company Ampex, Ellison met two other programmers, Bob Miner and Ed Oates.

After leaving Ampex, Ellison went to work for a small firm, the Precision Instrument Company, as the vice president for systems development, his first-ever executive-like position. One project Precision Instrument was involved in was building and trying to sell a new device for storing large amounts of data—either computer data in its earliest manifestation or subsequently pictures of data in the manner of a microfilm machine. To make the machine work, the company needed software and began soliciting bids from independent contractors. Ellison recruited his two friends, Miner and Oates, to put in a bid on the programming job. After they submitted the low bid, they were awarded the contract and in 1977 set up Software Development Laboratories to execute the contract. At the time, Ellison still worked for Precision Instrument, overseeing the execution of the contract by the new company of which he was the largest shareholder. Despite the appearance of a conflict of interests, the relationship was amicable.

With the money they were earning on the Precision Instrument contract, the three partners began to talk about the kind of company they would like to become once the contract was finished. Tired of contract programming, despite its lucrative fee structure, they set out to become a seller of packaged software products, a market just beginning to emerge in the late 1970s. Miner, the most academic of the trio, pointed out some articles about the idea for a new invention that research software engineers at IBM had come up with, a relational database management system. Before the contract with Precision Instrument was over, the three began writing code for a new product based on this invention. When the product was ready a few months later, they decided to name it Oracle after the project all three had worked on while in the employ of Ampex. Later they would change the name of the company to Oracle as well.

The young company moved into new offices in Silicon Valley and set out to sell their new database product. Their first sale came about almost completely by chance when they were approached by the Central Intelligence Agency (CIA), which was looking for a relational database system built from the IBM invention. (IBM itself was not prepared to sell its own product in this area.) The CIA asked the small company to supply it with the product ready to run on two different computers, a mid-sized IBM computer and the Digital Equipment VAX line of minicomputers. Following up on the initial sale to the CIA, Ellison sold the product to naval intelligence in San Diego. The navy wanted the product to run on yet another operating system, Unix. The young company suddenly had three orders for its new product—on three different computers. But the only existing version of its product worked on a fourth computer a Digital Equipment PDP-11, the machine the young company had had access to during its work for Precision Instrument.

To fulfill the requirements of the contracts, Ellison's people converted the program to the programming language C, which would run on any computer then available. This decision, made under the press of events, would turn out to be worth billions to the fledgling company. By 1989, twelve years after the company was founded, it had revenues of $583 million (just short of $800 million). Seven years later, these revenues had increased to $4.2 billion and the company had earned $603 million. By then Ellison was a billionaire.

What kind of company did Ellison and his colleagues build? The Oracle way, if there was such a thing, was to win. According to Mike Wilson, who chronicled the rise of the company, a joke went around Silicon Valley in the mid-1990s that involved describing a toaster as it would be made by any of a number of different companies. A Xerox toaster would reputedly produce toast that kept getting lighter and lighter with each subsequent slice. IBM would make only one toaster and require its customers to submit their bread for toasting overnight. If Oracle made a toaster, the pundits said, "they would claim that their toaster was compatible with all brands and styles of bread, but when you got it home, you would discover the Bagel Engine was still in development, the Croissant Extension was three years away, and indeed the whole appliance was just blowing smoke." Oracle's cavalier way with its commitments to its customers was one of the major factors in the coining of the term "vaporware" to describe planned but not yet complete software products. Ellison, the chief salesman responsible for most of the obligations not met, could not have cared less. He had become one of the richest men in the world, which is just about all he ever really wanted to do. The lessons of Ellison were not lost on others in the burgeoning high-tech start-up industry.

AOL: You've Got Mail

As start-up activity associated with high-tech companies expanded in the late 1970s and 1980s, the whole process of starting a company became easier. A new kind of investment company, the venture capital firm, began to recognize the enormous fortunes to be made in backing such businesses. These firms, which promised investors in their funds returns of 30+ percent a year on their money, sprang up in California to serve the needs of the Silicon Valley ventures and in Massachusetts to serve the needs of the Route 128 technology belt around Boston and most points in between. Most investors in most of these funds made out quite handily. Most but not all of the entrepreneurs who tapped into these funds made out even better. With experienced, professional investors in the loop, there was little doubt left that the purpose of entrepreneurship was to make money.

One of the entrepreneurs who did not make a lot of money despite being in on the ground floor of one of the megaventures of the late twentieth century was Bill Von Meister. The son of a successful entrepreneur in the chemicals industry, Von Meister was a tinkerer, an inventor, and a serial entrepreneur. He was so much a dyed-in-the-wool entrepreneur that he seldom hung around with his ventures long enough to cash in. Three of his early business inventions were the Telemail system of fax mail delivery for Western Union, the Light-Alert device to let security guards turn on the lights in a building, and the Ray-Alert device to warn people of radiation emissions from their TV sets. None of these ventures succeeded, but they whet Von Meister's appetite for bigger and better things.

In 1975 Von Meister found an engineer with a technology that could be used to route long-distance telephone calls on the least expensive circuits. The company they founded, TDX Systems, received venture backing of $500,000 ($1.6 million) from an established telecommunications company, Cable & Wireless (C&W), PLC. When Von Meister ran through this initial seed money too quickly, C&W invested again, this time forcing the young entrepreneur to relinquish his share in the company. The company went on to exceed $1 billion in revenue as a subsidiary of C&W.

By 1978 the undaunted Von Meister was back with a new venture; this one involved transmitting data over the FM broadcast band for banks and grocery stores. This venture went bust before it had time to realize its potential. Convinced that the future was in the combination of telephone and computer technology, Von Meister went on to found the Source—one of the earliest on-line services aimed at the consumer market. To fund this deal, Von Meister went to an early venture investor, Jack Taub, who raised a loan for the new company. By late 1979 Taub had ousted Von Meister; he later sold the company to the Readers Digest organization for millions of dollars. Von Meister moved on to found the Home Music Store, a way to download music from recording companies direct to consumer homes. This venture, too, fell apart when traditional music companies began to think through what the venture might mean for their stock-in-trade sales. With his source of supply dried up, Von Meister decided to try the same thing with video games, a hot technology of the moment.

While Von Meister was wooing investors in this latest venture, he would often talk about the potential he had explored once before of using the core on-line technology to download software, news, stock quotations, airline reservations, and any number of other products through this new medium. Bear in mind that this was 1982, ten years before the Internet appeared on the scene. His spiel was so persuasive that two leading venture capital companies backed him with an initial $400,000 (just over $700,000) of seed capital. With this money, Von Meister set up Control Video Corporation (CVC) behind a car dealership in Vienna, Virginia. A year later Von Meister was demonstrating his prototype receiving device at the consumer electronics show in Las Vegas.

One of the people who watched the show with growing excitement was Stephen McConnell Case, the brother of one of the venture capitalists who had initially backed Von Meister in this deal. Case was a young MBA learning his trade as a middle manager at Pepsi's Pizza Hut division in Wichita, Kansas. He soon signed on to work for the fledgling venture. As he was recruiting employees, Von Meister was convincing his venture backers to put more money into the company so they could bring their new service to market. Before long the venture money invested would run into the tens of millions of dollars. In the meantime, the video games market went into decline, the money the company had in hand got spent, and Von Meister was first kicked upstairs in the company and then ousted. He moved on to launch a number of other ventures, all of which failed, and eventually died relatively young with essentially nothing to his name.

The CVC that Von Meister left behind in 1983 was a disaster. It had a product and a technology that no one was particularly interested in and no way to get them to market anyway. Just when the investors in CVC were about to despair, CBS, IBM, and Sears announced a new venture called Prodigy, the kind of full-service, on-line, timesharing system Von Meister had been talking about for so long. Armed with the evidence that someone else thought this was a good idea, CVC convinced the regional phone company, Bell South, to give the company $5 million ($8.2 million) more to launch a similar service called Masterline. It would compete head on with Prodigy and an older service called CompuServe. The company had a new life. The business plan they sold to Bell South promised 1.5 million subscribers and revenues of $110 million ($150 million) by 1989. The plan didn't work, and Bell South, eager to get out, asked for its money back—too late; the money had already been spent.

Facing another crisis, the people trying to resuscitate CVC came up with another idea. It approached Commodore Computer and offered to become its vehicle for an on-line service dedicated to users of Commodore computers. Commodore signed on, but to get this business up and running a new round of venture funding was needed. Against all odds, the former CVC raised $5 million (around $8.5 million), mostly from the original investors in the company, and created Quantum Computer Services from the remains of CVC.

The service went on-line on November 1, 1985. By mid-1987 the new company had revenues of $8.6 million ($13 million) and was turning a small profit. Commodore's success in the computer market was tailing off, however, and in order to grow Quantum turned to Apple Computer, offering the same kind of exclusive on-line service to Apple users. Just after the deal was done with Apple, the company signed a similar contract with Tandy Corporation to provide service for users of that company's TRS computers. Apple was not pleased. But with these deals in hand the company raised another $5 million (just over $7.5 million) from venture backers and expanded its service base to cover the broader range of users.

The relationship with Apple continued to go sour, and on October 2, 1989, Apple withdrew from the deal with Quantum, paying it $2.5 million ($3.5 million) to relinquish rights. Confronted with this crisis, the company changed its name to America Online (AOL) and vowed to go forward on its own. The rest, as people say, is history. With the commercialization of the Internet in the early 1990s and AOL's leadership position in the industry, AOL went on to become the premiere on-line service, with in excess of 15 million subscribers. It became large enough and strong enough to buy out one of its chief early rivals, CompuServe. When its stock went public, it quickly set new standards for technology stocks, making Case and his colleagues from the early days of the company billionaires. In early 2000 the company used its high-flying stock to acquire the media giant Time Warner in the largest merger ever. Von Meister would have been proud of them.

Transformation in the Concept of Business

The first three chapters of this book have traced the evolution of business from its beginnings in the late nineteenth century through its blossoming in the age of the Internet start-up near the end of the millennium. Companies founded in the nineteenth and early twentieth century were started by family members working together. More often than not, their early expansion was funded by family members who dipped into their own pockets or reached out to close friends who believed in them. These companies functioned as vehicles for building family wealth and preserving family assets for generations to come. As family-oriented companies, they treated employees as extended members of the founding family, offering them cradle-to-grave security in return for long hours and loyal service. Given their orientation toward wealth preservation, they tended to take a long view of business and were often criticized for not leaping on opportunities laid in front of them.

As the companies outgrew the managerial abilities of the founding families, they imported professional managers to see them on to their next level of growth. But they insisted on a firm set of financial systems and controls that would allow the founders to monitor how their legacy was being cared for.

The companies founded around the time of World War II were different in character and concept, if no less successful than their progenitors. For the most part, these companies were created by technocrats—engineers and scientists on the one hand and experts at functional activities like retailing on the other. As technocratically oriented individuals, they surrounded themselves with other technocrats. Perhaps in reaction to the parochial nature of companies that had come before them, many of these companies actively discouraged any form of nepotism in their ranks, arguing for a new idea of meritocracy in place of family values.

As these companies grew, they pioneered many of the practices that together came to be common in modern management. For example, although decentralization had for years been a feature of General Motors as an accidental by-product of its founding, the new wave of companies practiced decentralization to respect the talents and independence of the professional managers they recruited to their ranks. To tie the decentralized parts of their organizations together, they adopted techniques like strategic planning (which was invented in its modern form in the venerable General Electric Company but became the raison d'être of management of these latter-day companies).

The companies founded by the technocrats were put in place to provide a living for their founders, as were the more family-oriented firms of the earlier era. Very often there were other influences at work as well. Many of these technocrats wanted to be their own bosses—out from under the supervision, and often stultification, of the large, older companies around them. They also wanted to see commercialized some product or idea they held dear. Much of their satisfaction came from seeing something they had conceived brought to fruition in their own labs, factories, or stores and scooped up by eager consumers. That they got rich from commercializing their ideas was a by-product, not the driving rationale, of their existence.

A book I wrote with Terry Deal, *The New Corporate Cultures*, documents the rise of the notion of shareholder value as the guiding ethic of business. This idea began to get a serious hearing in the 1970s, as a new breed of investment bankers saw in these theories a way to make a lot of money quickly. As these corporate raiders, as they came to be known, put their thinking into practice, the influence of their ideas spread across the ranks of managers as well. More and more, executive compensation schemes were adapted to include stock options for senior managers. With their pay tied to stock options, senior managers began to pay greater attention to stock price levels and began to manage their companies as though a higher and higher stock price was the only legitimate objective of management itself. The founders of companies one hundred years ago might have argued strenuously with them, but they were no longer around to state their case.

Major shifts in perception do not occur in a vacuum, of course. At the same time the idea of shareholder value was sweeping the world of corporate management, a new kind of company, the ilk profiled in this chapter, was arising. These companies were started with the express purpose of making lots of money for their founders and their early investors, usually venture capitalists who did little beyond searching out promising new ventures to invest in. With the robust economy of the 1990s and the stock market boom that coincided with it, many of these founders and investors became rich indeed. At the same time, corporate managers were becoming rich off the stock market as well. What goes around comes around. The rewards entrepreneurs and managers alike were reaping from the flourishing stock market became the justification in itself for the practices they were following. Making money, as much of it as possible as fast as possible, soon became the driving ethic of everyone in business. Even older companies that arguably should have known better got caught up in the fever. Maximizing shareholder value and the individual wealth of the lucky few was in. The Internet companies launched in the 1990s, like Amazon.com, Yahoo, Lycos, E-Bay, and PriceLine.com, represented only the last flowering of this movement, as their valuations soared into the stratosphere while their businesses experienced mostly profitless growth.

Was this the wave of the future? Were all the old rules for business success to be discarded and new ones written to capture the spirit of the age? Or was this the death rattle of a movement that had come too far too fast based on a set of ideas that had real limitations? The rest of this book examines this issue in detail—putting forth a vision of how the best of all the eras of business portrayed to date could come together in a new era of profitable growth for all.

PART TWO

The Impact of Shareholder Value

Shareholder value took hold as the driving ethic of business in the last two decades of the twentieth century. The bellwether for this shift was the venerable General Electric Company (GE) under the stewardship of its chairman, Jack Welch. Chapter 4 examines in some detail how shareholder value thinking has affected GE, not only its soaring stock price but its prospects for the future. The chapter then takes stock of the effect shareholder value thinking has had on the legion of older industrial companies that followed GE's lead. The chapter's conclusion, that all these companies appear to have mortgaged their futures in return for a higher stock price now, does not bode well for the economy at large.

Many observers of the economic scene, however, point to the emergence of the "new economy" as the engine of growth and renewal. Although there are as many definitions of what the new economy consists of as there are economic analysts, all would agree that the new economy is best epitomized by the companies founded in the final twenty years of the twentieth century, particularly those associated with the Internet. Chapter 5, therefore, looks at several of the most prominent of these new companies to see if they do indeed offer a promise for the future consonant with their stratospheric stock market valuations. Unfortunately, investors appear to be fooling themselves in their rush to buy their own piece of this future. Today's investors in Internet stocks will likely never receive value commensurate with the cost of their investments. In fact, the prices paid for these new-economy stocks bear a closer relationship to the prices investors paid for tulips in the 1630s before the tulip craze came to its inevitable demise. Chapter 5 concludes on the somber note that the rush to embrace shareholder value thinking has given rise to a stock market bubble while producing little of lasting value for the future.

CHAPTER 4

Mortgaging the Future

As we have seen, companies founded in different periods adopt characteristics of their times. Some of these characteristics they never shed. As times change, however, successful companies adapt to the circumstances and ideas around them. Thus, for example, some of the earliest adopters and most ardent adherents of so-called modern management practices were big companies founded around different ideas years earlier. As the twentieth century raced to its conclusion, the new philosophy of business was maximizing shareholder value. Succinctly put, this philosophy has come to entail getting as much as you can as fast as you can for shareholders, who almost always include (through options or direct shareholdings) managers of the enterprise itself. Although the most visible exponents of this philosophy were the raft of high-tech start-ups, particularly those involving the Internet, managers in older industrial companies were also quick to sign up. The shareholder value movement gave these managers the excuse, if not the mandate, to build enormous personal fortunes, typically in the hundreds of millions of dollars, on the back of their share options in the company. Prior to the emergence of the shareholder value movement, hired managers of large companies were lucky to end their careers modestly wealthy, perhaps worth as much as several million dollars, for their years of toil in the corporate vineyard. Who wouldn't be enthusiastic about a new philosophy that justified multiplying personal wealth by factors of ten or more?

Most of the high-tech exponents of the shareholder value ethic made their money by launching business ventures that brought new products and services to market. Although founding entrepreneurs often became wealthy simply by issuing stock in their ventures without ever proving the viability or efficacy of their concepts (to say nothing of earning a profit from the venture itself), the basis of their wealth was innovation (and as always, timing). This was not true for the managers of more mature companies who also made fortunes adopting the shareholder value ethic. They squeezed more earnings than anyone previously had thought possible out of their often moribund corporations. The means they used to do this almost always included a series of "management innovations" thrust on them by specialized academics and consultants. Chief among these were downsizing staff, outsourcing noncritical (and some critical) staff functions to lower-cost providers, and mergers (with, it seemed, virtually anyone and everyone for whom a good story could be put together to sell to Wall Street). Adoption of these management techniques undercut some of the most deeply held assumptions about corporate life, such as the notion that loyal and performing employees deserved employment for life. The result was skyrocketing stock prices, mounting personal fortunes for the managers who enthusiastically undertook these actions, and a massive widening of the gap between the haves and have-nots in society.

Was the journey worth it? Did the innovators in high-tech start-ups really add so much new wealth to society? Or were their innovations simply mispriced in the stock market? Did the reborn advocates of shareholder value in older industrial companies really take decisive steps late in life to ensure the long-term competitive viability of their companies? Or did they simply take the money available to them, regardless of the cost to others, and run? This chapter and the next focus on these questions.

GE Adopts Shareholder Value

The General Electric Company was founded near the end of the nineteenth century to exploit the commercialization of the major new technology of the day, electricity. Within thirty years of its founding, the company had become one of the largest in the world, manufacturing a range of basic electrical products, including turbines and generators, transformers, electric motors, light bulbs, and electrical appliances for the home. The heart of the company was its research laboratories in Schenectady, New York, which, under the direction of Charles Proteus Steinmetz, spit out the steady stream of inventions and innovations that propelled the company to its leadership status. In its early days, the company was also an innovator in the social realm. It pioneered the practice of extending benefits and pensions to its thousands of workers. If any one company represented the finest of traditional big business, it was GE.

GE was also an early adopter of shareholder value. Led by Jack Welch since 1981, GE came to epitomize the shareholder value era. It was the first company to initiate massive downsizing of its staff. It was the first to restructure itself by hiving off parts of the business deemed incapable of superior performance and replacing them with businesses positioned well in faster-growing and more profitable segments of the market. It has been a major acquirer and divestor of businesses. And it has seen its market valuation soar throughout the 1980s and 1990s to make it the largest market capitalization company in the world (until it was surpassed, recently, by the technological marvels Microsoft and Cisco). As a devotee of shareholder value, it has served its shareholders extremely well. Or has it?

Let's look at some of GE's positive achievements over almost two decades. Its revenue went from $25 billion in 1980 to $100 billion in 1998–300 percent growth over the period (about 130 percent in real terms, or 7 percent a year, after factoring in inflation during the period). Even more impressive, its net earnings went from $1.5 billion to $9.3 billion—a jump of 520 percent (250 percent in real terms, or almost 14 percent a year), almost but not quite twice the rate of its increase in revenue. (Since it consolidated the operations of its finance subsidiary, GE Financial Services (GEFS), in 1990, the revenue increase figures are likely inflated, further underscoring the earnings achievements of this shareholder-oriented management era in the company.) Total returns to shareholders were, of course, much higher, as the stock price soared during most of Welch's tenure as CEO: a total increase in excess of 1,200 percent overall.

How were these phenomenal gains achieved in an industrial behemoth like GE? What legacy has Jack Welch, the most shareholder-value-driven manager of his era, left to future investors in GE? What is the future for this great company once the Welch era is over?

The GE Agenda for Change

Welch pioneered the use of tools that became the kit bag of a whole generation of stock-price-oriented managers of the shareholder value era. Chief among these were restructuring and downsizing.

Restructuring

More than anything else, the era of Welch will be remembered for the transformation he wrought in the composition of GE's business. When he took over as CEO, Welch said he was committed to being in businesses that were number one or number two in their market segments. Immediately after taking over, Welch set out with a vengeance to make this happen. The flow of acquisitions and disposals was as follows:

1981   Acquisition of Intersil (semiconductors) for $235 million (plus six other smaller companies).
1982   Sale of central air conditioning business and parts of Utah International (mining); total disposals in 1981 and 1982

amounted to seventy-one businesses worth $500 million; total acquisitions in the same time period cost $1 billion.

1983   Acquisition of AMIC (mortgage insurer); acquisition of Tegas Systems, a computer-aided engineering software firm; announcement of intent to sell small appliances business.

1984   Sale of rest of Utah International for $2.4 billion; acquisition of Employers Reinsurance for $1.1 billion; sale of housewares division.

1986   Acquisition of RCA for $6.4 billion; acquisition of 80 percent interest in Kidder Peabody.

1987   Trade of consumer electronics businesses to Thomson in return for their medical equipment business; sale of parts of RCA; acquisition of Navistar Financial, Canada.

1988   Acquisition of Borg-Warner's chemical businesses for $2.3 billion; acquisition of Roper Corporation for $507 million; acquisition of Montgomery Ward Credit Corporation for $718 million; disposal of international construction and semiconductor businesses and seven radio stations.

1989   Acquisition of Bombardier's locomotive business and remaining 62 percent of FGIC Corporation.

1990   Acquisition of Tungsram lighting business in Hungary for $150 million; acquisition of several leasing businesses or portfolios for $666 million; sale of Ladd Petroleum for $542 million; acquisition of several other financial services businesses for a total of $526 million.

1991   Acquisition of engine overhaul business from British Airways for $483 million; acquisition of Thorn EMI lighting business in Britain; acquisition for several billions of a number of leasing businesses.

1992   Acquisition of Avis Europe's vehicle leasing business.

1993   Transfer of aerospace business to a company controlled by Martin Marietta, a transaction worth $3.3 billion; acquisition of GNA Corporation and Union Pacific Insurance Company.

1994   Closing down of Kidder Peabody.

1995   Acquisition of Frankona and Aachen Reinsurance in Europe and a number of financing businesses around the world.

1996   Acquisition of Union Fidelity Life Insurance Company, Life Insurance Company of Virginia, and First Colony Corporation.

1997   Acquisition of Colonial Penn (auto insurance) and a number of other interests.

1998   Acquisition of Eagle Star Reinsurance Company, Ltd., and several other financial services firms; acquisition of a number of medical equipment manufacturers; acquisition of a number of other small add-ons spread across GE's portfolio of businesses.

One reason acquisitions were so favored, especially in the latter years of Welch's tenure, was that they involved the balance sheet, not the operating statement of the company—that is, an acquisition properly done had no immediate earnings impact. The most important of Welch's disposals were his sale of Utah International and small appliance, consumer electronics, and aerospace businesses, although these larger examples of divestitures were only the tip of the iceberg in relation to the hundreds of businesses Welch disposed of during his stewardship. He also bought businesses to position the company for greater growth and profitability. If observers of Welch's recent acquisition activity were to comment that the scope of the acquisitions seemed rather small in scale, compared, for example, to the earlier acquisition of RCA, they would be correct. A recent *New York Times* article quoted Welch as being primarily interested in "niches" to support existing businesses. According to the article, Welch said the niches would give GE "high barriers to entry" by competitors, thereby enhancing profitability. Whether they will succeed in building a lasting future for GE remains to be seen.

Welch's recent reluctance to pursue major acquisitions may be due to his previous experience. Not all of his larger, early purchases succeeded, with notable failures and subsequent dispositions including Kidder Peabody and the consumer electronics elements of RCA. But several, including NBC (purchased as part of the RCA acquisition), the medical equipment businesses of Thomson (now included in GE's Medical Equipment Group) and the many acquisitions that spurred the growth of GE Financial Services, have had a lasting influence on the performance of the company.

When Welch took over GE in the early 1980s, the bulk of its operating profits were generated by traditional businesses like aircraft engines, major appliances, industrial products, power generation equipment, and so-called technical products (which included medical devices and plastics, Welch's former areas). By 1997 these businesses still contributed almost $4.8 billion in operating profits to GE—roughly 42 percent of GE's total operating profits for the year (comparable figures were not reported in 1998). The phenomenal GE Financial Services contributed another $4.4 billion (up from about $100 million in the last year of leadership by Reginald Jones, Welch's predecessor)—fully 38 percent of the company's operating profit that year. GEFS contributed 40.8 percent of GE's net income in 1998 because of the highly profitable nature of its activities. No doubt a lot of management was required to maintain the traditional business's contribution to GE's overall success, yet without the extraordinary growth and profitability of GEFS, GE would have just about stood still during the Welch era. When the incremental $1-billion earnings of NBC are added to the picture, Welch's restructuring success becomes clearer: He built financial services and acquired (and made profitable) a TV network as the main means of restructuring the company during his tenure in office—no mean achievement over a twenty-year term. With the traditional businesses of GE still continuing to contribute, the company surely is well poised for a successful future.

Downsizing

Welch inherited a company with just over 400,000 loyal and committed employees when he took over from Jones. One of his first priorities was to get this number down by getting rid of the deadwood. With the brief blip imposed by his acquisition of RCA in 1986, this he has done admirably, as shown in Figure 4.1. Given the modest growth in employment in the late 1990s, most of which occurred in GE's financial operations, Welch installed new management at GE Financial Services with a charter to get its costs down. Even with this increase, revenue productivity per employee rose from just over $62,000 in 1981 to $342,897 by 1998—a phenomenal jump by any measure. The net elimination of approximately 120,000 employees from the company during Welch's tenure probably saved the company around $5–7 billion in annual operating costs—savings for the most part extracted from GE's traditional manufacturing businesses. Put in this context, the $7.8 billion expansion in net earnings during the Welch era is not quite so impressive. The bulk of it was achieved on the backs of laid-off workers.

Milking the Traditional Businesses

Less visible than GE's successes under Welch are the prices paid to achieve these successes. Since its founding as a vehicle to commercialize Thomas Edison's inventions, GE has been one of the premier technology companies in the world. Most of this technology is embedded in its traditional businesses. R&D spending is the fuel that keeps this technology alive (little such investment is needed in the "new" businesses of financial services and TV). How has R&D fared under Welch?

R&D expenditures from the company's own funds (i.e., excluding research contracts primarily with the military) went from $760 million in 1981 to $1.54 billion in 1998—a rise of 102 percent (a bit less than 6 percent a year). In real terms, this increase is negligible—less than one-third of a percent a year. In relation to revenue, it marks a steep decline in R&D spending, as shown in Figure 4.2 (albeit with revenues distorted upward by

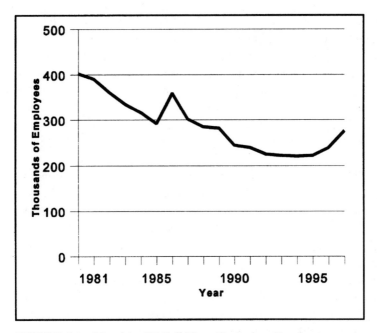

FIGURE 4.1   Trend in GE Full-Time-Equivalent Employment

SOURCE: GE Annual Reports.

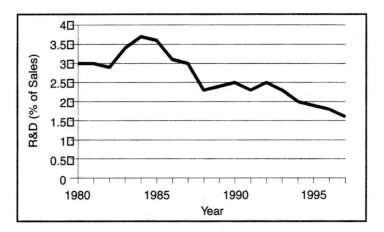

FIGURE 4.2   Trend in GE R&D Spending as a Percent of Revenue

SOURCE: GE Annual Reports.

the consolidation of GEFS in 1990). Had R&D expenditures kept pace with revenue, they would have totaled almost $3.1 billion in 1998—almost twice the level GE actually spent. Thus, about $1.5 billion of the jump in GE's operating earnings was in effect funded by cutting back on investment in R&D, the fuel that makes traditional manufacturing businesses grow.

Looked at in competitive terms, GE now spends about 1.6 percent of its revenue on R&D (not counting government R&D contracts, which fluctuate from year to year). This compares with average corporate R&D spending in the United States of 2.4 percent of revenue in 1988, the last year the National Science Foundation published such figures. GE of course counters that a large part of its business, broadcasting and financial services in particular, is not R&D intensive. Even allowing for this, GE still spends only about 3.3 percent of its manufacturing revenues on R&D. By contrast, Honda Motor Company of Japan spends 5 percent of its revenue on research, NEC of Japan spends 7 percent of its revenue, and high-tech companies like Microsoft spend as much as 10 percent of revenue on R&D. GE spokesperson Joyce Hergenhan was reported to have said about these R&D spending figures, "We are world leaders in medical imaging. We are world leaders in gas turbines. We are world leaders in plastics. Do we have to be in Walkmen and pantyhose as well?" Maybe not Walkmen and pantyhose, but there are certainly a lot of other exciting areas of technology GE might have considered investing in if it had not been so focused on immediate bottom-line results.

Not only has R&D spending, especially for traditional manufacturing businesses, been penurious under Welch, but the vast majority of the head-count reductions GE achieved during the Welch era came from these same, traditional businesses. It thus looks as if the increase in operating earnings realized by these businesses all came about from cuts—in their human capabilities and in the technology that underpinned them.

Although not conclusive by any means, the size of the cuts in these businesses suggests there may not be much left in them to spur future contributions. Surely GE's medical equipment and plastics businesses, both favorites of Welch, have state-of-the-art technology. Similarly, the aircraft engine business, one of three competitors in the global market, has enough technology left to be able to continue to compete effectively (although some critics questioned this after Welch forced massive layoffs in the engineering staffs of the division). GE's market-leading gas turbine technology, however, was developed in the 1970s, its steam turbine technology decades earlier. Cutbacks in both staffing and R&D spending in these businesses may well have seriously undermined their long-term competitive positions. But since most of these businesses operate in the electrical oligarchy, their competitors have also endured sizable cutbacks over the same time frame. This may mean that GE's traditional businesses, despite the severity of the cutbacks they have endured, are still competitively viable. But for how long?

Investment in Financial Services

While he was extracting costs of all kinds from GE's traditional manufacturing businesses, Welch invested heavily in financial services as a means to induce increased earnings for the company. These investments were spectacularly successful. GEFS's contribution to net income increased from just over $100 million in Jones's last year at the helm to $3.8 billion by 1998—just over 40 percent of GE's reported net. In operating profit terms, the bulk of these earnings ($3.7 billion in 1997) was derived from financing activities covering everything from credit cards to airplanes to freight containers around the world. The second biggest source of financial earnings came from the even more prosaic area of insurance, which contributed operating earnings of almost $1.3 billion in 1997. Although these appear to be attractive businesses for GE to participate in, GE has just about reached the limit of what it can achieve from the financial arena. If earnings from financial services continue to rise as a proportion of the whole, the market will come to see GE as the financial institution it increasingly is. But financial institutions in relatively mundane areas such as consumer finance, leasing, and insurance do not command the stock market premiums that diversified firms like GE do, as illustrated in Figure 4.3 on the next page. Most investment analysts, in fact, believe that a 40 percent contribution by a financial subsidiary to the parent's profit is about the limit. Further relative increases in financially derived earnings are unlikely to flow through to stock price levels as price-earnings ratios (P/Es) adjust downward to reflect the changing nature of the business and its risks.

The second major problem with GEFS's contribution to GE's recent success is the nature of the business itself. Earnings from GEFS soared through the 1990s, but so did the U.S. economy. In due course this unprecedented expansion will come to an end. During a recession, write-offs, particularly of consumer receivables, typically skyrocket. In 1998 GE wrote off a total of $1.6 billion in consumer receivables (1.3 percent of the receivables outstanding). In the recession of 1990 and 1991, not a particularly severe one by historical standards, GE's level of write-offs increased by about 45 percent. Other companies involved in consumer finance were less fortunate, with write-off increases ranging from a low of around 15 percent to a high of 125 percent. Write-offs, whatever their level, come right off the bottom line. Hence, in the not-too-distant future GEFS earnings are likely to suffer a

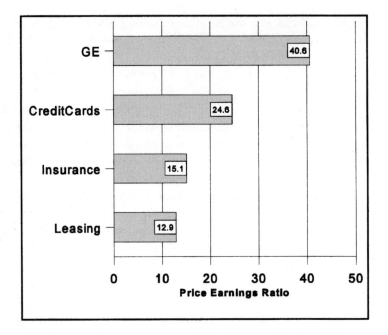

FIGURE 4.3   Financial Services P/E Ratios Compared to GE

SOURCE: Annual Reports, 1998 (comparisons based on averages of relevant companies).

decline on the order of $1 billion if GE repeats its own experience from the earlier recession or as much as $3–5 billion if GE's experience sours in line with that of others. Even ten years of positive momentum will be unable to hide such a massive—if temporary—setback.

Over the Welch years, GE has been reluctant to use write-offs as a way of clearing its books of bad debts. In 1983, when Tiger International (parent of North American Railcar) went belly up, instead of writing off the loans GE got into the railcar leasing business itself (and, to its credit, subsequently made it a profitable business for the company). When leased airplanes came off lease prematurely, leaving GE holding the bag, GE provided the seed capital to convert the planes for use as cargo vessels, which were in turn leased to its own newly started freight airline. When the Houston Astros baseball team defaulted on its loans, leading other banks in the lending consortium to write off the loans, GE decided to keep the loans on its books and run the team for a couple of years, until selling it to other investors.

GE's success in "managing" its way out of lending difficulties was so impressive that Nicholas Heymann of Prudential Securities was heard to opine,

"The old idea was that you shouldn't pay a premium for GE stock because nearly 40% of earnings come from financial services firms, a low P/E business. But the market is learning that Capital [GE Capital, the original name of GE Financial Services] is different from cyclical financial services firms, that its better than 15 percent growth is practically guaranteed." Although in keeping with the tenor of the times, this remark does not bear up under scrutiny over the longer term. The reason financial services companies trade at lower P/E ratios is because they cannot forever insulate themselves from cyclical downturns. GE is no different. When the next downturn comes, the proof of the pudding will be in the eating.

Thus, Welch's primary vehicle for increasing shareholder value during his tenure as CEO has about run out of steam. With the earnings of the nonfinancial parts of GE about at their natural limits—generated as they were by waves of cost-cutting—where can GE turn next for growth?

Investment in Service-Led Growth

Welch clearly recognized this impending dilemma some time ago and launched a major initiative in the rest of GE's businesses to spur growth in services—for manufacturing businesses, primarily in the aftermarket of their equipment sales. The growth of this segment of GE's business has been dramatic, as shown in Figure 4.4 on the next page.

The rise in service revenue, however, has not been able to keep up with the rise in overall revenue, despite Welch's frequent exhortations to his managers. This suggests that the strategy of emphasizing services in GE's traditional businesses, though sound, is not a substitute for the earnings windfall the company has seen from its financial services activity. Moreover, even though the profitability of these service revenues is rumored to be high compared to their underlying manufacturing parents, after-sales service, even when supported with clever technology, tends to be labor intensive. In the cost-conscious world of GE, one wonders how long these initiatives into service will continue to be the chairman's pets.

Investment in Stock Buybacks

The biggest single and sustained investment during the Welch era at GE was an investment in buying back GE stock in the stock market. At a time when Welch believed he could not afford to maintain employment levels or increase spending on R&D, he found the resources to purchase about $30 billion of GE stock. Although stock buybacks are an efficient method of returning capital to shareholders and a magnificent way of boosting stock price

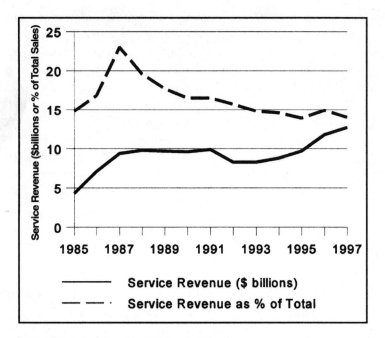

FIGURE 4.4   Trend in GE Service Revenue

SOURCE: GE Annual Reports.

levels for holders of stock options, by no means do they help provide a secure future for the company. But they do help to sustain a rising stock price level, the ultimate goal of any shareholder-value-oriented manager. Welch is conscious of this fact, of course. In a statement to security analysts accompanying his latest stock buyback announcement, Welch indicated that buying back stock was a better way to generate value for shareholders than taking a "wild swing" on an acquisition or investing in new technology.

The bottom line, therefore, is that GE, the old-line company most conspicuously managed by shareholder value rules, has just about run out of options. It has invested nearly as much as it can in the higher-margin/faster-growth financial arena without having its share multiple marked down. Its attempts to spur growth in services related to its traditional manufacturing businesses have been inadequate. And it appears to have milked these traditional businesses dry in its devotion to an ever-increasing share price. Despite his reputation as a manager, Welch laid off over a 100,000 people, presumably because he couldn't find anything useful for them to do, while holding R&D spending flat in real terms and investing heavily in stock buybacks. It is fair to wonder whether future share owners will give him high marks.

GE is of course in no danger of going bankrupt. It is a great company. It will continue to make its myriad products and sell its myriad services for the foreseeable future. But it will not likely be able to sustain either the revenue growth or even the level of earnings that did so much to push its share price to ever higher levels. With Welch in place until early 2001, there is little doubt he will find some way to keep up the earnings growth at least until he steps down. For example, he has already announced his intention to address costs in the financial services arm of GE's business portfolio. He has also indicated that he believes even more costs can be cut from GE's traditional manufacturing businesses. But what then? Pity his poor successor, who will have to find a new way to run the business in order to maintain GE's successful track record. What kind of a legacy is that?

What Is GE Really Worth?

Because of the long-lasting expansion of the U.S. economy, coupled with a steady growth in investable earnings on the part of individual investors, the stock market boomed throughout the 1990s. With its devotion to shareholder value maximization and its unending string of quarter-to-quarter earnings gains, GE has virtually led the way. GE's stock market gain has far outstripped its operating gains, however. This difference can be seen most directly in GE's ever-escalating price-earnings ratio on the market. At a P/E ratio in excess of 40, GE is now rated as a true growth stock by willing investors in the market.

A stock price and the P/E ratio it represents indicate the value investors place on a company's stock. In the classic terms of Benjamin Graham and David Dodd (the original gurus of security analysis), they are a measure of what investors eventually expect to get back from the company over the longer term. Although short-term stock market fluctuations may bring distortions, the basic concept is valid. An investor in any stock, GE included, expects to be paid back out of the future earnings stream of the company. To keep things simple, Graham, in his landmark book *The Intelligent Investor,* provided a formula by which investors could measure what a particular equity investment was worth to them. In essence this formula involves discounting future earnings streams as a way of validating the company's stock price (or its P/E ratio, depending on which one prefers to look at). Although modern followers of the stock market may pooh-pooh Graham and Dodd as being too conservative and old-fashioned, their benchmark formula is still useful in calibrating the relative worth of individual investments. How does GE fare against such a benchmark?

As discussed earlier, GE's current valuation in the stock market is already subject to a number of caveats. A lot of its earnings today come from financial services traditionally given a lower rating in the stock market because of their higher volatility. GE's present valuation does not really reflect this fact of life for the company. Moreover, under Welch's leadership GE has squeezed its costs and cut back its relative spending on R&D. This means it may find it difficult to sustain its record of steadily rising earnings in the future, independent of the overvaluation of the financial portion of its earnings stream. Let's consider how all these factors might play out in relation to the likely true value of GE's stock today. GE's P/E ratio at the time of writing was 40.6. In Graham and Dodd's terms, this suggests that GE will be able to increase its earnings year after year into the future by about 16–17 percent a year in perpetuity. But during Welch's tenure, earnings have increased at only around 12 percent a year. What impact would a continuation of this historical trend or other foreseeable developments have on GE's value in the market? Let's look at three possibilities:

> *GE's P/E ratio, according to Graham, would be around 30 if historical earnings trends prevailed (including a full valuation for GE Capital's faster-growing earnings stream).* In other words, a fair stock market price for GE would be about 75 percent of its current level, if Graham and Dodd's reasoning were to prevail. With all the arguments suggesting that Graham and Dodd are simply out-of-date, perhaps this one-third overvaluation of GE's stock today should be thought of as the Graham and Dodd premium, not an actual overvaluation of the company. (In technical terms, the one-third higher valuation can be explained by a decrease in the equity risk factor modern investors are willing to accept on their investments in equities.)
>
> *GE's P/E ratio would be around 20 if the market began to discount the value of its financial services earnings stream.* In other words, if GEFS's contribution to GE's earnings were valued in line with other financial services companies now traded on the market, GE's stock price today would be trading at about double its justifiable level, according to Graham and Dodd, if analysts started looking more carefully at where its earnings come from. If the Graham and Dodd premium were added back into GE's stock, raising its level by one-third, GE's stock price would still be trading today at a level one-third above its sustainable long-term level.
>
> *GE's P/E ratio could fall as far as 15 if GE's traditional businesses are unable to sustain their historical increases in earnings and if financial ser-*

vices earnings are downgraded by the market. This implies a stock price level of around one-third of its current price level for this venerable old-line company.

This all assumes that the current era of uninterrupted growth continues unabated. To test the effect of a recession, either severe (2 percent decline in gross domestic product, or GDP, followed by no growth for two years) or moderate (simply no economic growth for two years), I calculated how badly GE's stock price might be hit—with and without the Graham and Dodd premium. The results of these speculations are as follows:

In a more moderate recession, GE's P/E ratio could dip to 15. Figuring in the Graham and Dodd premium, this would still imply a stock price level at about half of today's level.

As a result of a severe recession, GE's P/E ratio might fall to 10. This would imply a stock price a couple of years down the road at about 25 percent of the heady levels of the late 1990s. Even with the Graham and Dodd premium taken into account, GE's stock price would be less than one-third of its current level.

If everything bad happened, GE's P/E ratio could crash to 7 or 8. This assumes a recession of some intensity. It also assumes GE's financial services earnings were downgraded by the market (which might well happen if large write-offs occurred as a result of the recession). It also assumes that GE's traditional manufacturing businesses would struggle to regain earnings momentum after the worst effects of the recession were over. The implication for GE: a stock price at about 15 to 20 percent what it is now.

I am not in the business of predicting future stock price levels; the calculations above are meant to be illustrative at best. But from what I know about the company, I find little reason to justify a scenario where GE's stock price goes any higher on a sustained basis. Perhaps—just perhaps—GE's adoption and pursuit of the shareholder value ethic has done a disservice to its long-term shareholders as senior managers took the money and ran. (Welch is expected to leave GE at the end of 2000 with personal wealth between $750 million and $1 billion as a result of cashing in his GE stock options.)

Where GE Treads, Others Follow

GE has always been a bit of a bellwether for corporate activity around the world. What was true in the 1960s when GE introduced strategic planning and most companies rushed to copy it, was true in the 1970s when GE CEO Reg Jones was the most respected businessman of his generation, and is true today when Welch's tenure is celebrated by a book with the title *Jack Welch Speaks*. It is not surprising, therefore, that a lot of companies followed GE's lead in embracing the shareholder value ethic.

Time did not permit me to make as extensive an analysis of all these other companies as I made for GE (and in any case an evaluation of stock market price levels and their justification is not the main purpose of this book). Instead, I used some crude measures of the extent to which other companies have followed GE's lead since the 1980s. Specifically, I checked

> *the extent to which these companies had downsized their organization:* GE under Welch cut out about 30 percent of its employees. Any company that substantially shrunk its workforce seemed to warrant inclusion in the GE shareholder value fan club.
>
> *the extent to which companies had reduced real spending on R&D:* GE's spending on R&D was flat in real terms during Welch's tenure. I included in my analysis any other company that showed flat or declining R&D (as well as reduced head count).
>
> *the extent to which companies engaged in wholesale restructuring activities involving the acquisition and disposal of parts of their operations:* GE was extremely aggressive in this arena; I looked only for evidence that others were pursuing a similar route.
>
> *the extent to which companies were investing heavily in stock buyback programs:* Again, the measure I used was simply an indication of repeated buybacks rather than a quantification of buybacks in relationship to total capitalization.

Using this screening, I found that almost one-third of the hundred largest market capitalization companies in the United States followed GE's lead in pursuing shareholder value maximization, employing the same tools GE found so useful in its own quest. The companies that met this test include a lot of household names:

General Motors
IBM
Sears
K-Mart
Boeing
Hewlett-Packard (surprisingly)
United Technologies

Caterpillar
Xerox
International Paper
Dow Chemical
Allied Signal
Pepsico
3M
Gillette
Colgate
Procter & Gamble

Most on this list are traditional companies like GE (the exceptions being a handful of companies, like 3M, Xerox, and Hewlett-Packard that Roger Trapp, the respected British business journalist, says were ruefully thankful for the "help" they received from Wall Street in managing their companies). Combined, the revenues of these companies exceed $500 billion—well over 5 percent of the U.S. GDP. (Weighing the total revenue of a collection of multinational companies against GDP is hardly comparing apples to apples, but the comparison does give some idea of how big a portion of the economy may be caught in the shareholder value trap. My guess is that if the analysis had covered more than the top one hundred companies in terms of market capitalization, the extent of the economic exposure would be on the order of 10–20 percent of GDP.) If these followers of GE's lead were in a similar position to GE—having apparently mortgaged their long-term future in support of a higher immediate stock price level—just how much overinflation might be built into the stock prices of these companies today? Although I recognize the limitations of using Graham and Dodd's techniques to value stocks in today's era, these seemed as good a metric as any for computing relative valuations—adjusted, as suggested above, for the Graham and Dodd premium (that is, my estimate for how much Graham and Dodd's methodology understates the current value of stocks on the market). The results of this exercise show that

> the average GE follower is today valued at approximately *twice* its Graham and Dodd predicted valuation
> adjusting for the Graham and Dodd premium, current valuations are at least *one-third too high*
> if a modest recession were to hit and affect these companies' performance accordingly, current market valuations would be *three times higher* than could be justified using Graham and Dodd's methodology, even correcting for the Graham and Dodd premium

The pursuit of shareholder value maximization following the lead of a company like GE appears to have produced a stock market valuation for old-line companies almost twice as high as can be justified by conservative financial analysis principles under reasonable assumptions about how the economy will unfold over the next few years. This certainly represents the attainment of high levels of shareholder value for current shareholders who have ridden these stocks up to such dizzy heights. But what of people who buy the stocks today?

The overvaluation of stocks is simply a symptom of the failure of the shareholder value ethic to produce anything of lasting value. The real problem is in the details of what companies have done to achieve inflated stock price levels. Across the board, companies have cut back on staffing. Some of the staff cuts undoubtedly involved trimming fat that had accumulated over the years and hampered the competitiveness of the companies. Others, however, involved reductions in the human capital companies will likely need to build a profitable and sustainable future.

Along with slashing human capital, companies have cut heavily into their R&D spending in pursuit of higher profits and a higher stock price now. Although difficult to measure directly, reductions in R&D spending in due course restrict the flow of ideas for future products and technologies. (Of course without the human capital to pursue these new ideas a decline in the idea pipeline may be a moot point. Who would execute the ideas if they had been developed?) Without new products and technologies, any business will eventually stagnate.

Defenders of the shareholder value movement argue that the "new economy" is rewriting the rules by which companies and the economy should be run. The next chapter looks at these arguments in detail but finds little of comfort to assuage concerns about the future.

CHAPTER 5

New Economy or
False Dawn?

Defenders of the shareholder value movement and the surging stock market that accompanied it argue strenuously that the changes in business in the last two decades of the twentieth century were essential for its long-term viability. The downsizings, outsourcings, and restructurings companies undertook were necessary for them to regain their competitive edge in increasingly global markets, these exponents claim. When making this argument, most people conveniently forget that major competitors around the world, particularly the Japanese and Asian tigers, were mostly on their uppers as the century rushed to a close. If they do acknowledge this, they cite the renewed competitiveness of American business as a key factor.

The run-up in stock prices that accompanied the changes in individual businesses was justified, these defenders say, by the demonstrably improved performance of companies, as evidenced by steadily rising quarterly earnings. That these earnings increases may have been achieved at the expense of long-term growth and viability is seldom mentioned. When stock market valuations of companies like General Electric and its Dow-Jones industrial average peers began to climb to indefensible levels in the late 1990s, despite comments about "irrational exuberance" from Alan Greenspan, the respected head of the Federal Reserve Bank, defenders of the new ethic of business found another justification for their optimism. This justification was the emergence of the "new economy," as epitomized by the Internet and the fundamental changes in the patterns of future business it promised. Enthusiasm for the new economy was most evident in the valuations afforded Internet-related start-up companies like Yahoo and Amazon.com when they came to market in the latter half of the 1990s. Indeed, the Internet boom carried the stock market to even higher record levels than those Greenspan criticized earlier in the decade. Following the old Wall Street adage "Never argue with the tape" (i.e., the stock market ticker), Greenspan himself turned silent as the market set record after record.

There is very little doubt that the advent and rapid acceptance of the Internet is one of the most important technological changes ever to affect business. With its promise of universal access to all (who are well-off enough to have access to an Internet-capable computer), the Internet is dramatically changing the face of business. Just as the steam engine powered the industrial revolution in the early nineteenth century and the adoption of electricity and the telephone powered the growth of big business in the early twentieth century, the Internet will (and in some instances already has) change forever how virtually all companies do business. E-commerce applications for consumers are making traditional investment in bricks and mortar obsolete for retailers. Internet-enabled order-entry systems have already changed the face of business-to-business commerce around the world. The instant accessibility of information of all kinds over the Internet is making libraries obsolete—as fast as their contents can be rendered into digital format and stored on Internet-accessible file servers.

But how fast will change occur? It was almost seventy years after the invention of the steam engine that the industrial revolution took hold. It was nearly fifty years after the discovery of electricity before major cities around the world were wired for light. It took almost as long after the invention of modern computers before their real power was unleashed on desktops around the world. Are the Internet and the merger of computer and communications technology it represents really that much different that they will instantaneously, in economic terms, revolutionize how the world works? Even if the Internet's potential for change is real (and I strongly suspect it is), will the new-economy companies it spawns justify the promise of their early market capitalizations?

Advocates of shareholder value thinking who are so enthusiastic about new-economy developments argue that the motivation of maximizing shareholder value will spur these new companies to heretofore unheard-of rates of expansion that will sweep aside older forms of enterprise. For once, the advent of a major new technology and the business philosophy to enable its rapid exploitation seem to be in perfect synchrony. In this chapter I explore the promise of the new economy, the companies that epitomize it, and its potential for turning traditional assumptions upside down. Will the new economy triumph over more traditional business approaches, or is the promotion of Internet-based companies simply the last successful hype to support an overextended stock market?

The leading-edge companies typical of the new economy, most of which are tied to the Internet in some way or another, have no basis in underlying economic realities to support the kinds of stock price levels they are currently commanding. But as the preceding chapter showed, Internet-related stocks are not the only ones suffering in today's market from indefensible stock price levels. Many of the older industrial and service companies, which are still the mainstay of the U.S. economy, have signed on to the precepts of shareholder value and done everything they can think of to inflate their current stock price levels (and, not at all coincidentally, inflate the value of the stock options held by the managers responsible for this slavish devotion to the new mantra of business). In doing so, to a greater or lesser degree, these older companies have mortgaged their futures in return for payback now.

Amazon.com: Impressive Growth at an Even More Impressive Cost

In 1994 thirty-year-old Jeff Bezos was the youngest senior vice president investment banker D. E. Shaw had ever had. It seems appropriate that his job was to search for companies involved with the Internet that might be interesting to invest in. While surfing the Net one day, he came across a Web site that said that Web population was growing at 2,300 percent a year. Without a second thought, he quit his job, jumped into a car with his wife, and drove to Seattle to start his own e-commerce firm. The company he founded was Amazon.com. By April 1999 the company had a stock market valuation of $36 billion, and Bezos's own net worth was approaching $13 billion. This was the new economy at work.

With the explosive growth the Internet was experiencing, Bezos reasoned that the door was wide open to someone positioned to sell to this amazing market. He initially made a list of twenty possible product categories he thought would sell well over this new medium, including compact discs, computer hardware, computer software, videos, and books. He decided on books because of the huge market and wide variety of products that were by their nature self-branding. The economics also seemed right. When the Web site was launched in July 1995, it listed over one million titles for sale. It quickly became the number-one bookseller and soon the number-one retailer on the World Wide Web.

To become the premiere retailer on the Web, Bezos and Amazon had to be innovators along a number of dimensions. First, to make sure he could offer low prices as an inducement to buyers, Bezos carried virtually no inventory of books (he had approximately 2,000 titles compared to an average of tens if not hundreds of thousands of titles for the typical bricks-and-mortar retailers whose business he hoped to take away). The start-up company was headquartered in Seattle partly because this put it in close proximity to

Ingram Book Group's Oregon warehouse, which supplied Bezos with almost 40 percent of the titles he shipped in his early days of operation. This allowed Amazon to offer three- to seven-day shipping to customers using the services of established carriers. To cover the extra cost of shipping and attract customers, Bezos offered discounts of about 40 percent off the list price of the books he sold.

The company was a pioneer in other ways, too. It introduced one-click shopping and offered secure means for customers to pay for their purchases with credit cards. It analyzed customer purchase patterns and made recommendations tailored to individual customers based on their prior purchases from the site. Besides providing standard best-seller lists and details on books reviewed in the press, Amazon encouraged customers to comment on books they liked and carried these customer reviews as part of each book's display record. It also maintained its own version of the best-seller list, the Amazon.com relative sales ranking, which customers and authors alike could use to track the popularity of individual titles. It pioneered links with other sites of "associates," who could recommend books they liked and then link directly to Amazon, where the interested viewer could buy the book—with a rebate going to the associate for the referral. From its first day, the site featured a robust and quick search capability to allow browsers to zero in on particular titles. With so many innovations in place, the Web site was a hit from its first day. Customers and browsers flocked to it. By October 1997 Amazon was able to announce that it was the first Web retailer to have tallied one million customers. Earlier that year, in May, the company had its initial public offering of 3 million shares.

As the trailblazing Web-based retailer, Amazon's revenue and stock price soared almost from the beginning. So did its operating losses, as shown in Table 5.1. At its peak stock price level in 1999, Amazon's market valuation was $36 billion. This level was almost twice the stock market valuation put on the venerable Sears Roebuck & Company and some twenty times the level of its nearest, traditional bookselling competitor, Barnes and Noble. Even as its stock price soared, its operating results continued to get worse. In the first quarter of 1999, the company reported a loss of $61.7 million on revenues of $293.6 million. Although analysts still predicted revenues of $1 billion for 1999 and $2 billion for 2000, the stock began to fall off because no one seemed able to estimate when the company would show a profit. What in the world was going on here?

The simplest explanation for the downturn in interest in Amazon.com's prospects was that its growth rate was slowing in its core bookselling business and the steps the company was taking to offset this slowdown were driving its costs through the roof. As Figure 5.1 shows, though still impressive,

TABLE 5.1   Trend in Amazon.com Revenues, Stock Price and Operating Income

Category	1995	1996	1997	1998
Revenues ($ millions)	$0.5	$15.7	$148.0	$610.0
Highest Stock Price (Dollars)	–	–	$10	$221
Operating Income ($ millions)	($0.3)	($5.7)	($25.8)	($52.1)

SOURCE: Standard & Poor's Stock Report, 08 May, 1999.

Amazon's sales were definitely cooling. Bookselling revenue growth was tailing off because after four years of pioneering, Amazon was facing competition from at least three other major on-line booksellers, at least one of which, BuyBooks.com, sold books at prices lower than those of Amazon. In addition to these Web-based booksellers, the search engine Lycos identified at least 500 other Web sites offering books. Amazon may have pioneered the formula and got its basics right, but it surely faces a lot of competition going

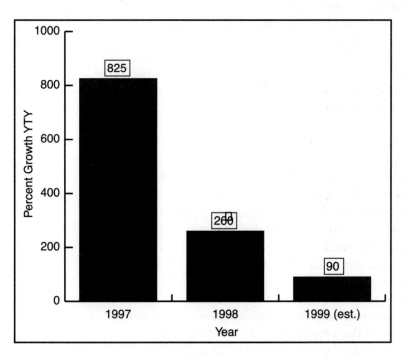

FIGURE 5.1   Trend in Book-Selling Revenue Growth—Amazon.com

SOURCE: Jacqueline Doherty, "Amazon.bomb," (*Barrons,* May 31, 1999), page 25.

forward. The beauty of the Internet is that it allows someone to reach a lot of potential customers quickly without a major investment in infrastructure, especially bricks and mortar. Its downside is equally apparent. New competitors can easily enter and undercut an established competitor like Amazon.

Recognizing this downside early, Amazon quickly moved to establish itself as the largest multicategory retailer on the Internet. It added music sales in 1998, which put it in direct competition with early music e-vendors like CD-Now. It expanded into movie videos and gifts later the same year. In early 1999 it entered the new glamour field of on-line auctions, positioning itself to compete head-to-head with another early Internet success, E-Bay. Yet all of these actions cost the company money. By early 1999, in order to lure customers to its widening array of retail offerings and services, Amazon was spending almost 24 cents per dollar of revenue generated, compared to about 4 cents per dollar for a conventional bookseller (though, to be fair, Amazon was rapidly diversifying away from this business arena).

The real question for a company like Amazon is whether there is sufficient margin in its business model to allow it ever to make a profit. On the surface Amazon's economics look attractive. The company buys books from publishers or wholesalers at around 50 percent of their normal retail price (conceivably even less as Amazon's volumes get larger and it is able to command bigger discounts). Of this total potential margin on the sale of 50 percent, Amazon immediately offers a discount to its customers of at least 30 percent of the normal retail price; this discount is necessary for Amazon to remain competitive with bookstores since Amazon passes along to customers the cost of shipping, which pretty much wipes out the value of the discount. From the remaining 20 percentage points of margin (assuming the selling price = 100 as a starting point), Amazon has to pay for marketing and operations. Of each sales dollar it has, Amazon currently spends almost 25 cents on marketing, more than erasing the remaining margin. Its cost of operations (e.g., computers, software, communications, physical handling, overhead) consumes almost another 100 percent of "margin." Given today's volumes, Amazon is bound to operate in the red for some time.

At much-expanded volumes, however, it is conceivable that Amazon's economics could look better. For example, if Amazon could increase its sales volumes to around $3 billion and keep all other gross cost fixed in dollar amounts (and therefore declining in percentage terms), there would be room in its business model to make some money, as we can see:

selling price = 100
available margin to Amazon = 50
discount = 30

operating expenses = 10
marketing expenses = 5
potential profit on each sale = 5

Unfortunately, the assumptions required to make this model work are extremely generous. First, it assumes a major increase in revenue with no increase in expense, something very few companies have been able to pull off and Amazon has shown no talent for addressing. Second, it assumes this greater volume is available to Amazon at its standard price—that is, that no further price discounting is required to retain volume. Given the ease of entry to the Internet and the tendency of shoppers everywhere, not just on the Internet, to gravitate toward low prices, this assumption is dubious indeed. As a result, Amazon's profit economics look shaky for the foreseeable future.

Amazon's theory, of course, which it was only too pleased to espouse to the investing public, was that its investments were designed to position itself as the retailer of choice across a broad number of categories on the Internet. Once it had claimed that position, Amazon could presumably raise its prices to the levels required to make its economics work. But in the meantime others are positioning themselves as well. Bertelsmann, a major book publisher, took a substantial stake in Barnesandnoble.com, the Internet outlet of the traditional bookseller. Two major music companies, BMG (the music publishing division of Bertelsmann) and Universal Music (a division of Seagram's), announced a venture to allow customers to download music directly from the Internet. Since Amazon functions only as an intermediary in the markets it serves, buying products from manufacturers or, more typically, wholesalers and passing them on to consumers, it is inherently disadvantaged when facing direct competition on-line from the manufacturers themselves. As it faced new and stiffer competition in its core markets, Amazon, a company that embodies the high-productivity and low-cost approach of the new economy, was busy building warehouses to improve its service delivery to customers. The costs of these facilities and of the mounting inventory that Amazon is carrying on its own books are further aggravating the company's economics.

Will Amazon ever show a profit? Will it even survive as competition mounts in its core retail segments? The stock market is betting yes. Although Amazon's stock has fallen from the giddy levels it reached at the start of 1999, its total market capitalization at the end of the year was still almost $20 billion. The company certainly has some substantial assets it can bring to bear—market-leading technology, a unique service orientation, brand recognition—to maintain and enhance its top position in the new economy. Its expenditures on marketing have also been helping. Its last published statement indicated that

Amazon had 8 million customers on its rolls. Still, few investment analysts are willing to go out on a limb and predict when, if ever, the company will turn a profit.

Mark Anderson, the technology consultant and publisher of the *Strategic News Service* newsletter, recently commented, "The idea of making it up on volume when you are losing on every product line is a tried-and-true recipe for something other than success. Indeed, the harder one looks, from weird stock valuations to venture funding mania to basic business models, the more one begins to feel that from a financial perspective, there is no 'there' there." Anderson calls the Internet stock game a "scam." As a heavy and devoted user of Amazon.com's bookselling operations, I certainly hope they succeed and prosper. If they are the cutting edge of what the new economy has to offer, however, even I have to admit they come up woefully short.

But what of some of the other new-economy companies that are potentially more insulated from the direct competition Amazon is suffering under? Do they offer hope of a renaissance of business sufficient to justify the stock market's ebullience?

Oh, to Be a Portal: The Yahoo Story

The best companies seem disproportionately to be those with the best stories to tell about their origins. Who can forget the tales of Bill Hewlett and Dave Packard tinkering in a garage to create products they would use to build the company bearing their names? Or what about Alexander Graham Bell and his strained, "Come here, please, Mr. Watson. I need you"—the signal of successful invention that would soon lead to the Bell Telephone Companies? And what about the story of Sam Walton dropping prices in his first general merchandise store and discovering that the resultant volume far offset the loss in revenue from lower prices? Great companies have great start-up stories, even if these tales are post hoc rationalizations for why they became great in the first place.

In the annals of Internet companies, people will look long and hard to find a launch story to rival that of Yahoo. Imagine two bored electrical engineering graduate students, Jerry Yang and David Filo, surfing the Net to put off working on their theses. The year was 1994 and the university they attended was Stanford. Imagine that they had so much fun discovering new things on the emerging Net that they decided to set up their own Web site called "Jerry's Guide to the World Wide Web" as a way of sharing their experience with others. Imagine that so many people liked their list of favorite Web sites that they began to build a substantial database of their finds and developed a "search engine," a new kind of tool for finding out what was in their database, that would increase access for others to their favorite sites. Imagine that the pair simply got tired of the name of their Web site and decided late one night to rename it Yahoo—"Yet Another Hierarchical Officious Oracle"—which seemed suitably rude and uncouth to suit their tastes. Finally, imagine that all of this was happening on their computer workstations at Stanford University. When you have this picture firmly in mind, you will have imagined the start-up of Yahoo, the most important single site on the Web.

Yang and Filo's tinkering proved so successful that before long Stanford's computers could not easily keep up with the incoming Web traffic they were generating. In early 1995 the two engineers took their act with them when they relocated to a new venue at Netscape Communications. There, overwhelmed by the growing traffic on their site, they began selling advertising, simple banner ads that flashed across their Web pages when users accessed them, as a means of generating funds to expand the scope of their database and search capabilities. With money coming in, Yang and Filo realized that they needed help to stay on top of their unusual enterprise. So they hired some experienced (by Internet standards) managers to help them with the commercial side of their operation. As growth continued at a prodigious rate, it should surprise no one that in less than a year, by early 1996, the fledgling company was taken public. It might surprise some to find out that on its first day of trading Yahoo was given a stock market valuation of $300 million—this for a company whose revenues in its first quarter of public trading would be slightly over $1 million. But this is the Internet, after all.

From its beginning as a public company, Yahoo's mission (and slogan) has been the same: "It is the only place anyone has to go to get connected to anything or anybody." If statistics can tell such a rich story, the principals of Yahoo have succeeded beyond any reasonable measure. The average daily (Web) page views at the Yahoo site by early 1999 exceeded 235 million, having grown inexorably from levels of several million at the time of the public flotation of the company. In its 1998 annual report, the company estimated it had over 50 million unique users worldwide. By the end of March 1999, more than 47 million of these users were registered with Yahoo and thus were recorded in the company's databases. By any measure, for any new technology, these numbers are staggering. These levels of recognition and use are a tribute to both the vision and persistence of the founders and their partners in the business.

When Yahoo started out, it was to be a search engine that would provide visitors to its site access to other areas of interest on the World Wide Web. Soon after launching the company, its founders decided that to fulfill their stated mission they would have to do more: They would have to become a "portal," a site Web users would not only visit as their first preference but stay at because the site could meet so many of their interests and desires. To make the transition to portal status, Yahoo began adding services and features to its site at a furious pace. Some of these Yahoo developed itself; others it acquired along with other fledgling Internet companies of interest. The end result for Yahoo is a site so rich that it legitimately attracts the huge number of people who visit it every day. For example, Yahoo today offers real-time news (which visitors can tailor to their own interests), stock quotes and access to stock research services, sports scores with links to other sites of interest to sports fans around the world, weather information, maps, and access to vendor services ranging from travel services to books to virtually anything else readily available for sale over the Net. To further cement visitors to its site, Yahoo offers free e-mail services to anyone who signs up. It also provides access to specialized chat services, mirroring AOL's original attraction for its initial customers. It truly is the only place anyone has to go to get connected to anything or anybody.

Even more impressive than the sheer numbers is that Yahoo has achieved these levels of penetration while still (as of the end of 1999) earning a profit. Advertising, for which it charges from $6 to $90 per thousand impressions (views on the Web page), is the company's main source of revenue. At the end of 1998, the company reported that it had 2,225 advertisers who paid an average of $34,000 each for the privilege. No one of these advertisers generated more than 10 percent of the company's revenue in that year. In addition to money from advertising, the company receives payments in cash or in kind for referring viewers to merchants who sell them products or services—in effect, a commission for the referral. Referrals accounted for less than 10 percent of the company's total revenue in 1998. Yahoo also gets paid for helping companies design their own Web pages and linkages.

The end result for Yahoo is as impressive a set of operating results and stock market performance as can be found on the Web, as shown in Table 5.2. Because of its stellar achievement of turning the corner on profitability in 1998, its stock price rose even higher at the start of 1999. At its peak in April, the stock market liked Yahoo's promise so much that it accorded it a valuation of $30 billion. And why shouldn't it? In Yahoo's own 1998 annual report, the company notes that the total market for Internet advertising is projected to grow to $7.7 billion by 2002. As the leading destination site on the World Wide Web, with a proven ability to sell space on its pages, Yahoo can expect to gain a sizable share of this advertising. Moreover, Web usage itself was projected by Yahoo to rise from 97 million people in 1998 to almost 320 million people by 2002. Yahoo would attract a large number of these new users to its pages, thereby increasing the value of advertising on its pages. Finally, Yahoo projected that Web-based e-commerce would jump

TABLE 5.2   Trend in Yahoo Revenues, Stock Price and Operating Income

Category	1995	1996	1997	1998
Revenues ($ milions)	$1.4	$19.1	$67.4	$203.0
Highest Stock Price (Dollars)	–	$7	$17	$147
Operating Income ($ millions)	($0.6)	($6.4)	($0.9)	$58.4

SOURCE: Standard & Poor's Stock Report, 08 May, 1999.

from $32.4 billion in 1998 to $426.7 billion in 2002. If Yahoo was just getting its feet wet in earning commissions from the 300 merchants affiliated with its site in 1998, surely it would gain massively from this expanding market as well. Perhaps here finally is the new-economy company we are looking for—a company perfectly positioned to participate fully in the explosive growth of a new medium and to reap the economic benefits from doing so.

What's wrong with this picture? A lot. First, Yahoo is not the only portal on the Web, only the most successful one to date. Recognizing the potential threat the Web poses to their core businesses, a number of leading media companies, most notably Disney and NBC, the broadcasting arm of General Electric, are moving aggressively to build their own portal businesses. Their efforts are being matched by Microsoft, which is likewise convinced the Internet holds the key to its future and is therefore investing heavily to build up its MSN Network portal site capabilities. AOL, with its acquisition of Netscape and its existing loyal group of millions of fee-paying subscribers, is also battling for a share of future traffic on the Internet and with its acquisition of Time Warner looks likely to set the standard for content as well. In short, although Yahoo is to be commended for taking the lead, the race is hardly over.

What is more, the promise of a rapidly growing advertising market, Yahoo's main source of revenue today, may not materialize. Participants in the advertising industry are increasingly questioning the efficacy of banner ads carried on Web sites. Most advertising on the Internet today is sold based on page views, the number of times people call up the page in question. Many, if not most, Web surfers ignore banner ads as they surf; in fact, if the advertiser has the bad luck to have its banner ad located at the bottom of a particular page, there is no guarantee that (and no way of measuring if) the typical browser of the Web will bother to scroll down the page to see the ad. The only other way to ensure a particular ad is being seen by potential customers is to measure click-throughs, that is, the number of people who actually click on the ad and go forward to look at the advertiser's Web site.

Only about 3 percent of all banner ads are actually clicked through, and a click-through is a guarantee only that someone is seeing the ad, not making a purchase.

Although it is too early to tell whether critics of Internet advertising are right, there is some tangible evidence that their criticism is not far off the mark. In its report in early April 1999 (covering the quarter ended the previous December), Yahoo noted that page views were up an impressive 41.7 percent for the quarter. But revenues were up only 12.7 percent in the same period. This suggests that revenue per page was down by almost 20 percent in the last quarter of 1999. One quarter's results are not enough to judge an overall trend in the making; however, some of the optimism about Yahoo as the star of the new-economy companies must be tempered by the reality that results are not living up to promises.

Finally, although overall Internet usage will undoubtedly grow, it is not clear that it will ever reach the levels forecast by Yahoo or that Yahoo will ever reap the benefits of this upsurge. First, most of the growth forecast for Internet usage will likely come outside of the United States. Already almost a half of U.S. families are regular Internet users, a percentage much higher than in most other parts of the world. Yahoo's home base is the United States; its highest return from the development of the new medium is likely to come from its position as a leading U.S. company serving the needs of U.S. consumers. Although Yahoo has invested abroad to cover this contingency—it has local language sites operating in most of Scandinavia, the UK, Germany, Japan, Korea, and several other areas—there are no guarantees that users in these countries will flock to Yahoo the way American and early users around the globe have.

What do all these factors suggest about Yahoo's future and the sustainability of its impressive stock market valuation of $30 billion? They suggest that Yahoo probably has a robust and profitable future to look forward to, but that future is unlikely to bring returns to shareholders of anything like $30 billion. Every new market or technology goes through a life cycle as it matures. The use of the Internet is unlikely to be different. Not all markets around the world, however, reach the same degree of penetration of any new technology, and not all do it at the same speed. If we take into account these factors, we see that though the Internet should experience explosive growth over the next few years, its growth will not be as great as the most optimistic forecasts (see Figure 5.2).

For the variety of reasons discussed earlier, Yahoo's ability to reap the benefits of whatever expansion occurs is likely to diminish, not increase, over time. A realistic forecast of future revenue and earnings for Yahoo may well be attractive but far below what the company has achieved to date, as illus-

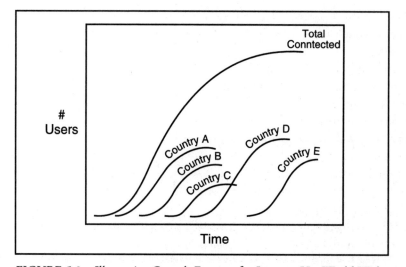

FIGURE 5.2   Illustrative Growth Forecast for Internet Use World Wide

SOURCE: Author illustration.

trated in Table 5.3 on page 80. The result of these forecasts suggests that a $4-billion turnover company would earn around $1 billion a year by 2005 and grow at around 15 percent a year. Such a company could be much admired but not worth anywhere near Yahoo's current market valuation.

Why is this important? Because it illustrates once again that the relentless search for shareholder value, which has so dominated the business world since the mid-1980s, has lost touch with reality in its final efforts to justify higher and higher share prices—even for a company as triumphant as Yahoo. But perhaps the choice of Yahoo to study in detail was flawed. What about the prospects for the network builders, the people supplying the infrastructure to make the new economy work? Cisco is widely thought to be the best and most successful of these companies. What are its prospects?

The Race for Bandwidth: Cisco Systems

Cisco Systems was founded in 1984 on the back of an experimental piece of technology created by a husband-and-wife team at Stanford University. Leonard Bosack was the manager of the Computer Science Department's laboratory. His wife, Sandra Lerner, was in charge of computer operations for Stanford's prestigious business school. Bosack developed a device that combined hardware and software to enable the computer networks in their two respective parts of Stanford to talk to one another.

TABLE 5.3   Illustrative Forecast of Yahoo Growth

	Web Users (millions)	Yahoo Page Views (millions)	Yahoo Revenues ($ millions)	Yahoo Operating Expenses ($ millions)	Yahoo Net Income ($ millions)
1995	N.A.	N.A.	$1.4	$2.4	($1.0)
1996	N.A.	25	19.1 +1264%	27.7 +1054%	(6.4)
1997	68.7	68 +172%	67.4 +253%	90.3 +226%	(25.5)
1998	97.3 +41.6%	165 +142%	203.0 +201%	147.8 +64%	25.6
1999	131.6 +26.1%	347 +110%	507.5 +150%	221.7 +50%	143.0
2000	157.9 +20%	624 +80%	1,030.0 +100%	332.6 +50%	349.0
2001	187.9 +19%	936 +50%	1,522.5 +50%	498.8 +50%	512.0
2002	221.8 +18%	1,216 +30%	2,131.5 +40%	698.3 +40%	716.6
2003	259.4 +17%	1,520 +25%	2,771.0 +30%	907.8 +30%	931.6
2004	301.0 +16%	1,824 +20%	3,325.1 +20%	1,089.4 +20%	1,117.8
2005	346.0 +15%	2,097 +15%	3,823.9 +15%	1,252.8 +15%	1,285.6

SOURCE: Author calculations, assumptions shown; all data up to and including 1998 from Yahoo Annual Report.

In 1984, the dark ages of the modern computer era, computers were just beginning to be networked. Networking allowed computers tied together to share files and peripheral resources, thus making overall operation more productive. There were two primary kinds of networks around in those days— local area networks known as LANs (which usually involved hooking together with some form of cable all the computers in one circumscribed geographic area) and wide area networks known as WANs (which typically tied together computers in geographically dispersed areas over telephone lines). The key to making these networks function was an agreement (among the engineers who designed the systems) on the ground rules or protocols by which data could be moved from one device to another in the network. There were many such protocols around even then and more to come on the scene as engineers everywhere looked for ways to make computer-to-computer communications ever more efficient. Bosack's innovation allowed two separate LANs to talk to one another, appropriately referred to as internetworking technology.

At around this same time, the biggest network of its kind was an academic network called ARPANET, developed with funding from various branches of the U.S. government. ARPANET tied together computers at major universities so that research scientists could collaborate on major research projects from remote sites around the country and, in due course, the world. One of the major technological innovations that allowed ARPANET to work was packet switching, which clumped data together in dense little packets that could be shipped down a telephone line, decoded, and reassembled in their original form at the other end. This invention allowed much more data to be transmitted over telephone lines than was previously possible, with much more flexibility in the way it was routed from the sender to the receiver. ARPANET and the technology that enabled it was so powerful that it was to become the basis of the World Wide Web (the Internet) some ten years later when it was brought out of the academic world and made available to users everywhere.

Convinced that Bosack's invention had applications outside of Stanford University, Lerner and Bosack first tried to sell it to existing computer companies. None of them were interested. So with some techie friends the couple set up a new company, Cisco Systems, and set out to sell the new invention directly to end users, typically large corporations that could benefit from having their computers talk to one another. Cisco was started on a shoestring: Lerner and Bosack had to mortgage their home and run up credit card debt to get the company off the ground. Even two years after its founding, Lerner held a full-time outside job to keep food on the table.

In Cisco's infancy, its primary product was a router, a hardware device incorporating software that selected the best path for data to follow in moving from one network to another. As its customer base grew, the small company kept adding to the number of different data protocols it could interface with. Two years after its founding, it introduced the first multiprotocol router, which could be programmed to handle the wide variety of network configurations it might encounter. In the year ending July 1987, sales of Cisco were running at $1.5 million. The company had only eight employees at the time.

As demand for its innovative technology grew, so did the company. To finance the growth, the founding couple turned to a venture capital firm, Sequoia Capital, which provided the money in return for a controlling interest in the company. It brought in new management to oversee the rapid expansion of the firm—pushing the founders aside in the process. In 1990 Sequoia took Cisco public at a time when annual sales were approaching $70 million a year. The two founders, Lerner and Bosack, immediately began selling their stock in the newly public firm. In August 1990, when Lerner was fired by the managers Sequoia had hired, the founders cashed in the rest of their ownership of the company and severed their ties with it. In total, they extracted almost $200 million from their entrepreneurship (most of which they subsequently donated to charity)—a handsome payoff but insignificant in light of the future value of Cisco. Though true innovators in the Silicon Valley tradition, Lerner and Bosack were outsiders, not fully bought-in to the get-all-you-can-as-fast-as-you-can ethic. Had the founders hung around, they would have been billionaires many times over by the end of the 1990s.

Left to their own devices, the management team that inherited Cisco continued to set the pace for the mushrooming data communications market. In 1992 the company introduced products designed to interface with IBM's proprietary Systems Network Architecture. In its 1994 fiscal year, Cisco introduced the first data switch for the emerging asynchronous transfer mode (ATM) technology. Around the same time, it aggressively entered the international market by setting up sales offices around the world and opening distribution deals with major local players, such as British Telecom, Alcatel, Siemens, and Olivetti. It also pursued strategic alliances with other major players in the fast-growing market, such as Microsoft and Novell. In 1993 and 1994, Cisco made the first two of what was to be a series of technology-motivated acquisitions, buying first Crescendo Communications and then Newport Systems Solutions. Cisco recognized that no one firm could likely dominate the field on its own, so it adopted a policy of keeping in-house R&D expenditures to modest levels while aggressively seeking to acquire small firms that were at the forefront of technological development.

All of these actions spurred the dramatic increase in sales for the company and the even more dramatic rise of its stock price and stock market valuation, as shown on Figure 5.3. By early 2000 Cisco had become the second largest market capitalization company in the world. With average annual sales and profit growth of 150 percent and 120 percent, respectively, throughout the 1990s (albeit from a fairly low base), Cisco certainly seemed to have earned such an exalted valuation in the market. Market valuation shot up at an average annual rate of 2,000 percent during the same decade—more than ten times the rate of increase in sales and earnings—as the rush to ever higher shareholder values drove Cisco's valuation into the stratosphere.

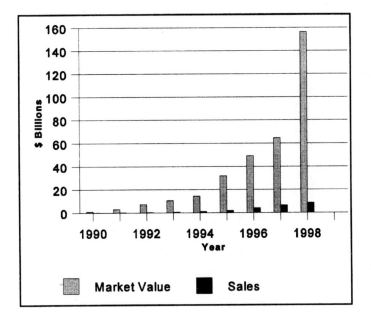

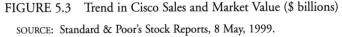

FIGURE 5.3   Trend in Cisco Sales and Market Value ($ billions)

SOURCE: Standard & Poor's Stock Reports, 8 May, 1999.

The remarkable increase in Cisco's sales and earnings during the 1990s masked a gradual and inevitable maturation of the business as the decade advanced, as shown on Figure 5.4 (see page 84). Growth in excess of 30 percent, as Cisco experienced between 1998 and 1999, is far from shabby, of course. In financial terms, however, it is less than one-third of the growth rate required to support Cisco's price-earnings ratio of 100+. Is the slowdown in growth signaling something fundamental about the prospects for Cisco's business? Or is it only a temporary adjustment on the path toward an even more glorious future?

An article by Seth Schiesel in the *New York Times* on July 11, 1999, summarized the dilemma facing companies like Cisco. The article, titled "Jumping Off the Bandwidth Wagon: Long-Distance Carriers Regroup," documented the increasing commoditization of bandwidth with the rapid and duplicative construction of long-distance fiber-optic networks across the United States and around the world. The giant leap in communications activity, particularly data traffic facilitated by equipment from companies like Cisco, led a number of companies—AT&T, MCI, Sprint, Qwest, Level 3 Communications, ITXC, and the communications subsidiaries of Williams

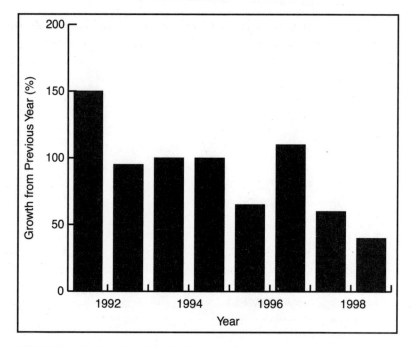

FIGURE 5.4   Trend in Cisco's Annual Sales Growth

SOURCE: Standard & Poor's Stock Reports, 8 May, 1999.

Companies and Enron—to build new fiber-optic networks to handle the traffic. A fiber-optic network has almost 160 times the theoretical capacity of a traditional copper-cable network. In addition, advances in the use of fiber optics have further expanded the capacity of the new networks. For example, in 1985 it took six fibers in a fiber-optic line to carry one American football game for television broadcast; by 1999 one fiber was capable of handling 700 games simultaneously. With the proliferation of networks, total capacity available to transport data around the world has expanded by millions of times—far in excess of any near-term foreseeable increase in traffic on these networks. The result has been a glut of transmission capability, causing prices to plummet and companies that had invested in these networks to refocus their strategies.

' Every time a new network is built and every time someone (a large corporate user, for example) wants to connect to one of them, Cisco and its competitors in the internetworking equipment business sell gear. That's what they do for a living. But with such an overabundance of bandwidth, few new networks are likely to be built in the near future. Moreover, most large and many small businesses, the core of Cisco's business base, are already connected to these networks. Even with overall Internet traffic projected to grow at 50+ percent a year in the years ahead, this growth is unlikely to translate into the demand for as many new connections as in the early to mid-1990s. Big surprise: Cisco's market is maturing, as most markets do over time.

The implication of this maturation of Cisco's core markets is that the recent slowdown in growth rates experienced by the company is likely to be a sign of an upcoming trend, not a onetime anomaly. Without a doubt Cisco is an enormously innovative company. In 1999 almost 80 percent of the company's orders were transmitted to it electronically; over 70 percent of customer service inquiries were handled on-line. The bulk of these transactions are processed without the intervention of human hands, giving Cisco levels of sustainable productivity that make it the envy of companies everywhere. This high productivity translates directly into high gross margins, turning Cisco into one of the most profitable companies of its ilk in the world. But no amount of efficiency and profitability can substitute for demand. With the slowdown in Cisco's core markets already becoming apparent, its day in the sun may already be over.

What of its stock market valuation, then? If Cisco's core business, albeit still robust, is slowing down, will its stock price continue to be able to set new highs with each move forward in the market? Will its lofty valuation in the stock market ever repay investors for their bet on the company's future? The truth is no. If Cisco continued to increase its earnings at 30 percent a year for the foreseeable future, a prospect that looks daunting in light of market trends, and paid all of these earnings back to investors as dividends, investors today might reasonably expect to collect as much as $30 billion from the company on a discounted cash-flow basis (i.e., valuing future payouts in today's dollars). Cisco's market capitalization is in excess of $150 billion, however. Based on the future earnings capacity of the company, it seems today's investors may be lucky to get back 20 cents on every dollar they invest in this finest of the new-economy companies. Although this may far exceed what they might hope to get back from other high-flying firms such as Amazon.com, it hardly looks like the kind of investment most punters would rush out to make.

The only hope investors have for getting their money back, therefore, is to sell their investment to another investor willing to take a fling on the stock. By definition, that is what a bubble is. All markets have some aspect of a bubble about them most of the time. As a matter of politesse, we are accustomed to referring to this as market liquidity. But when the only recourse for buyers is to find greater fools to unload their holdings on, that is pure bubble.

The Shareholder Value Bubble

In the 1630s, the usually calm and sober Dutch people went mad about tulips, a new flower recently imported from Turkey. At the height of the so-called tulip craze, the price of individual bulbs was bid up to 6,000 florins (equivalent to about $20,000–$25,000 today). Foreigners eager to get in on the action began buying tulip bulb futures for as much as $1 million. When the bubble broke in 1637, a lot of people went bankrupt.

Human nature being what it is, almost one hundred years passed before the next major bubble appeared on the scene. This one was set in motion in 1720 across the English Channel from the Netherlands when the Earl of Oxford floated stock in a new company he had dreamed up, the South Sea Company, whose purpose was to exploit the advantages of having sole trading rights to the newly discovered Americas (most of which were under Spanish, not English, dominion at the time). Within months, stock in the new company rose from an initial offering price of £128 to £1,000 (in today's dollars from about $5,000 to about $40,000). When the insiders to the speculation sold out their positions later that year, the bubble collapsed, and even the likes of Isaac Newton lost substantial sums of money.

It took almost 120 years for the investing public to recapture its enthusiasm for speculative ventures. But recapture enthusiasm it did in 1847 in the UK, when investors flocked to buy shares in the new technology of the era that was promising to revolutionize the world of commerce: railroads. One hundred and eighteen railroad companies were floated in a brief period, attracting over £350 million (about $35 billion in today's dollars) in total investment capital. Most went bust in 1847 when the economy turned sour. The British government had to intervene to see that the rights of consumers, if not investors, were protected.

The bubble leading up to the great stock market crash of 1929 is probably the only one most people are even vaguely aware of today (the time necessary for human folly to reassert itself apparently having once again passed). Buoyed by an economy finally freed from the ravages of World War I, the Dow-Jones industrial average surged from a level of 100 in 1924 to a level of 400 in 1929 (a move roughly equivalent to the movement of the Dow-Jones average during the expansion of the 1990s). Even in 1929, at the height of the precrash market, individuals were rushing to buy stocks despite their inflated valuations. It took twenty-six years for the Dow to recover after the market declined by 89 percent from its 1929 highs.

Of course the most recent bubble to afflict investors is that of the late 1990s. In 1997 the stock market dallied briefly in the 7,500 range on the Dow-Jones industrial average; by mid-1999 the market had surged above

11,000 with hardly a glance backward. Because new Internet offerings have been the most prominent feature of the market and because Internet stocks (or more generally, new-economy stocks) have tended to lead each subsequent advance of the market, many skeptics of the market's staying power at these levels have dubbed the phenomenon the "Internet bubble." Yet the currently insupportable levels in the stock market should be known as the shareholder value bubble. Commitment to the primacy of shareholders to the exclusion of all other stakeholders, which led to the mentality of get-all-you-can-as-fast-as-you-can, is the real engine driving the stock market to its ever higher and indefensible levels.

Like all bubbles throughout history, the shareholder value bubble will burst, too. Forecasting such events is neither productive nor within the scope of this book. Nevertheless, I am tempted to predict that the rupture will come soon.

PART THREE

Stakeholder Response

Shareholder value thinking transformed the face of business and made a lot of senior managers and investors wealthy in the last decade of the twentieth century. But what impact did shareholder value thinking have on other, less-favored stakeholders in the corporate world—employees, governments and communities, suppliers, and customers/consumers? How have these stakeholders responded to their exclusion from the central corporate equation? This part of the book profiles both the effects on each group of stakeholders and their efforts to defend themselves.

Chapter 6 looks at employees. Their corporate employers have downsized, outsourced, merged, globalized, and automated them beyond recognition. As a result, employees have lost their sense of identification with their employers and have begun to look out almost exclusively for themselves. An astonishing and growing number even retain lawyers to negotiate deals with the companies that hire them. Instead of a loyal and motivated labor force, corporations increasingly have to deal with self-motivated and self-interested free agents.

Chapter 7 examines the changes occurring between governments and corporations. Since this arena is so large, the chapter focuses exclusively on the field of government incentives for companies to invest. Where once corporations ruled the roost and played competing jurisdictions off against each other to garner the best deal they could get in return for opening a new factory or call center, governments around the world today are banding together to level the playing field among themselves. The days of the sweetheart deal for a corporate investor are nearly over.

Chapter 8 explores the effect of the shareholder value era on suppliers, corporations themselves. Many suppliers have fallen by the wayside under pressure for reduced costs and increased services from their major customers. Those that have survived have responded in the only way they knew how: by consolidating with their counterparts to achieve a scale that their major customers would envy. In many industries today, the supplier is in the driver's seat vis-à-vis their major customers.

Chapter 9 ends Part 3 by exploring the changed relationship between corporations and their customers. Again because of the scope of the subject, the chapter concentrates primarily on consumers and their reaction to the corporations they buy from. In the pursuit of profit, corporations have exploited their customers just as badly as they have treated their own employees. Customers have responded by withdrawing their loyalty from corporations and brands and shopping for the lowest-priced goods within their reach. With the advent of the Internet, corporations are just beginning to see how this loss of customer loyalty will hit them.

Action produces reaction. Corporations favored their shareholders to the exclusion and exploitation of other stakeholders. So these other stakeholders are fighting back. The already gloomy future of corporations looks even worse as a result.

CHAPTER 6

Employees Strike Back

In the blind rush of corporations everywhere to raise shareholder value by doing everything they can think of to increase their stock prices, other stakeholders have been left on the sidelines. Employees, the stakeholders who have the most frequent and regular contact with the people who run business, are subject to arbitrary downsizings and the outsourcing of their work as company after company seeks to plug holes in its forecast earnings stream. Governments who for decades bent over backward to attract corporations and the jobs they bring with them see their communities devastated by plant closures. Suppliers whose livelihood depends on serving the needs of their major corporate customers watch as their businesses are so squeezed by arbitrary price cuts that their future viability is threatened. Customers who ought to have been benefiting from the near maniacal pursuit of efficiency find to their dismay that prices have risen as soon as weaker competitors are driven from the market. For all of these primary stakeholders in any business, the shareholder value revolution has been a disaster—a way for corporate executives and a handful of investors to get rich while every other stakeholder suffers. A revolution is stirring among the ranks of the disaffected stakeholders, however. Companies smart enough to see what is going on around them will have to figure out a new mode of operation in order to survive and prosper.

Employees Under the Gun

In the 1980s and especially the 1990s, corporations that adopted the shareholder value ethic attempted to increase their stock price levels by any means available. The tools corporate managers found most effective in this pursuit were downsizing, outsourcing, and restructuring, usually through mergers and disposal of parts of the business. All these managerial actions had a profound effect on employees, who were the first to bear the consequences. Many long-term employees lost their jobs. Many more found themselves working for a new employer, often with benefits eliminated and wages cut. Still others saw their position in the workplace subordinated to the interests of new owners. The psychological damage was even more severe. Employees who had labored, often for decades, under the implicit assumption that they would receive lifetime job security in return for a loyal and satisfactory effort on behalf of their employers discovered that their most basic assumptions about life at work were no longer valid.

With the rapid rise of downsizing and its closely related twin, outsourcing, the very nature of the job market began to change. Suddenly, millions of people could find work only as temporary or contract workers. Growth in the companies that supplied such workers was phenomenal. People still performed tasks for companies, but the companies that paid their salaries were no longer the companies they worked for. When they did the natural human thing and attempted to transfer their loyalty from their old, lifetime employers to their new masters, they found that other than receiving paychecks from these employers, they had no meaningful relationships with them. Millions of workers had become fungible commodities available for sale or rent in the transitory job market.

Along with changes in the basic terms and conditions of employment, the work environment itself was changing rapidly. In almost all areas, the workplace became automated. Those who were unable to master the new skills required to function in the automated workplace were soon cast aside. The mix of workers also changed significantly. More and more women found employment on a permanent basis as a way of supplementing family incomes. And with a booming economy many more ethnic minorities and racially and ethnically diverse immigrants entered the workforce. Although many of these trends had been occurring for some time, they all reached maturity during the 1990s, as downsizing reshaped the corporate world.

If the world of work was changing around them, the approach people took to work would have to change as well. So change it did. Employees could band together in organizations like trade unions to increase their bargaining strength against newly hostile employers. Indeed, transformations of management and employment practices seem to have breathed new life into the labor movement in countries like France and Germany. Alternatively, employees could shoulder the burden on their own. In the United States, the bastion of individualism, this is what happened, with individual employees revising their attitudes toward work and, as a result, their approaches to work itself. A new era in employee relations was to emerge, the era of market-based employment practices.

Those workers in a position to exploit the market-based job environment have done so with a vengeance. They are the select many who happen to have skills that are in high demand (computer and networking expertise, for example). This group includes many of the better-educated members of the workforce—MBAs, for example, still have little difficulty landing plum jobs. It also includes huge swatches from the high-tech industry, especially from those parts of the industry associated with start-up Internet businesses, where an overenthusiastic stock market is spawning millionaires and even billionaires at a record pace. It certainly also includes most members of senior corporate management who have taken advantage of the movement toward shareholder value to position themselves as a new elite in society (a massive change from the nameless and faceless ranks of dull people in gray flannel suits who seemed to characterize earlier eras). All these people are the winners in the new economy and job marketplace—winners so intent on personal gain that they seldom notice that their ranks exclude a large number of people. It is these winners who are driving the market-based employment arena by demanding more and more to keep them satisfied at work.

Unfortunately, there are a lot of losers in the new market-based employment environment as well. The ranks of losers include the millions who have been downsized out of once secure jobs. They include the legions of older workers who were forced into early retirement by company restructuring initiatives. They include most of the almost 20 million American workers who are in temporary or contract work situations against their will, often put there by corporations eager to outsource functions to lower their cost bases. The ranks of losers include millions of blue-collar workers who toil away in less-than-satisfactory working environments in so-called right-to-work states, where companies have relocated their factories to avoid having to deal with unions. On a global basis, the ranks of the losers certainly include many of the millions in Third World countries who work in near sweat-shop conditions for deplorable wages producing goods for consumption in the wealthy economies of the developed world. Despite the unprecedented growth in the United States during the 1990s, the losers in the new economy are so numerous that their existence in effect keeps a cap on the total wage bill companies have to pay to attract labor. At a time of unparalleled wealth creation in society, the real wages of these losers have been declining, and their status is such that they are in danger of forming a permanent underclass. It is a sign of the selfish times that no one seems to care much.

Corporations Rewrite the Rules

Employees did not lead the movement to put shareholders' interests above those of all other stakeholders. Nor did they initiate the actions that would rewrite forever the rules governing employee-employer relations. Corporations did. In the early days of the shareholder value movement, the new rules of employment were neither explicitly stated nor fully apparent. Before long they were to become so. The new rules of employment are as follows:

1. *Employment no longer implies job security.* A 1997 Conference Board survey of employment practices found that only 6 percent of all companies that responded to the poll offered job security as part of the deal. Fully 67 percent of the companies said the employment "compact" had changed; 27 percent said job security had never been part of the deal in the first place. The General Electric Company under the leadership of Jack Welch probably put it most bluntly: "The only job security is a successful business."

2. *With no lifetime jobs, corporate commitment to developing employees is on the decline.* Companies simply cannot afford to invest in employees who might be with them for only a short period. Whereas flagship companies like IBM used to boast of the high levels of training they provided to their employees, these same companies now emphasize hiring the talent they need from the outside market (including, in IBM's case, bringing experienced salespeople into its legendary sales force). In high-turnover, high-tech Silicon Valley, few companies even give lip service to training their employees. It is cheaper and more practical to poach the needed skills from nearby companies or competitors.

3. *With no lifetime jobs and little investment in people, it follows that most of the risks associated with a career are being pushed back onto employees.* Managers put a positive spin on their new criteria for job applicants; they emphasize personal ambition as the key attribute they require. A 1997 survey in *Training* magazine showed that only 2 percent of managers valued the commitment of the employee versus 56 percent who valued ambition. A favorite saying of corporate executives in this new era is, "You want loyalty, get a dog." Welch of GE goes even further by referring to loyalty to a corporation as "nonsense." The new era of employment relations forces employees into the status of free agents—responsible for themselves and to themselves.

The new deal that employers began offering employees under the guise of shareholder value was inherently contradictory. On the one hand, companies wanted motivated, hardworking employees who would devote their every effort, at least for a time, to the pursuit of company objectives. On the other hand, by refusing to offer these employees any kind of job security and with fewer and fewer opportunities for career development within the firm, companies were implicitly telling employees to look out for themselves. Employees soon did.

The New Employee Attitude Toward Work

In most areas of life, nothing short of being hit over the head with a bat will change individuals' attitudes toward things they hold dear. A job can be one such thing. With employers delivering the blow to their employees in terms of unexpected layoffs, employees were quick to rethink their relationships to their jobs.

The first to react were the people directly affected by the management changes imposed on them. Those who had been downsized, outsourced, or merged into an alien (to them) environment withdrew their loyalty (and in fact their respect) from their former employers. When other employment opportunities arose, these people were reluctant to invest the same kind of emotional energy in their new employers. Who could blame them? Having been victimized once, often blindsided by the turn in corporate direction, they stayed skeptical about work and those who employed them.

A similar shift in attitude occurred among the children of the generation most directly affected by corporate actions in the 1990s. In some respects the different attitude of those just entering the workforce may turn out to have been even more lasting than the new perspective of seasoned workers. As employees now see it, employers are not to be trusted, and all employers are alike. The only difference is the degree to which any individual employer will victimize its employees. Getting ahead on one's own terms is all that matters. In a surprisingly short time by historical standards, then, the entire workforce dramatically revised its approach to work and employers.

A major survey of employee attitudes conducted in 1997 revealed that fully 94 percent of survey respondents saw themselves, not employers, as responsible for their employability—no cradle-to-grave coddling for this workforce, no reliance on a paternalistic company to provide the training necessary to keep job skills sharp and relevant to the evolving job market. Workers (or at least 94 percent of them) regarded their career and job prospects as being in their own hands, for better or worse.

What are some of the key aspects of this new approach to work and employment? One should be obvious: Loyalty to the company that employs you is dead, deader than any of the executives who so derided it could ever have imagined. In its place is loyalty to one's profession or job function. Ed McCabe, a longtime human resources executive of Chemical Bank, described the phenomenon: "I always thought of myself as a Chemical Bank manager who happened to be in human resources. The new generation of managers think of themselves as human resource managers who happen to be at Chemical."

Along with a lack of loyalty to any company, the new employee attitude emphasizes

- self-management and the related personal skills this requires
- self-reliance in all aspects of one's career (More than a quarter of all students attending community colleges in northern California already hold a baccalaureate degree: They are there for self-improvement.)
- an increased willingness to switch employers if another job appears to offer advantages (One study estimated that 80 percent of the electrical engineers in Silicon Valley who quit their jobs in the region went to work for competitors, something unheard of in an earlier era.)

In addition to being more willing to assume responsibility for their own careers, employees are more demanding in virtually every other way that matters to them. They want more money and they want it now, not after they have earned their spurs in the company or job market. They want more perks—benefits programs, flexible working conditions, opportunities to develop outside contacts and interests. They want more challenging jobs now, not as a reward for years of faithful service. Figure 6.1 shows the full array of what the newly enlightened worker wants as documented by the Conference Board in its landmark 1997 survey. The shoe fits, and employees with a new attitude toward work are comfortable in it. In the future all companies will have to meet their demands if they want to employ them productively. But how can employees maximize their own chances of getting what they want? Corporations have shown them how.

Companies Provide the Model at the Top

During the recession of the early 1990s, an unprecedented number of Fortune 500 corporations fired their CEOs for their failure, in the eyes of their boards of directors, to produce adequate returns for their shareholders. This phenomenon was so important that I return to it in Chapter 10. Here I would like simply to cite this development as a seminal event that began the transformation of employment and compensation practices across all of American industry in the 1990s. Not for the first time in the last quarter of the twentieth century, corporations seemed blissfully unaware of the forces they were unleashing.

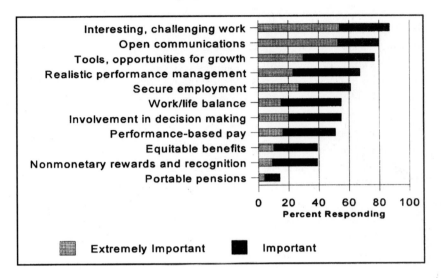

FIGURE 6.1   What Employees Expect From Companies

SOURCE: *HR Executive Review: Implementing the New Employment Contract,* (Conference Board, 1997).

The problem with firing a CEO in a large company is that you have to find a new one to replace him (until recently, unfortunately, all CEOs of Fortune 500 companies were men). If you can find a suitable replacement candidate within the company, the elevation of the candidate can be relatively smooth. If you have to go to the outside world for a new CEO, as IBM felt it needed to do, you have embarked on an expensive mission. Talented CEO-level managers have always been in short supply, and a company looking to recruit one must be willing to pay the price. IBM, which attracted a superb one in Lou Gerstner, is a good case in point. To lure Gerstner away from his previous job as CEO of RJR Nabisco, IBM had to offer him a package that included

- a signing bonus of just under $5 million to make up for the loss of compensation, current and deferred, he had coming from RJR Nabisco
- a substantial pay packet consisting of a base salary of $2 million and a guaranteed bonus of $1.5 million
- 500,000 stock options worth an estimated $10.8 million to tie his motivation directly to the interests of investors; if the stock went up, Gerstner's total pay would go up as the value of his options increased

- a guarantee that his cash-out on RJR stock options would yield him $9.9 million—that is, protection for Gerstner from any decline in RJR's stock price up until he made the switch
- a series of perks that, generally speaking, are part of any self-respecting CEO's package in this day and age, such as use of company airplanes, cars, and drivers; security appropriate to the head of the world's largest computer company; generous health and disability benefits; retirement benefits; and in Gerstner's case paying the fee of $25,000 he had incurred for financial planning advice while he was at RJR Nabisco

The total value of Gerstner's package for joining IBM was estimated at $21.9 million. I include the component amounts because the specifics are generally interesting and were widely published, but such details are irrelevant. Certainly, IBM got its money's worth. For employees everywhere, not just at the top of major corporations, it was the nature of the package and the publicity attendant on its acceptance that was the seminal event. All of a sudden the sky was the limit—or at least as much of the sky as an individual could negotiate in head-to-head dealings with a prospective employer. Another element of Gerstner's deal foretold future trends: The deal was so complicated that he employed a high-priced lawyer from a New York firm, Joe Bachelder, to negotiate the package for him. And IBM paid the lawyer's fees.

Bachelder, a little-known figure except in corporate boardrooms, played a major role in changing both CEO and eventually all employee compensation practices in the latter stages of the twentieth century. A Harvard-trained tax lawyer, Bachelder was hired by McKinsey & Company (the world's leading management consulting firm, where he likely met Gerstner and other future clients) in 1971 to help it figure out the ramifications of President Richard Nixon's newly imposed pay freeze. After a stint in Washington advising the president's pay board, he returned to New York and the practice of corporate law. By 1982 his unique understanding of pay-related tax consequences was so great that he started his own boutique law firm to specialize in this emerging area. From the beginning, he was one of the loudest exponents of tying executive pay to stock options in order to align top management incentives with the interests of shareholders. Over the years he has left his mark on virtually every aspect of executive pay practices. Most notably, he is known as the inventor of "hold harmless" provisions in contracts that institutionalized signing bonuses as part of executive recruitment packages.

In a typical year, by his own account, Bachelder advises about seventy executive clients and turns away about one-third again as many. He also advises twenty to twenty-five corporations in a typical year—in effect, crossing over to sit on the other side of the negotiating table. His fees of $650 an hour are almost always paid by the corporation he is negotiating for or against, not the CEO who hired him. His success at the top of the executive-advising-league table has spawned a slew of imitators across the United States and around the world.

The Rise of the Third-Party Agent

Consider, for example, the case of Robert Adelson. Adelson was a young corporate lawyer in his native Boston in the early 1990s. Struggling to build a practice, he spent a good deal of his time calling on the high-tech companies that had sprung up in the Boston suburbs, asking them to consider his firm for their next major piece of corporate legal work. One day in 1992, one of the executives he was calling on in a software company pulled him aside after the meeting was over and sought his counsel on a personal matter. The executive was about to take a job with a rival firm and wondered if Adelson could represent him in the negotiations with his prospective employer. Adelson, who was well grounded in tax issues, readily agreed. After he had successfully completed this initial assignment, Adelson got a call from an executive in a biotech firm who was similarly changing jobs. Then he heard from another and another. Although Adelson's fees may not be as high as Bachelder's and his client list not quite so famous in the business press (his clients earn upward of $70,000 a year in base salary, with most comfortably in the six-figure area), he has created a thriving and lucrative practice in one of the fastest-growing areas of corporate law. Today Adelson represents around twenty or thirty executives a year involved in job switches and another twenty or so companies that have come to respect his expertise at the negotiating table. One of the beauties of the practice is that it encourages repeat business with little or no effort on Adelson's part. An executive pleased with the first package Adelson negotiated for him is almost certain to return to him the next time a job switch opportunity appears. With turnover rates in executive ranks nearing 30 percent, Adelson's future is secure.

Adelson is not alone. Every major law firm in Boston (and every major city across America) and many smaller firms as well have lawyers representing clients negotiating for new jobs. Executive search and human resource consulting firms are also getting in on the trend. There is now even a Web site (http://www.salarymaster.com) that offers to take on all comers involved in computer-related professions, and as part of its service it provides links to other Web sites that give details of wages paid for various kinds of technical jobs across the country.

Intrigued by these developments in the job market, some colleagues and I conducted a survey to pinpoint where third-party agents were most active and how many people were involved. The survey covered laws firms in New York, Chicago, Boston, San Francisco, Dallas, Atlanta, Philadelphia, and Seattle—but also such places as Raleigh, Phoenix, Richmond, Houston, San Diego, and New Orleans. We came away from the survey convinced that the practice is national in scope: At least 1,000 law firms across the country take part in third-party employment negotiations.

We interviewed about fifty of the firms, both large and small. From these interviews we estimate that approximately 100,000 to 200,000 people in the United States receive third-party assistance every year, most of them at the upper ends of the earnings spectrum. If this extrapolation from a modest sample is accurate, it suggests that between 5 and 10 percent of all high-level job switches are being negotiated by third-party agents on behalf of the job-switching employees. Moreover, according to the participants in our survey, the number of people who turn to agents to negotiate their employment deals is growing at between 30 and 50 percent a year nationwide.

Third-party agents are active in virtually every industry. Without a doubt, employees in the high-tech sector have been the most aggressive users of agents. Other industries where the practice seems widespread include health care, banking, securities, media and entertainment, consumer packaged goods companies, the oil and gas industry, insurance, and even the public and not-for-profit sector. In terms of functional areas involved, engineers—both hardware and software—are well represented. So are salespeople in a variety of industries. Doctors and lawyers, not too surprisingly, often seek such representation, as do senior financial executives. The impression we developed overall was that executives, or those who fancy the hat, in virtually all areas were seeking help in negotiating their next employment deal.

Despite the use of the term "executive" to characterize users of agents, pay statistics suggest that the practice reaches well beyond the board room. Of the firms we talked with, the average salary involved for one of their clients was around $150,000 a year. The lowest salary these firms dealt with, however, ranged from $50,000 to $70,000 a year, hardly the province of senior executives. In rank order of their importance in the interviews, the key issues these negotiations were involved with were: (1) severance or change-of-ownership provisions, (2) stock and stock option arrangements, (3) noncompete and confidentiality agreements, and (4) signing bonuses or make-whole provisions, which compensate job switchers for monies left behind at their old employers. Other areas of frequent concern mentioned included benefits, relocation packages, and vacation provisions. Obviously, central to most discussions were the connected issues of job scope and responsibilities and basic salary and bonuses.

Bachelder may have set the trend in motion by his headline-making deals for famous executives. There is almost no doubt that early adopters of the practice of hiring lawyers to negotiate employment contracts outside of the top executive levels were motivated in large part by a desire to get their fair share of whatever was on offer. The growth in the business of third-party agents was spurred by the ever-tightening job market occasioned by the long economic expansion of the 1990s. Wherever shortages occur, the use of third-party agents soon follows. Once hooked by the benefits of having someone else negotiate their pay and employment packages, people are not likely to forgo the use of agents in the future.

Employers Cave In

The actions of CEOs at the top and a tight labor market, particularly for workers with special skills, have led to a rapid escalation of the number and array of options for people changing jobs. Some companies have tried to get ahead of the pressures on the job market by inaugurating what are now widely known as work/life programs, which offer a bevy of benefits to entice employees at a cost lower to the company than pay and bonus arrangements. The American Compensation Association in 1999 conducted a survey that indicated that 18 percent of the companies polled had some form of work/life program in place. These programs tend to draw people for a time but are so quickly emulated by competing companies that their unique appeal is often limited. Nevertheless, the very existence of these programs is evidence enough of what is going on in large parts of the job market. Some of the specific items on offer are

- employee assistance programs that provide counseling and financial planning services
- casual-dress days or even policies, especially at high-tech companies
- paid personal days for employees to deal with family-related issues
- on-site day care facilities
- child care referral services
- sick-child care services
- backup child care services
- job-sharing programs to allow individuals more flexibility in when they work
- telecommuting options for appropriate groups of workers
- paid or unpaid educational sabbaticals
- formal mentoring programs
- flex time and lactation programs for nursing mothers

- provision of personal convenience services at the workplace such as ATMs, dry-cleaning outlets, barber shops, hairdressers, and shoe repair shops
- concierge services
- company-negotiated group auto and homeowner insurance
- assistance in home buying
- free breakfasts, coffee, and so on
- subsidized cafeterias, often selling take-home meals
- use of company planes for family emergencies
- unlimited accumulation of vacation time
- group prepaid legal services
- tuition reimbursement programs for training undertaken by individuals on their own initiative
- wellness and fitness programs at work
- career counseling services for employees (covering options within the company and outside)

The list is limited only by the imagination of the people inventing or asking for these options. Some of the wackier entries on the list, mostly from Silicon Valley, include the right to bring pets into the office and free massage services at work to relieve workplace tension.

Make no mistake, these workplace benefits are real and becoming more widespread all the time. For example, about 10 percent of companies now provide financial planning assistance to at least some of their employees; experts in the area project its use to rise to about 30 percent of companies in the next few years. Among large companies, almost 40 percent offer some of their employees individual financial planning assistance today. Some 18 percent of companies offer long-term care insurance; its use is predicted to increase to almost half of companies over the next three years. The proliferation of benefits has become a permanent part of the employment landscape in America.

CEOs who started the movement toward richer pay packages and more and more perks are not left out in the rush to entice employees. More and more companies give their senior executives lifetime executive perks. These include access to company airplanes for the executive and his family (available to Jack Welch of GE when he retires), provision of company cars and drivers, access to company residential properties (i.e., apartments) for temporary stays, and use of an office and secretarial support in perpetuity. Former CEOs, including the legendary Walter Wriston of Citibank, publicly rue the fact that they finished their working careers too soon. Bob Holland, the former CEO of Ben and Jerry's Homemade, the ice cream people, received free ice cream for life as a parting gesture of goodwill from the company when he left because of a dispute over strategic policy. Given the multiplicity of formal and informal elements that go into making up an employment agreement today, it is hardly surprising that about one-third of large U.S. companies now sign a formal employment contract with their employees—a practice long common in Europe but only recently arrived on American shores. The only people not participating in the bonanza are the have-nots in the employment market. The shareholder-value-driven society of the 1990s has abandoned them to their fates.

What the Future Holds

The changes in the workers' attitude toward work are likely to be permanent, barring another cataclysm in the corporate world. Too much of the workforce has benefited from the tight labor market of the late 1990s to do a volte face and give up what it has so recently gained. Moreover, developments like the use of third-party agents to negotiate employment deals for individuals have in a sense institutionalized the new arrangements in the job market. The new and increasingly universal information environment offered by the Internet will virtually guarantee greater employee knowledge about the options they have and the means available to most to capitalize on these options.

Various commentators have labeled the new employment environment the "market-driven workforce" or the "new working community of free agents." In light of broader trends affecting the business environment, I prefer to call this development in the job market "employees strike back," since the changes have shifted power to the side of employees at the expense of employers who created the situation in the first place by their cavalier withdrawal of the safety net they once provided.

What, then, are the implications of this new environment at work? What can we expect to see in the future? The simple answer is more and more of what is already visible now, until much of the job market closely resembles the one in Silicon Valley today. Specifically:

- *Benefits and perks once offered will be very difficult to remove.* Look for companies everywhere to begin to adopt many of the work/life programs that are a prevalent feature of life in the Valley.
- *The clamor for more real ownership stakes in companies will grow and grow.* By 2010 most companies will be offering stock or stock options to all employees as a matter of course.
- *More and more people will move into near-permanent contract employee status.* Working as contractors will allow them to maximize their return from the job market of the day. Despite their status as contractors, these mobile employees will ask for and receive all the benefits

and perks available to more conventional employees (or they will take their in-demand skills elsewhere).

- *Flatter organizations structured around temporary project lines will become the norm as a fundamental adaptation to the new workforce.* Silicon Valley in effect works that way now.
- *Staff turnover will likely increase steadily until it stabilizes at a high level.* But this level will not be as inflated as that in the Valley, where the skills in demand really are very scarce. Turnover rates in Silicon Valley typically run between 35 and 50 percent of the workforce per year, with only a handful of exceptions (such as at the venerable Hewlett-Packard Company, which garners exceptional staff loyalty). A nationwide norm is more likely to be around 20 to 30 percent per year, almost double the rate most companies now experience. This will be expensive for companies to cope with but will become a cost of doing business, because turnover is the key to employees' maximizing their returns from the job market.
- *The use of third-party agents to negotiate employment deals will continue to grow.* In due course, perhaps by 2010, virtually all employees earning over, say, $100,000 in base compensation a year will have agents negotiate their job packages for them. People below this level of earnings or without the specialized skills that place them in demand will negotiate their own deals, but will do so armed with much more knowledge because of the availability of salary surveys and other information on the Internet. The implications for corporate recruiters are clear: They will be facing tough negotiators across the table all the time.

All of these changes will be dramatic, making the jobs of human resource managers in particular much more difficult. But in a sense the changes will be liberating as well. For centuries, employees have been relatively helpless pawns in the job market. They have had neither the knowledge nor the resources to match up fairly with their corporate bosses. That formula is changing. The change will take time, and it will likely be uneven across the sectors of the economy. But the forces now at work in the employment marketplace are altering fundamentally the nature of jobs and the meaning of careers. Taken to their logical extreme, these forces could lead us all back to a kind of medieval marketplace of craftspeople and artists, where participants bring to the employment market their own skills and initiative and are rewarded appropriately. This is a far cry from the recently deceased corporate paternalism and a step in the right direction for the liberation of the human spirit. Finally, the employee gets to call the shots. Employers beware.

CHAPTER 7

Government
Tightens the Screws

As the intermediary between individuals and institutions in society, government has many interactions with corporations every day. Through the laws it enacts or announces, government lays down the rules by which corporations have to live. Although corporations sometimes evade their responsibilities under relevant laws (and suffer the consequences), for the most part the rule of law is so well established that the relationship between business and government works smoothly, with corporations obeying relevant laws.

A much more contentious area of interaction between governments and corporations is in income and wealth distribution. Governments impose taxes to fund their own operations and to move money between one segment of society and another (usually from the wealthy to those less favored). No one likes taxes, and corporations are no different in this respect from individuals. Occasional public skirmishes about elements of proposed tax legislation aside, however, interactions between corporations and governments around the issue of taxes, too, are mostly routine. Like individuals, most corporations try to avoid paying taxes they can legally justify not paying. Every once in a while a corporation succeeds so well in this respect that it draws the ire (and likely secret admiration) of the public and, as a result, the attention of the public's representatives in government. A prominent case in point involves the activities of Rupert Murdoch's News Corporation, which despite its position as one of the leading media firms in the world manages to pay virtually no taxes anywhere. This has caused consternation in many circles, but to date the company's efforts at tax minimization have been found to be perfectly legal, and it continues to operate with impunity around the world.

Governments are also very large consumers of the goods and services that corporations sell. State and local government in the United States accounts for almost 14 percent of the gross national product (GNP) of the country. The

U.S. federal government contributes a share of GNP almost twice this level. Even excluding transfer payments to individuals that make up government expenditures at all levels, the government as customer is a major factor in the market. The nature of government procurement is such, however, that not all corporations are attracted to this potentially lucrative source of revenue, leaving the job in the hands of specialized companies generally referred to as government contractors. Now and then the public will be regaled with stories about abuses that occur when the government becomes a customer (the defense contractor nightmares of $600 toilet seats being a classic example). But for the most part government procurement proceeds smoothly and the buyer-seller relationship between governments and corporations works smoothly.

The push by corporations to maximize shareholder value undoubtedly caused friction at all of the normally benign interfaces with government outlined above. For example, a shareholder-value-driven company would look harder and longer at ways to avoid the most stringent and costly provisions of new laws (such as environmental protection laws) that might affect its bottom line than would a company less caught up in the shareholder value movement. A shareholder-value-driven company would likely be even more intent on minimizing its tax bill than another, less-motivated company. A shareholder-value-driven company would work even harder than most to maximize profits from the government contracts it held. But the tension between governments and corporations on these issues would be part of the normal give-and-take between adversaries. Ray Vernon aptly described the friction as he reflected on his own foresight in talking about the growth of multinational corporations in his book *Sovereignty at Bay:* "'The manifest technical advantages of large enterprises and strong governments will lead men in the future to insist on both.' I saw two systems, therefore, each legitimated by popular consent, each potentially useful to the other, yet each containing features antagonistic to the other."

With government influence and interaction with corporations so pervasive, there were bound to be other areas where more tensions would arise as a result of the push for shareholder value. One of the most significant, if little publicized, of these concerns government subsidies to business, particularly subsidies related to new investment projects. This area I examine in some detail for the lessons it can teach us about how the interface between governments and corporations is changing.

Companies on the Take

Because of its size, government influences economic development in virtually everything it does. By spending money on schools, government prepares a workforce to be active participants in commerce; by investing in police forces and other security measures, government creates the kind of social environment conducive to economic activity; by funding infrastructure like roads and bridges, government provides the means by which private firms can get their goods to market; by its own expenditures in the community, government helps determine which firms thrive and which fail. Most of these routine acts of government are benign (or meant to be) in economic development terms.

For centuries, however, government has taken a direct hand in trying to stimulate economic development as well. When railroads and roads were built in the nineteenth century, the public funds spent on these projects acted as direct subsidies to industries (including agriculture) that followed in their wake. These were not typically labeled as investments in economic development, although it is clear that is exactly what they were. The direct investments were not the only means used to stimulate growth in those early days. Ingenious tax assessors usually found ways to abate or waive taxes on properties owned by friends close to these major infrastructure investments as a way to increase the value of their friends' investments. Abuse was so rife in this area that by the turn of the twentieth century most state legislatures had enacted laws or amended their constitutions specifically to prohibit loans or grants to private parties. No doubt clever administrators and businesspeople found little-publicized ways around these restrictions over time.

The first formal program of subsidies to attract investment occurred in Mississippi in 1936, when that state (soon emulated by neighboring Kentucky in 1946 and Tennessee and Alabama in 1951), enacted a law under its "Balance Agriculture with Industry" program, which used state and local government borrowing powers to raise money for specific plant investment projects. By the end of the 1950s, this use of industrial revenue bonds (IRBs) had extended across most of the states in the Union.

But the real flood of investment incentives to business did not hit until the 1970s, when manufacturing firms, particularly those located in the Midwest rust belt, began an aggressive program to relocate their factories to lower-cost venues. The primary motivator for this movement was not just the age and obsolescence of factories. The movement was driven by the desire of many managers to escape from the highly unionized and highly paid Midwest workforce to nonunionized, business-friendly locations in the southern states. With so much potential business investment available, states everywhere began to pull out the stops, inventing subsidy program after subsidy program in an effort to win a disproportionate share of the relocating operations. Once it was started, there was no way to stop the movement to subsidize business, as states rushed to make sure they could compete with all other jurisdictions. By 1991 a fifty-state survey of financial incentives on offer took almost 800 pages to document the scope of the phenomenon.

For all the sound and fury associated with the movement to lure investment projects, the subsidies fell into a handful of major categories:

- capital subsidies, including subsidized credit in the form of direct loans, loan guarantees, and (most commonly) the pass-through of the federal income tax exemption
- grants, typically to intermediaries, to finance site preparation costs and other capital costs
- subsidies of other inputs, including training costs, research and development costs, marketing and promotion costs, and site search costs
- tax preferences
- enterprise zones, where a variety of incentives are available, often on a more generous basis than elsewhere in the state or city
- promotion of the state, region, or city as a good place to locate or visit
- opening of overseas export promotion offices to help firms from a locality find export markets for their goods
- provision of venture capital funds to encourage the launch of high-tech ventures

The most advanced of these kinds of programs involved the entrepreneurial outreach of communities to the companies they most wanted to attract, armed with an array of community-enhancing incentive options. This so-called new wave of economic development programs became prominent in the late 1980s and early 1990s as localities sought ways to protect themselves from the ever-escalating cost of direct financial subsidies. Throughout, however, the most visible incentive scheme was the provision of direct loans and grants to projects. These continued in use even when the new-wave programs began to fall by the wayside because of lack of demonstrable proof of their efficacy.

With so much on offer from so many places, it should not be surprising that corporations responded enthusiastically. According to Dick Netzer, the respected academic and public finance economist, "A large share of what has been said and written about economic development consists of belaboring the obvious. Of course, no firm will turn down gifts, even ones of small value, and any firm will say that a gift will persuade it to do nice things." State and local officials responsible for administering the various incentive programs are eager to announce how well their own programs make good things happen, so the bandwagon of economic development incentives keeps rolling on year by year. Thousands of companies, both large and small, have benefited from these incentive programs, some many times over and in many different locales. Figuring the value of available incentives into investment deals has become a standard part of any company's operating procedures.

Site Selection magazine each year picks the top ten incentive awards to various companies. Some recent examples illustrate how important incentive programs have become:

- Boeing: $80 million in incentives (mainly in the form of tax concessions) to build a $400-million plant in Decatur, Alabama, to house, eventually, 3,000 workers in its space sciences division
- Chrysler Corporation: $223 million in incentives to encourage it to keep its Jeep-manufacturing plant in Toledo, Ohio. The plant will employ a total of 4,900 people and is an overall investment of $1.2 billion for Chrysler
- Gateway: $80,000–$200,000 in financial incentives plus assistance in employee recruitment and training for it to locate a computer assembly facility in Salt Lake City, Utah, projected to employ 1,350 people. The overall attractiveness of the business situation in Salt Lake was said to tilt the deal in the city's favor without requiring massive subsidization of the $20-million project.
- Hankook Synthetics (of Korea): $1 million in site preparation monies plus free land and training for 500 workers to attract a $1.2 billion synthetic fibers plant employing 1,800 people to Augusta, Georgia. (One can only speculate that the deal might have included a free pass to the prestigious Masters Golf Tournament.)
- IBM: $178 million in incentives and an additional $135 million in investment tax credits to encourage IBM to keep its 3,290-person chip-making facility in East Fishkill, New York
- MCI: $12.5 million in incentives against a projected cost of $43 million for a high-tech facility in St. Louis, Missouri. The incentives were broken into $5.8 million in funds for training, $4 million for infrastructure around the new facility, and $2.3 million in loans and tax credits.

These are, of course, only a handful of the deals done in recent years. The variations in the amounts and types of subsidies provided reflect the unique situation of each investment proposal and environment. For example, MCI was said to have looked at twenty different sites across the United States before finalizing the deal with St. Louis; IBM had its corporate headquarters in

New York State and had long operated around the East Fishkill area. Both firms, however, given the temper of the times, were motivated to negotiate the best deal they could with state and local authorities before finalizing their commitment to the facilities. In other highly publicized incentive deals, the determining issue was simply the amount of money local governments were willing to put on the table to attract a plant. Alabama reputedly paid over $200,000 per job created to Mercedes to get it to build its North American assembly plant in the state. Not to be outdone, Iowa is reputed to have paid $250,000 per job to bring a steel mill to its confines. With monies like this on offer, it is no wonder companies negotiate hard before deciding where to put their facilities.

The Globalization of Investment Incentives

Investment incentive programs were never a uniquely American phenomenon. Countries around the world have for many years used a full gamut of incentive programs to attract investment, especially foreign direct investment (FDI). As sovereign states, individual countries have an even wider array of instruments at their disposal to make themselves attractive to potential investors: They can manipulate their currency exchange rates, their import and export regulations, wage and price control policies, and virtually any other aspect of their own economy. As one leading example of the kinds of debates that occur at the national and supranational level, the United Kingdom initially opted out of the Social Chapter of the European Union (EU), which sets a variety of conditions on the treatment and use of labor (extensive maternity leave provisions for both parents of a newborn child, as one example) because it believed its more flexible labor laws would make it more tempting to investors. The Labour government of Tony Blair reversed this decision and opted back into the Social Chapter.

Competition for investments and the jobs that go with them occurs on a truly global basis. As Table 7.1 shows, 80 percent of the countries around the world offer income tax reductions to foreign investors, 65 percent offer some form of tax holiday, 61 percent offer their investors waivers from import duties, and around 45 percent offer either accelerated depreciation on capital assets or some other kind of special tax deductions or both. Countries are chasing investors hard. Is it any surprise that companies everywhere are taking them up on their offers?

In addition to various kinds of financial inducements, countries around the world tender a large number of nonfinancial incentives to potential investors. Chief among these are

TABLE 7.1   Fiscal Incentives for Foreign Investors, early 1990s

Incentive	Africa	SEA	Latin America	North America	West Europe	East Europe	Other
# of countries	23	17	12	2	20	25	4
Reduced Income Tax	18	13	12	2	16	20	2
Tax Holiday	16	13	8	2	7	19	2
Accelerated Depreciation	12	8	6	2	10	6	3
Investment Allowance	4	5	9	–	5	3	–
Reduced SS Tax	2	1	2	–	5	2	–
Special Tax Deductions	14	12	6	2	9	2	–
Exemption From Duties	5	13	11	2	7	13	2
Duty Drawback	10	8	10	1	6	12	2

SOURCE: *Incentives and Foreign Direct Investment* (United Nations, 1996), Table III.2, page 21.

- *Subsidized infrastructure:* It has become the norm for countries eager to attract investors to pave the way for them by building special investment zones or sites in preferred areas that include all of the amenities a new investor might ask for. Scotland, one of the more aggressive and successful FDI chasers, has even opened branches of universities as the centerpieces of industrial areas in order to appeal to high-tech foreign investors.
- *Subsidized services:* In addition to preparing the physical plant for investors, many countries are now offering specialized services designed to help potential investors settle on sites within their jurisdictions. These services include consulting on site-selection alternatives, preparing lists of possible suppliers and acting as the facilitator of early contacts with potential investors, providing advice on manufacturing processes, and offering training for new employees to be hired at the site.
- *Market preferences:* Many countries will try to lure new investors by promising them preferential access to government contracts, where appropriate, or by protecting them for designated periods from competition from imports. These kinds of arrangements are most prevalent for big-ticket investment projects like automobile assembly facilities.
- *Foreign exchange services:* Since concern over the effects of currency movements are prevalent among foreign investors, many countries offer protection to investors to limit their currency exposure risks.

The kinds of incentives range from simple foreign exchange rate guarantees to agreements on the repatriation of profits earned on the investment.

Albeit technically nonfinancial in their nature, all these kinds of incentives have a clear financial value to a potential investor. Companies contemplating an investment overseas negotiate hard to get the best deal they can under such circumstances. Without a doubt, these incentive programs have been effective. Some examples of recent projects documented by the United Nations Conference on Trade and Development (UNCTAD) include

- a Korean electronics venture in northeast England, which was given a grant of £58 million ($100 million) by the British government (possibly topped up by another £20 million—$35 million—from local government authorities), an amount equal to just less than 20 percent of the project's capital cost, or £20,000 ($30,000–$35,000) per job, for a plant expected to employ around 3,000 workers
- a U.S. automotive component company, which was given a grant of £500,000 ($0.8 million)—or £4,500 ($7,500) per job—to build a plant in the English Midlands
- a German-Swiss car-making investment amounting to $473 million in France attracted by subsidies equal to about 23 percent of the plant's cost and a tax holiday for five years after the plant was up and running
- a U.S. electronic assembly facility in Ireland landed by grants of I£12 million (30 percent of the plant's cost and equal to about I£15,000–$20,000 per job created)
- a German-American car assembly facility drawn to Portugal by a grant equal to about 22 percent of the cost of the plant

These are only examples, of course, of the thousands of deals done every year to bring in foreign investors. The scale of the projects alone is enough to explain, if not justify, the countries' interest in snapping up such investments.

The proliferation of foreign investment incentive programs around the world has had its own unintended but perfectly predictable consequence: Any new form of subsidy initiated in one part of the world and found to be attractive to potential investors is rapidly adopted in other countries. Thus the business of pulling in foreign investors has become a costly exercise for most countries—an ever-escalating process of giving companies what they want (or at least as much as any serious competitive country is willing to offer). In their frustration over this price war, politicians and administrators involved in investment-attracting schema have begun to work behind the scenes to stop the incentives race for advantage. The seeds of this movement are just now beginning to grow, of which more anon.

Do Investment Incentive Programs Work?

Many economists who have looked at the question of investment incentives have come away with the conclusion that they simply do not work. No company is going to decide to build a plant simply because there is an incentive on offer. Moreover, the amount involved in even the largest incentives is small enough relative to the overall value of the investment the company is making (usually around 20 percent) that it will not precipitate a decision— although it will influence one. True, an incentive that moves a plant to one location instead of another can have a small distorting effect on the economies of the two competing jurisdictions, imposing a small cost on one location in return for the small benefit it realizes for the other. But in the increasingly borderless world we live in, even these small costs and benefits are mitigated almost immediately by the benefits consumers derive from buying a product more cheaply because it was made in a low-cost location. The net effect, therefore, is that paying incentives to firms to locate somewhere is essentially a zero-sum game (or even, as the economist Dick Netzer would argue, a negative-sum game) for society once all of the economic effects of the incentive program are taken into account.

This high-level perspective on the economics of investment subsidies is widely known and accepted, including by officials of most of the major subsidy-granting agencies around the world. Although these economics are correct, they miss the point. A community that attracts a major operation to its locale at an acceptable cost is a big winner, just as a community that bids sensibly for a major investment project and loses is a loser. A successful investment project generates jobs, corporate and individual tax payments, increased spending in the local community, and lower levels of social expenditures. Economic development officials know this and do careful cost-benefit analyses before they decide on the level of incentive to offer. The officials who work for economic development agencies are paid to win projects, however. If they don't succeed in doing so, they soon lose their jobs. Moreover, politicians in areas that have won a number of big investment projects typically get reelected. People put to work in a spanking clean new plant are almost always grateful for the leg up the job has given them and vote to support the people who got the project for them in the first place. So the human side of the debate on incentives is quite clear: Incentives for business to invest in a particular location are a good thing—even if the economics are questionable. Thus, the endless cycle of beggar-thy-neighbor competition for jobs continues. Companies around the world know this and take the money without hesitation. It's a sellers' market, and companies with jobs are the sellers. The buyers, the governments at all levels around the world, are the losers in the deal. And they all know it.

A Winning Example: Ireland

In the world race to capture foreign investment, Ireland knows no peers. For a country of 4 million people (only about 1 percent of the European population), tucked on the corner of Europe, Ireland attracts 13 percent of all mobile foreign investment going into Europe, garners fully 26 percent of all U.S. investment projects going into Europe, and holds the number-one position in Europe as the locale of choice for foreign investments focused on international services. Almost two-thirds of the output of Ireland's manufacturing sector is produced by foreign companies operating in Ireland, 80 percent of which is exported every year. Almost half of the 230,000 people in manufacturing in Ireland work for these foreign investors. How has such a small and insignificant (except for its beauty, wit, and culture) country managed to capture a lion's share of the world's foreign investment? Has it always been a magnet for foreign investment, or has the movement of foreign firms to its shores been a recent phenomenon? What role have foreign investment incentives played in its success? What does the future hold with respect to a continuation of its success?

Ireland finally won its independence from its longtime colonial master, the United Kingdom, in 1922. For the next forty-five years, it was one of the most protectionist of countries around the globe. High tariff barriers discouraged imports and protected Ireland's domestic companies from competition from abroad. This protectionism was justified in Irish minds by the need to build up indigenous Irish industry in place of companies operating as branches of British firms from across the Irish Sea. The result of the policy, however, was to create dinosaur industries in the republic and produce an economy and standard of living that were among the poorest in Europe (GDP per capita in Ireland was just over 60 percent of the average for all of Europe in 1960). In 1966 this long-standing policy was abandoned when Ireland negotiated the Anglo-Irish Free Trade Agreement with its former colonial master and began a twelve-year process of eliminating the tariffs that had previously sheltered Irish firms from competition. Recognizing that the elimination of tariffs would cause immediate economic distress, Ireland in 1969 set up the Industrial Development Authority (IDA) to seek out foreign investors to fill the gap. This agency virtually invented most of the leading-edge practices associated with attracting foreign investment in the thirty years it struggled to bring Ireland to its top position in the industry.

From the beginning, the Irish Parliament gave IDA two kinds of incentives it could use to attract foreign firms: an automatic tax holiday on profits earned from exports out of the country and the ability to offer grants to investing companies up to certain limits. In the earliest days of the program, grants were specifically tied to investments in capital equipment. As Irish officials increasingly came to recognize that their interest was in jobs, the basis of the grants was shifted explicitly to job creation, with monies disbursed to investing companies only after the workers were in place. Similarly, as a member of the EU (Ireland joined in 1973), Ireland had to amend its tax holiday provisions because by focusing on exports only they were by definition a barrier to free trade—free trade being the mantra under which the EU had been formed. Ireland's response was to offer a 10 percent corporate income tax rate to all manufacturing companies in Ireland, a position it maintained through 1999 (the rate is slated to rise to 12.5 percent in early 2000), still by orders of magnitude the lowest rate of corporate taxation in Europe. From the beginning, the Irish officials responsible for IDA set out to be selective and proactive in their efforts to lure foreign investment. They deliberately targeted the fast-growing electronics and pharmaceutical sectors as the likely best source for firms. As time went on, IDA amended this focus to reflect developments in the world economy—but only after Ireland had achieved preemptive success.

Not content simply to respond to requests from potential foreign investors, Irish officials analyzed the industries they were targeting and made direct contact with the leading firms in each industry. Even this direct approach was insufficient. Irish infrastructure, particularly roads and telecommunications, was so deficient that many of the firms they first approached were dissuaded from investing. Working closely with other government officials in the relevant areas, IDA gradually overcame these obstacles, especially in the area around Dublin, and a trickle of new investment projects began. The trickle gradually turned into a flood following Intel's decision in the late 1980s to build a major semiconductor factory on the island, a factory that today employs more than 4,000 workers.

Let's look at the success IDA and Ireland have achieved. By the end of 1998, IDA was supporting 1,140 companies that employed 115,981 full-time workers. Total corporate tax receipts in 1998 were estimated at I£800 million ($1.1 billion) despite Ireland's low corporate tax rate, in contrast to the I£138 million ($200 million) in grants issued by IDA in the same year. Getting to this level of return was a rocky road, however, as illustrated in Figure 7.1 on the next page. Perhaps more important for Ireland has been

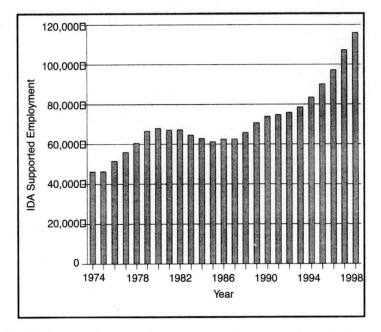

FIGURE 7.1   Total Employment in IDA Supported Companies

SOURCE: IDA Ireland Annual Report, 1998.

the tremendous increase in the productivity of the money it has used as grants to attract new jobs to Ireland, as shown in Figure 7.2. Between the mid-1980s and the end of the century, the amount of subsidy Ireland had to dole out to attract a job was cut in half.

The economic effect of IDA's efforts has been substantial. Ireland's GDP per capita, once the laggard, is now almost on a par with the rest of Europe, as shown in Figure 7.3. Ireland has been growing at a rate three or four times faster than its fellow EU members. Ireland's unemployment rate is approximately half that of major countries in Europe like France and Germany, even though the island nation has been welcoming immigrants back into the country from the Irish diaspora created by the potato famine and its aftermath.

With such an enviable record, it would not be surprising if IDA were resting on its laurels or even scaling back its efforts. Not likely. With employment booming, especially around Dublin, IDA is now trying to channel investments into the relatively depressed western part of the country. It has increasingly concentrated on winning higher-level jobs for Irish workers (who are no longer among the ranks of the poorly paid in Europe, eliminating the low-wage appeal Ireland once had for investors). In 1998 IDA hired

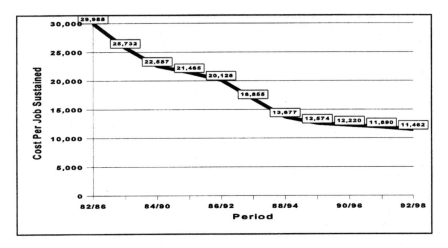

FIGURE 7.2   Cost to Ireland of Job Sustained

SOURCE: IDA Ireland Annual Report, 1998.
NOTE: Data calculated only for jobs sustained during entire period.

consultants to advise it and train its people on how to persuade subsidiary plant managers to upgrade their plants to make higher value-added products and make them more secure parts of the Irish economy. IDA also has in place systems to encourage new investors to buy from existing Irish firms in

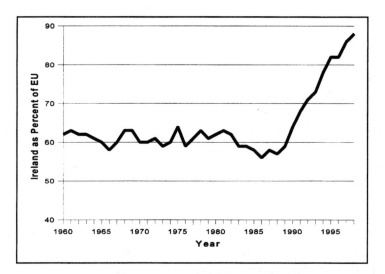

FIGURE 7.3   Ireland GDP Per Capita Compared to EU

SOURCE: *National Investment Priorities For The Period 2000–2006,* (ESRI, 1999), page 32.

an attempt to improve the domestic economy through its success with foreign investors. Although still in its early stages, this program has shown some
promise in areas such as software. Having taken the lead in attracting foreign
investors, Ireland is determined to build on its strengths and use its considerable expertise to push the Irish economy to the next level of performance.
Few outside observers would expect the country to fail in this endeavor.

When Companies Misbehave:
The Downside of Incentive Programs

If Ireland's incentive programs are such a triumph, why shouldn't every jurisdiction seek to have their own equally successful programs? Why aren't incentives the way to go? A lot of the answer has to do with how companies use
incentives and misuse public officials in the process. A furniture company in
North Carolina accepts $230,000 and other incentives to open a factory in
the state that would employ 200 workers. Within weeks after accepting the
grant, the company, This End Up, closes a similar factory only a few miles
away and lays off its 150 workers. Quaker Oats receives a modest $98,000
for opening a factory intended to employ ninety-eight workers and shuts another nearby factory with a payroll of seventy to justify the move. American
Hoist and Derrick Company gets a $4 million, federally funded grant to
build a new crane factory in North Carolina and in effect closes down production at its plant in St. Paul, Minnesota, to transfer the work south. After
months of acrimonious controversy, Amhoist is finally forced to pay back
$2.8 million of the grant since it had illegally used federal money to move
jobs from one state to another. The laid-off workers in St. Paul get essentially
nothing to compensate them for their loss.

Not all misuses of public incentive monies are so blatant, although the end
result is the same. Navistar Corporation (previously called International
Harvester) decides to get out of a steel mill operation in Wisconsin. To avoid
liability for unfunded pension costs of $65 million, Navistar devises a com-
plex sellout of the mill to a holding company. The holding company approaches Wisconsin's economic development authorities for assistance in
arranging an industrial revenue bond of $90 million, which they intend to
invest in the facility. Once the loan is approved and the investment made,
Navistar decides to accept a strike in its main agricultural equipment plants
in order to lower their costs. When the strike drags on for six months, the
holding company that had bought the steel mill goes bankrupt, since 40 percent of the output of the mill normally went directly to Navistar, its former
owner. A comedy of errors and miscalculations? An example of a corporation's thinking that it is due any monies available to it in one part of its op-

erations while somewhere else in the corporation a whole new strategy is being undertaken that will contradict the reason the money was given to the
company in the first place? Or a deliberate abuse of government subsidies? At
the end of the day, it almost doesn't matter. Abuses occur for whatever reason, and the public, represented by its government, ends up paying. In a system where all of the negotiating power is on one side of the bargaining table,
such as is the case in the use of investment incentives to attract companies,
abuses are bound to occur with disquieting regularity.

The abuses against government incentive programs occur everywhere, not
just in the rust belt towns of America. IBM takes subsidies from IDA Ireland
to open a small plant. Within a few years, the production of this plant is consolidated in IBM's even more heavily subsidized Scottish operation, where
the incentives used to attract IBM included building a special train line and
stop to serve the new plant. (IBM continues, however, to be a substantial
employer in Ireland.) Mitsubishi takes subsidies from Locate in Scotland,
Scotland's IDA equivalent, to build a very successful color TV plant in
Haddington. After eighteen years of operating the plant, Mitsubishi announces its closure and the loss of 850 jobs because of unspecified "market
difficulties." Shortly thereafter it opens a TV plant using low-cost labor in
Eastern Europe. The subsidies it received for the new facility were not documented for the public. A printed circuit board manufacturer, Exacta, takes
£12 million ($20 million) in subsidies to open a plant employing 200 work-
ers in the Borders area of Scotland. Three years later the company sells itself
to a larger rival, Viasystems, which closes the plant and transfers the work to
one of its facilities south of the Scottish border. The ability to move this
work and realize savings was undoubtedly a factor in Viasystems' decision to
buy Exacta. And the Scottish government was left empty-handed.

On August 6, 1995, the front page of the *Financial Times* features a story
about the Siemens company's plan to invest £1 billion ($1.7 billion) in a mi-
crochip plant in the depressed Tyneside area of England. The investment was
so important to Tyneside that the announcement warranted a favorable edi-
torial from the *Times*. Attracting the big investment from Siemens cost the
UK government in excess of £200 million ($330 million) in subsidies and
involved negotiations that went all the way to the top of the government
then in power in return for the guarantee of upward of 2,000 new jobs.
Response was somewhat more muted in August 1998 when Siemens said it
was closing the factory to save $200 million a year because of the low prices
for the memory chips the plant was making. When questions were raised
about what happened to the subsidy money, Siemens claimed it had kept its
side of the bargain by refunding the £18 million ($30 million) unequivocally
due back to the government. Very few even bothered to mention that in

January of that year Siemens had announced that it was taking a $200-million subsidy from the free state of Saxony to open a joint-venture chip-making facility with its U.S. rival, Motorola. A sweetener in the deal for Siemens was a contract to build the power plant for the high-tech zone in Dresden where the new chip plant was to be located.

Confusion in strategy, changing market conditions, changes of ownership and hence priorities all can cause companies to go back on their decisions to invest in new plants. Some of this is truly unavoidable and out of the control of the company. Some of it, however, is simply a matter of companies' taking advantage of local governments too willing to court the firms for the jobs they bring with them. Whatever the reason, it is a big problem for government officials concerned with economic development. Economists William Keating and Tom Keane estimated from government statistics that 24 percent of the jobs IDA attracted to Ireland by 1979 were lost to plant closures by 1986. Contraction of employment in ongoing plants cut another 18 percent of jobs. The net result is that for the period studied, 1979 to 1986, just about 50 percent of the subsidized jobs created were lost. The study period is, of course, an artificiality; the process is ongoing. IDA has to generate two manufacturing jobs for every one it wants to keep. But each new manufacturing job creates about one additional job in the service sector, as the newly hired worker goes about upgrading his or her life-style. If job loss is an ongoing concern, then, it is not such a dire concern overall. Other studies of the Irish economy, especially one by Mary O'Sullivan published as a chapter in the book *The Economy of Ireland,* suggest that even greater job churning was required to achieve the net job gains cited by IDA; although this is likely so, the reality is that Ireland's economy has been undergoing a substantial transformation in recent decades, and this transformation alone is a major contributor to the upheaval in jobs in the republic.

In addition to jobs lost, many have expressed concerns about the quality of the jobs created by economic development incentive schemes. For example, O'Sullivan, has written about the tendency of foreign investors in Ireland to bring in "McJobs," low-level jobs requiring only rudimentary skill levels and offering little hope for career advancement. O'Sullivan makes the point that "foreign-owned parent companies . . . have had little incentive to invest in new learning processes in Ireland to sustain advantage"—advantage based on skills learned and kept in home-country operations. As evidence in support of her claim, she notes the relatively low level of R&D spending undertaken by foreign investors in Ireland. She also cites investments in telemarketing call centers and electronic assembly facilities.

Her case is buttressed by a detailed study of the Irish software industry by Seán Ó Riain. Foreign multinationals use Ireland as a base for porting software from one platform to another or simply copying and distributing software developed elsewhere. By contrast, indigenous Irish software firms engage in more fundamental software development and need to hire more qualified software engineers. The statistics Ó Riain develops are quite compelling, since the indigenous software industry in Ireland is about the same size as the foreign-owned segment of the industry. He quotes the chief executive officer of one domestically owned software firm as saying, "The other thing I'd like is someone to go out to Dublin Port and put up a sign saying 'We're Closed'" to foreign software firms who come into Ireland to lessen competition for the already scarce software engineers in the country.

Development officials in Ireland (and indeed other jurisdictions) are aware of these criticisms of their past efforts and the performance of the foreign companies they recruit. The response of these same officials is to change the targeting of their recruitment efforts and tilt the grant-making process to attract companies that offer higher-level jobs to the local population. Viewed as an ongoing process, this response is perfectly valid. It does nothing to naysay the criticism levied against the companies taking grants for locating in a particular area. Many companies who take investment incentives fail to deliver on the number of jobs they promise and offer only the lowest-level jobs they can get away with. The worst of the lot simply take the money and run—to another jurisdiction advertising even bigger incentives to relocate.

Government Responds

In democratic and pluralistic societies, government tends to move slowly to adjust its policies to reflect new realities. In the case of the use and misuse of investment incentives, an area the public generally supports because of the apparent job-creation benefits of the programs, the movement to tighten subsidy arrangements to eliminate the most egregious offenses has been slow indeed. As time has passed and the behavior of companies attracted to these subsidies has become even more transparently self-interested, governments have, however, responded. The full story for what the ultimate government response will be has not yet been told, but its outlines are becoming increasingly clear. Companies that partake of investment subsidies in the future will be bound to adhere to more stringent performance criteria for the life of the contract they sign with the subsidizing government. The seller's market in investment incentives that historically favored the company selling its jobs is gradually transforming itself into a legitimate and balanced market of informed buyers and ever more cautious sellers willing to take the incentives on offer only after carefully thinking through all the consequences, short- and long-term, of their actions. The world may well be a better place as a result.

The movement to tighten the terms and conditions of incentive contracts with companies began in Europe in the mid-1980s. The first visible steps appear to have occurred in Ireland, appropriately enough, when Irish authorities changed the basis of their incentive grants from capital spending subsidies to subsidies for employment created. Before long, concerned about companies' walking away from commitments they had made or failing to live up to the full extent of their commitments (e.g., by delivering fewer jobs than promised), IDA started making grant disbursement contingent on the actual delivery of the jobs pledged. By holding back grant money until the jobs were in place, IDA was able to protect its economic interests at least at the margin. When other subsidized firms simply closed, IDA took them to court to get the grant monies back. Following the example of Ireland and even improving on it, other countries rushed to revise the fine print associated with their investment incentive programs.

By the beginning of the 1990s, it was the norm across Europe for investment incentive contracts between governments and companies to include a whole range of provisions designed to protect the position of the government in the deal. These typically included

- rescission terms by which the contract could be canceled if certain conditions were not met
- clawback provisions that allowed for the recovery of all or part of the subsidy costs if the company did not keep up its side of the bargain
- penalty clauses that imposed specific charges for nonperformance or premature relocation of a facility
- recalibration provisions through which subsidy amounts could be adjusted to reflect changing business conditions and performance

These tighter contract provisions were coupled with a greatly increased willingness to litigate to ensure that the provisions were met. What began in Europe quickly spread to the United States and other parts of the world as jurisdictions everywhere tried to rein in the worst of the corporate behavior they were seeing. By 1993 the *Wall Street Journal* was reporting, "Recently legislators have become more savvy in their dealings with companies. Louisiana, Ohio and Texas, as well as some municipalities, have passed laws requiring companies to compensate municipalities for financial inducements if they move out of town prematurely. The long term commitments and reimbursement obligations are set forth in carefully drafted contracts. Other states and communities will probably follow their example." How right they were.

Writing tougher contracts and enforcing them does not address the problem of the economic inefficiencies of subsidies per se. Once again, Europe is in the lead in attempting to do something about this core issue, although movement is under way in the United States as well. In Europe the main bodies for setting European policy are the European Parliament, the European Commission, and the Council of Ministers. In 1995 the European Commission's Directorate-General for External Economic Relations issued a report called "A Level Playing Field for Direct Investment World-Wide," outlining the commission's long-term policy goals of leaving the management of foreign investment at the local level while working at the central level to eliminate anything that might distort investment patterns, including investment subsidies. In its 1997 report on competition policy, the European Commission's Directorate-General for Competition published guidelines that included a series of provisions aimed at greater transparency in the use of state aid to industry designed to "lessen the distortions of competition caused by aid." It also stipulated that "aided investments and jobs must remain in the region for at least five years." The same year, another directorate concerned with taxation called for a voluntary code of conduct among its member states to "tackle harmful tax competition" and inappropriate use of state fiscal aid. The following year the commission called for member submissions on guidelines for the future of state aid to industry, including the vexing question of investment subsidies. All of this may sound torturous, but by EU standards this is the equivalent of a freight train moving down the tracks at 100 miles an hour. The European Commission is preparing to take action and is working hard to build the kind of consensus it needs among its member states to enable that movement to take place.

Even more interesting than the machinations in Brussels is the response of member states. Every one of the fifteen economic development officials I interviewed across the EU indicated that their submission on the question of state aid would call for the elimination of all subsidies. Even IDA Ireland, which arguably has the best track record in making subsidies work for its own good, says in its 1998 annual report, "The EU itself is changing and adopting new strategies and policies which will have significant impact on Ireland. . . . The IDA welcomes the decisions reached at European and Irish Government level." In private conversations I had with IDA and other economic development agencies across Europe, the universal theme was in favor of the EU's abolishing subsidies because individual countries could not do so on their own without incurring a backlash from industry. In all likelihood, given the leadership of the government officials responsible for investment incentive programs, the general population in Europe will throw its weight behind these steps toward reform. (To be thorough, I should note that there is no equivalent consensus around issues of corporate taxation. Countries like Ireland and the United Kingdom are adamant about being left the freedom to set their own policies in the tax arena in order to continue to be attractive to business investors.)

Whereas the EU is taking the governmental lead in the direct assault on investment incentive programs, an equivalent movement in the United States is occurring more at a grassroots level. It is still too early to tell what the ultimate outcome of this movement will be. In May 1996 the National Academy of Sciences held a conference in Washington, D.C., with the theme "the economic war among the states." This conference, attended by over one hundred representatives of all parts of society, including government and academia, took a very strong position against the continuation of state and local investment incentive programs. Since the proceedings of the conference were published, the relevant journals have been full of articles arguing the case against subsidies. Because of the complex politics involved, however, no major political figure has jumped on the issue. Perhaps the EU's laborious efforts toward an actionable coalition against subsidies are not so byzantine after all. In any case, only time will tell where the various policy debates will come out. The direction in which policy is moving is quite clear, however: fewer or no subsidies, with tighter control over their use and abuse by corporations.

My own point of view on the subject is that subsidies will never be totally eliminated because there will always be some rogue jurisdiction willing to offer inducements to companies to invest (Germany as it rebuilds the east German economy is the current leading candidate for this role). But the use of subsidies to attract investment will be much less than it has been historically. Governments everywhere will work much harder and from an enhanced position of knowledge to make sure they get their money's worth from any such incentives they give. The day of the free ride for companies at the expense of government is over.

The whole debate about subsidies is metaphoric for the shift in attitude in the government sector toward corporations. Since the late 1970s, corporations have had a free hand to do pretty much what they wanted to do around the world. Obsessed with doing whatever it might take to increase earnings and win a higher market valuation for their shareholders, corporations have taken advantage of this freedom. In particular, they have run roughshod over government interests in pursuit of their own selfish objectives. No more. Governments everywhere are waking up to what has been going on and are working hard behind the scenes to shorten the leash on corporations and make them conform to larger community interests. This movement is not just evident in the area of investment subsidies, as discussed in detail in this chapter. It can be seen in the gradual strengthening of environmental laws. It can be seen in combined government and consumer actions to write and enforce new rules of behavior in relationship to the use of child labor. It can be seen in the increasingly litigious government relations with tobacco companies and possibly even companies that make guns. Government moves slowly and in fits and starts. But the direction of movement is clear: Corporations are going to have to treat governments as equal partners or pay the price. The successful companies of tomorrow will recognize this trend and modify the way they work.

CHAPTER 8

Suppliers Circle the Wagons
(or Get Picked Off)

The public, as represented by communities and employees, were not the only ones exploited by corporations in their rush to achieve higher stock prices now. They were not even the first to receive critical scrutiny from corporate managers. This privilege was reserved for entities even more closely entwined in the day-to-day affairs of large companies, their suppliers. Although it probably didn't feel like it at the time, by putting suppliers first many companies may have inadvertently done them a favor. Of all major stakeholders, suppliers have made the greatest strides toward recapturing a viable, in some cases even superior, negotiating posture vis-à-vis their corporate masters. This chapter chronicles the evolution supplier relations went through in the last twenty years of the twentieth century. The lessons for any corporate executive are clear: Beware what you unleash, for you may find it turning on you in the future.

The Discovery of Japanese Management Techniques

The 1970s were a troubled decade for business in the United States and Western Europe. Shortly after the decade began, a then unknown OPEC announced a drastic increase in the price of its main export, triggering a world recession and panic in the minds of many Western businesspeople. As companies slowly pulled themselves out of the recession, another threat appeared on the horizon. This threat was tangible. It consisted of a whole raft of carefully engineered and superbly manufactured products emanating from a new source, Japan. Suddenly, industry after industry, ranging from office equipment to automobiles, was confronted with competition at price points often well below the manufacturing costs of an equivalent American or European product. When these products also turned out to be higher quality than the equivalent domestic products, panic became widespread. How was it that a country like Japan, which had been totally devastated in World War II, could so soon thereafter produce superior goods at lower costs than U.S. or European companies?

The search for answers moved into high gear. Young researchers at American business schools went to Japan to try to find out the secrets of Japanese success. Their early publications in journals like the *Harvard Business Review* attracted enough attention that they were soon asked to produce books on the subject. These books, most notably, Bill Ouchi's *Theory Z* and Tony Athos and Richard Pascale's *Art of Japanese Management*, became the first of a string of best-sellers on the previously arcane subject of business.

These initial books on the Japanese attempted to explain their success by focusing on what came to be known as the soft side of Japanese management practices. The authors, therefore, put great emphasis on such aspects of the Japanese system as lifetime employment and consensus-oriented decision-making processes as the primary reason Japan appeared to be manufacturing such superior products at such incredibly low prices. In zeroing in on lifetime employment, they missed the point that this practice seemed to apply only in the major Japanese firms and did not extend through the network of suppliers who were so integral to the Japanese success story. Nor did the focus on consensual decisionmaking reach out to encompass the single-minded and obsessive behavior of post–World-War II Japanese entrepreneurs. Understanding of these aspects was to come later. Still, the books received a ready audience and were widely discussed in the boardrooms of America and Europe by managers eager to find some way out of the economic doldrums they were in as a result of Japanese competition.

In an appendix to his book, Ouchi had a brief description of the Japanese approach to quality control and the extensive use of "quality circles." He even mentioned that these techniques were not new but had been imported to Japan shortly after the war primarily by two American academics, W. Edward Deming and Joe Juran. For people in the trenches of American business, this rediscovery of Deming and Juran was a major breakthrough. For example, in the late 1970s, I was working as a consultant for the Xerox Corporation in its U.S. manufacturing facility in Webster, New York. Engineers there had taken apart copiers made in Japan, noted the fine engineering and quality control, and were trying to figure out how they could achieve comparable standards in their U.S. operations. They had visited Japan (Xerox had a long-standing relationship with Fuji Xerox), heard about Deming and Juran, and were among the first closely to examine Deming's *Quality, Productivity and Competitive Position* and Juran's *Quality Planning and Analysis: From Product Development Through Usage,* published in 1982 and 1970 (the latter having been republished at the end of the decade after being ignored in its first incarnation). It was these quality engineers and their counterparts in manufacturing who launched the first serious assault on suppliers in the early 1980s, having learned all they could about how the Japanese went about making products.

The Japanese system of manufacturing had developed logically, if almost by chance, out of the circumstances facing Japanese manufacturers in the postwar era. When the Japanese began to rebuild their industrial base in, for example, automobiles, they realized they did not have the scale in the Japanese market to match that of their much larger Western competitors. They could not hope to set up dedicated production lines for one model of car like GM and Ford did in the United States. Instead, they would have to assemble all the models they produced on one line and find some other way of achieving the cost savings their larger competitors enjoyed because of economies of scale. One thing was clear immediately: If multiple models were to be built on one line, there was no room for excess inventory related to any one model next to the line. So the Japanese invented *kanban,* known more commonly in the West as just-in-time (JIT) inventory practices. Under *kanban,* the legion of smaller suppliers of parts for cars (or copiers or any other product the Japanese were making) would have to send small and frequent shipments of required parts, each shipment arriving just in time for use in the assembly operation. This would eliminate excess inventory on the floor of the assembly plant and enable the mixed-line production to flow freely. It also moved a lot of inventory off the books of the major assemblers and left it on the books of the suppliers until it was ready to be shipped—a bit of a moot point in Japan, where the suppliers were often so closely affiliated with larger companies that it was financially irrelevant where the inventory sat on the books. Not so in America, however.

Just-in-time inventory practices were one of many production innovations the Japanese introduced. In order to claw back some of the scale advantages they were losing, the Japanese pioneered as well the use of common components across multiple product lines. Although the primary manufacturer might not have scale in any one model, it could gain from the scale advantages afforded by buying common components offered to several manufacturers by its suppliers, which were usually sibling companies tightly tied to the all-powerful parent. Similarly, because of the frequent changeovers from one model to another on these early production lines and because the employees of large Japanese companies were assumed to have employment for life, the Japanese set up programs of worker involvement such as quality circles and all its myriad variants. By involving committed workers meaningfully in the ongoing production process, the Japanese were able to achieve efficiencies unheard of in other parts of the world. It all made sense in the context of the Japanese system, and it worked well in terms of allowing them to move rapidly to become fearsome competitors in a number of world markets.

When American and other Western manufacturing and procurement specialists descended on Japan in droves in the late 1970s and early 1980s to learn what the Japanese were doing to make them so competitive in world markets, they were amazed by what they found—so amazed, in fact, that they rushed home to put the best of the Japanese practices in place in their home countries. Thus, the assault on suppliers began even while the first stirrings of the shareholder value movement were just starting to gain a wider audience.

But why suppliers first? Why not install all of these Japanese innovations in your own plants before trying to force them on suppliers? The answer is simple. It is hard to change practices in the arena of real work such as manufacturing. It can take months to rejigger systems and retrain workforces to accept new operating procedures. In contrast, given the superior-inferior relationship between manufacturers and their suppliers so prevalent around 1980, it was and still often is easier to demand that your suppliers change what they are doing in order to retain their share of your business. So it happened that the idea of just-in-time inventory came to America in the early 1980s in many industries.

The American version of JIT should have been called "YKI" for "you keep it," because in the United States, where most suppliers were independent companies with their own balance sheets and operating statements, one of the immediate gains from moving to a JIT system was a sudden reduction in the inventory costs of the company that made the switch. These inventory costs did not really go away; they just transferred to someone else's balance sheet (until or unless that company could push the practice further down the line onto its own suppliers). Nevertheless, this transfer resulted in an immediate (accepting that nothing happens immediately in the world of manufacturing) gain in the operating results of the primary manufacturer. These operating gains were not lost on the senior managers of companies newly embracing the shareholder value ethic. "Give me more of the same," they said to their manufacturing specialists as they rushed to take the gains into profits to add another fillip to their efforts to achieve a higher stock price. This revolution in supplier relations has continued more or less unabated to this day.

Suppliers Feel the Squeeze

The net effect of this movement to force suppliers to lower costs in virtually every area of their operations was a devastation of supplier economics—until they, too, read the writing on the wall and began to get their own acts together. Let's look at some of the practices that evolved. Perhaps the most famous of the cost cutters during the era of the most intense pressures on suppliers was GM's Jose Ignacio Lopez de Arriortua. As reported in the trade publication *Ward's Autoworld,* "Lopez and Co. would select a small group of finalists [to supply some component to GM's vast assembly operation], and then set a target price well below even the lowest bid [they had received]. The 'winning' supplier would leave the process wondering how his company could possibly make a profit at that price." This was the world of the supplier in the late 1980s and early 1990s, a very uncomfortable world indeed. (As most readers will know, despite his successes at GM, Lopez later became a figure of controversy when he took over worldwide procurement for Volkswagen. His switch in allegiance triggered a massive lawsuit in which GM accused Lopez of taking trade secrets to elope with a major competitor; this subsequently led to his dismissal from VW.)

As an example of the kind of damage done by such purchasing policies on the affairs of major supplier companies, let's look for a minute at the Dana Corporation. In existence since the early days of the automobile industry in North America, Dana in the 1980s was thought by many (this author included) to be the cream of the automobile supply companies. Dana makes a broad array of supplies, including drivetrain components, engine parts, filtration products, structural components, and chassis products. As one of the best-run companies anywhere, not just in the automotive supply industry, Dana had established an enviable track record of steadily rising sales and profits. Figure 8.1 (page 132) shows what happened to Dana with the onslaught of new purchasing and manufacturing practices in the auto industry in the 1980s and 1990s. Dana's sales and profits grew steadily until about 1988, with most of the fluctuations that occurred the result of demand changes in the highly cyclical auto industry. After 1988, however, Dana's sales hit a plateau, and its earnings plummeted in this time of the most intense pressure on suppliers by the automobile industry purchasing moguls. It should be noted that Dana dramatically outperformed its peers in the auto supply sector during this period.

The push to cut costs on supply contracts was not the only initiative automobile companies undertook in their search for more and more economies. Again taking the lead from the Japanese, all of the auto companies started programs of supplier consolidation in the early 1990s. For example, Chrysler Corporation, the least vertically integrated of the major automobile companies in the United States (i.e., it depends on suppliers for a higher percentage of the final value of the car than does Ford or GM), shrunk its supplier base from 2,500 to 1,140 companies between 1989 and

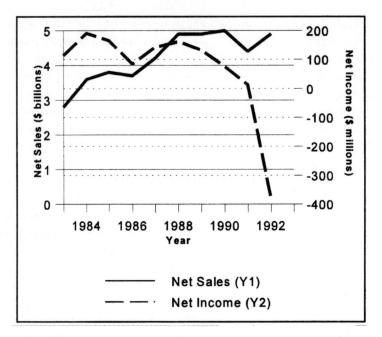

FIGURE 8.1   Trend in Dana Corporation Sales and Net Income

SOURCE: Dana Corporation Annual Reports.

1996. Its stated intention is to shrink the base even further in the years ahead to a target of only 150 companies by the early 2000s. These astonishing figures are slightly misleading, however. Although Chrysler is shrinking its supply base to a more limited number of companies that have become known as first-tier suppliers, other firms find themselves competing for business from these companies. From Chrysler's point of view, they gain by reducing the number of people they have to deal with and by having the ability to source larger and larger subsystems with these first-tier suppliers. Indeed, the trend in the industry, foreshadowed in some overseas plants, is to have first-tier suppliers come directly on the assembly floor, where their responsibility extends to installing the entire subsystem in the car as it passes through.

With the reduction in the number of suppliers on their lists, Chrysler and the other major auto companies can demand more from them. For example, Chrysler suppliers are rated annually on product quality, delivery, performance, cost, and technology. Chrysler requires its suppliers to comply with the stringent QS 9000 quality standards, which are increasingly the norm for the auto industry. If you cannot meet this standard as a supplier, you are dropped from Chrysler's list. Most major manufacturers are also demanding that all their suppliers establish electronic data interchange (EDI) links with them. This move to e-commerce to cut costs and expedite information flows forces supplier firms to invest in expensive information technology infrastructure at a time when they are feeling the squeeze across their entire business systems. Along with requiring suppliers to meet standards, firms like Chrysler are increasingly looking to their suppliers to take an active part in the car design process. This not only saves money for Chrysler but also shortens the length of the development cycle for new cars, which can be worth millions to an auto company.

In return for all the extra responsibilities car companies are placing on the shoulders of their suppliers, they are rewarding them with long-term contracts—in effect, contracts that are the suppliers' to lose in contrast to the original bid-as-you-go system. This is intended to allow suppliers to plan ahead, knowing that the level of business they will have is secure. These long-term supply contracts are not quite the good deal they appear to be, however. *New Steel,* a trade magazine for the steel industry, recently reported on a long-term supply contract between General Motors and a group of steel companies. The editors of the magazine asked, "If a steel company negotiates when the price is low and the price rises in four years, is it stuck with that lower price?" The immediate response from GM's director of steel purchasing, Ron Schuster, was, "Yes; and if prices go lower, we'll retain the same price." When the magazine editors pointed out that prices were already at historically low levels and unlikely to drop any further, the GM spokesperson responded about the strategic advantages of a long-term contract. Uh-huh. A separate article a few months earlier had reported that GM allegedly rebid a whole series of long-term material supply contracts demanding and getting 20 percent price cuts from each of its suppliers.

The price pressures on suppliers and the demands that they meet higher and higher standards of service and quality have put small firms at a tremendous competitive disadvantage. *Purchasing* magazine reported in August 1999 that the burden on small suppliers was devastating minority-owned supplier firms. In a special story on minority supplier development, Brian Milligan reported that "the typically small minority- or women-owned businesses are falling by the wayside as newly merged mega-companies are drastically consolidating their supply bases . . . Small suppliers, who may not be able to afford the latest in computer technology, are missing out on growing e-commerce activity." Although the story goes on to report special efforts to protect the role of minority-owned suppliers, the overall message is clear: Changes in the relationship between major companies and their suppliers in the United States are wiping out years of progress achieved under affirmative action laws.

The automobile industry has been the focus of the discussion so far because it is so large and so dependent on suppliers. This industry was not alone in rewriting its deal with its supplier base. Rank Xerox, the American company's UK affiliate, reduced its base of suppliers from 5,000 in 1981 to just over 300 in 1987. (Xerox, as noted earlier, was an early mover in efforts to cut costs out of purchasing and manufacturing.) In an entirely different but highly analogous sector, discount stores were squeezing their distributors by charging back to them penalties for any errors in labeling, packaging, or delivery. They were also substantially reducing the number of distributors they were willing to deal with. The move to cut costs and consolidate the supply base was near universal across American industry in the 1990s.

Suppliers Strike Back

If you were a supplier subjected to repeated demands for price rollbacks from your main customer, price rollbacks so severe that you were hardly able to make a profit on the business, what would you do? In all probability, you would do anything you could to strengthen your negotiating position. You might also try to do everything you could to pass some of the price cuts down the line to your own network of suppliers. That's exactly what suppliers did.

The most visible manifestation of the attempt to regain negotiating power is the explosion of merger and acquisition activity among supply companies. Within the automotive sector alone, from the beginning of 1998 until mid-1999 fourteen major acquisitions occurred and one major joint venture was announced:

- Dana merged with Echlin and subsequently bought parts of Federal-Mogul's bearing operations.
- Eaton Corporation acquired Aeroquip-Vickers.
- Federal-Mogul bought Fel-Pro, T&N PLC, and the automotive division of Cooper Industries.
- Johnson Controls bought Becker Group.
- Arvin Industries bought Purolator's filter business, Mark IV.
- Lear bought United Technologies' automotive business.
- MascoTech bought TriMas (combining two firms with multicapital names).
- Meritor bought Volvo's axle manufacturing facility and LucasVarity's heavy vehicle braking systems business.
- TRW subsequently bought all that was left of LucasVarity.

- A firm called Venture Holdings bought Peguform of Germany.
- Goodyear Tire and Rubber entered into a long-term joint venture with Sumitomo Rubber Industries.

Most of the companies listed above are hardly household names because their primary business is as suppliers to major manufacturers. Even without widespread name recognition, it is clear the major players in this industry were thinking along the same lines. Most of the consolidation going on was aimed at building scale—share of purchase, in effect—in critical car subassembly areas. For example, one company, Johnson Controls, spent over $500 million in the 1990s in Europe expanding its position in the car seat supply market. Some of the merger activity involved diversification, however, as suppliers pursued the lucrative aftermarket for automotive components.

Of the approximately 5,000 U.S. automotive supply companies in existence in 1990, almost half of them had disappeared by 1999. In selected product areas, the consolidation has been even more dramatic. Between them, Lear Corporation and Johnson Controls control nearly 80 percent of the car seat market in the United States; in Europe they share that market with one other supplier, a subsidiary of Peugeot. As one industry analyst remarked, "Lear was essentially a sleepy little seat company in the 1980s that has repositioned itself as a full interior systems supplier [by 1999]." Other areas that have experienced similar consolidation include brakes, airbags, transmissions, frames, tires, wheels, engine valves, seals, pistons, and wire harnesses. In none of these major product areas are there more than four or five major suppliers in Europe or North America. By contrast, there are still almost a dozen companies making cars on each of these two continents.

These consolidations have had a huge impact on the economics of automotive supply companies. As shown in Figure 8.2 (page 136), from its low point in 1992 Dana Corporation's fortunes have turned around completely. After its merger with Echlin in 1998, Dana reported all-time record sales and earnings for the combined companies in 1998, despite taking a write-off in relation to the merger. Automotive supply continues to be a tough business in which to prosper. Its record results notwithstanding, at the end of 1998 Dana reported plans to lay off 3,500 people and close fifteen plants. An observer of the industry interviewed in a special edition of the *Wall Street Transcript* noted he was more likely to put aside for his children the stock of an auto supply company than he was to buy stock in an automobile company itself. The balance of power between suppliers and the companies they serve had surely shifted.

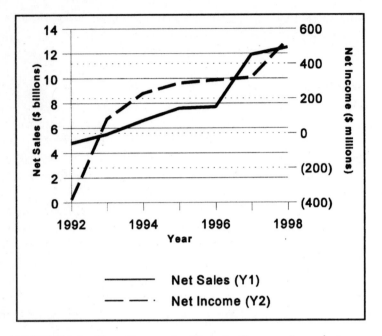

FIGURE 8.2   Dana Corporation Turns Its Fortunes Around

SOURCE: Dana Corporation Annual Reports.

A Case in Point: The Mouse That Squeaked, Loudly

If any one company embodies the changes going on in the relationship between large companies and their suppliers, it is the company now known as
the Lear Corporation (its name has changed somewhat over the years). The
original Lear Seating Company was founded in 1917 to make seat frames for
Ford and General Motors. By 1983 its sales had grown to $159.8 million,
which represented a $12 share of each car it sold seat frames to. Under pres-
sure from its major car company customers, Lear introduced a JIT system of
manufacturing all the way back in 1983, when it operated as a division of
Lear Siegler, a publicly listed company.

Lear Siegler continued to operate the company until 1988, when the lever-
aged buyout specialists at Kidder Peabody, then a subsidiary of GE, bought
it out from its parent and took the company private. When the recession of
the early 1990s hit, these early investors also had to be bailed out, this time
by another LBO investor, the Lehman Funds, who paid GE Credit
Corporation (GECC) $75 million to take over all of the stock in the com-
pany and to assume its outstanding debt. GECC facilitated the deal by of-

fering the new entity a $20-million mortgage on its plants and machinery. What a purchase for Lehman Funds that turned out to be.

Emerging from the recession, the still private Lear Seating Company began to build its position in the auto supply sector by acquisition. In November 1993 it bought Ford's own seat cover business for $173.4 million. The terms of the purchase agreement guaranteed that Lear would supply seat covers to the bulk of Ford's North American cars for at least five years. One might say that Ford's former seat cover business fit nicely with Lear's traditional seat frame operations. Five months after the acquisition from Ford, the company was refloated on the New York stock exchange at $18.50 a share, valuing the company at about $1 billion at that time.

With the acquisition from Ford under its belt and the successful stock market flotation behind it, in December 1994 Lear greatly expanded its presence in Europe by acquiring the car seat operations of Fiat in a deal very similar to the Ford deal. Less than a year later, it acquired all of the stock of Automotive Industries Holdings, positioning itself solidly in car interiors (e.g., door panels and headliners) to complement its already strong position in seats. In 1996 it acquired Masland Corporation, adding capabilities in acoustical systems and materials for cars, and bought out Borealis Industrie, a major European supplier of instrument panels and door panels. In 1997 it bought three major companies, Dunlop in Britain, Keiper Seating in Germany, and ITT Automotive in the United States. In 1998 it bought out the GM car seat facilities from its A. C. Delco subsidiary.

While it was making these acquisitions, Lear was investing either on its own or in joint ventures with local companies in Brazil, Argentina, Venezuela, South Africa, Poland, Spain, Turkey, Thailand, India, Indonesia, Australia, and Japan in a series of operations related to its core businesses. By the end of 1997, Lear sold seats or interior components to twenty-seven automobile companies around the globe. Its products are an integral component of most of the leading car brands, including

BMW (Z3 and M Roadster)
Chrysler (Cirrus, Concorde, LHS, Sebring, Town and Country)
Dodge (Avenger, Caravan, Dakota, Durango, Intrepid, Neon, Ram, Stratus)
Ford (Escort, Expedition, F-Series, Mustang, Ranger, Taurus, Windstar)
Saturn
Cadillac (Catera, DeVille, Eldorado/Seville)
Lincoln (Continental, Navigator, Town Car)
Pontiac (Bonneville, Firebird, Grand Am, Grand Prix, Sunfire, Tran Sport)

Mercury (Grand Marquis, Mountaineer, Mystique, Sable, Tracer, Villager)

Buick (Century, LeSabre, Park Avenue, Regal, Riviera, Skylark)

Chevrolet (Metro, Monte Carlo, Prizm, S 10, Suburban, Swing, Tahoe, Venture)

GMC (Jimmy, Safari, Savana, Sierra, Sonoma, Suburban, Top-Kick, Yukon)

Oldsmobile (88, Achieve, Aurora, Bravada, Cutlass, Intrigue, Silhouette)

Honda (Accord, Acura, Civic, Passport)

Mazda (626, B-Series, MX-6)

Mitsubishi (Eclipse, Galant)

Nissan (Altima, Frontier, Quest, Sentra)

Subaru/Isuzu (Rodeo, Legacy)

Jeep (Cherokee, Wrangler)

Suzuki (Sidekick, Swift)

Toyota (Avalon, Camry, Corolla, Sienna, Tacoma)

Volkswagen (Cabrio, Golf, GPA Minivan, Jetta)

Volvo (S/V 70)

Alfa Romeo (145, 146, 936, Coupe/GTV, Giuletta, Spider)

Audi (A3, A4, A6, A8, Cabriolet)

Citroën (Berlingo, Saxo)

Ferrari (F355 Berlinetta, F355 Spider, S50 Maranello)

Fiat (Barchetta, Bravo/Brava, Coupe, Ducato, Marea, Panda, Punto)

Jaguar (XJ Saloon, XK8)

Lancia (Dedra, Delta, Kappa, Y)

Mercedes (A-class, C-class, E-class, SL, SLK)

Opel (Astra, Calibra, Corsa, Frontera, Omega, Vectra)

Porsche (911, Boxster)

Peugeot (306, 406, 406 Coupe)

Renault (Cabrio, Clio, Express, Laguna, Megane, Safrane, Scenic, Twingo)

Rolls Royce

It is no surprise that Lear is the market leader in seats and car interiors in both the United States and Europe. In 1997 its systems accounted for almost $320 of the final purchase price of cars it supplied.

The effect of all this activity on its revenue and earnings was, needless to say, dramatic. On the basis of the performance illustrated in Figure 8.3, Lear's market valuation had increased to $3.3 billion by September 1999.

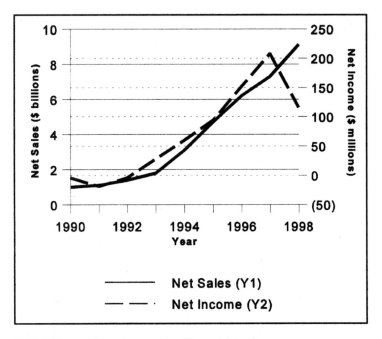

FIGURE 8.3   Lear Corporation Financial Performance

SOURCE: Dana Corporation Annual Reports and Standard & Poor's Stock Report, 19 June, 1999.

Lear's corporate strategy is clear, and it is not afraid to state it boldly in its annual report: It wants to expand its position as the world's top supplier of automotive interior systems. Lear currently has a substantial if not always leading spot in all five major categories of car interiors (seat systems, floor and acoustic systems, door panels, instrument panels, and headliners). It intends to grow by enhancing its already strong relationships with the manufacturers; building up its presence in emerging markets; taking advantage of new outsourcing opportunities as they arise; investing in product technology and design capability; capitalizing on its worldwide JIT manufacturing capabilities to set service standards so high they are hard for others to meet; and selectively acquiring other firms to expand its footprint in the industry.

As one of the ten largest auto supply companies in the world and a major first-tier supplier to most of the major car makers, Lear has invested heavily in engineering and design capability related to its areas of expertise. It holds several significant patents closely connected to the components it supplies. In short, it is in a position to dictate the direction car interiors take over the next number of years by designing and supplying the interiors likely to be found in most major brands. Lear's is hardly the tale of a beaten-down supplier but a story beginning to echo across the ranks of suppliers in many industries.

Think what has really happened in the automotive supply sector. The major automotive companies used to be highly vertically integrated, making the bulk of their supplies in house. No more. GM spun off its supply subsidiary, A. C. Delco, and publicly proclaimed its intent to rely more on third-party suppliers. Moreover, where automobile companies used to deal with thousands of suppliers, they are all on record and in the process of reducing this number to a mere handful by historical standards. These remaining few supply larger and larger parts of the finished car; take far more responsibility for the design, quality, and delivery of the completed assembly; and operate in an industry sector that is far more concentrated and therefore controlling than the automobile industry itself. If that isn't the functional equivalent of giving away the store, I don't know what is.

The automobile industry is not alone. The same process of supplier consolidation has occurred in the office equipment market, the telecommunications industry, the computer industry, retailing, and even airplane manufacturing, to list just a sampling of industries going through the same process. For example, in the airplane market, a once tiny company, Precision Castparts, has bought up virtually all of the suppliers of forged metal components to Boeing, the dominant plane maker in the United States. If any of these consolidating industries wants a peek at the future, they might just well look at the computer industry and notice what clout Microsoft and Intel exercise even though their main products are components of the final product shipped to consumers.

Major Companies (Try to) Fight Back

The shift in the balance of power between major companies and their suppliers is, of course, still under way, with some supplier companies in most industries showing the way. Among major companies that rely on suppliers, the shift is beginning to cause consternation, as the smartest of these begin to realize what they have done to themselves by their repeated pressures on suppliers to cut costs and take on broader responsibilities. Already both the rhetoric and the actions of these companies are changing to accommodate the new reality of the marketplace. Companies heavily reliant on suppliers are increasingly using terms like "supplier voice" and "partnerships." Such nomenclature may sound better to most ears, but it is unlikely to restore the old balance of power between firms and their suppliers.

Despite giving away the store so readily, large companies are nothing if not responsive to changes in their circumstances. General Motors, not widely acclaimed for its quickness of feet, gave a supplier-of-the-year award in 1997 to BBK. What does BBK "supply" to GM? It consults with GM's suppliers to help them meet GM's requirements more easily. In a different industry, Nortel, the telecommunications equipment giant, talks about its "shared savings" partnership program with its suppliers. Even in the notoriously hard-nosed retail industry, major players are beginning to change their traditional posture toward their suppliers. Paul Mason, the VP of logistics and human resources for ASDA (the UK supermarket chain bought out by Wal-Mart), is on record as saying, "Retailers have to be more even-handed [with their suppliers]. . . . We should be talking about partner shift, not partner shaft."

Susan Helper, a professor at Case Western Reserve University, refers to the evolving relationships between suppliers and their customers as "face" relationships, which she characterizes as ones in which the partners share information and ideas to sort out problems as they arise. This kind of relationship is in stark contrast to the "exit" relationships that used to so dominate supplier-customer interactions, in which the customer made a take-it-or-leave-it offer and that was the end of the discussion. In a series of widely read articles based on her surveys of the automobile industry, Helper claims that these new-style relationships are creating economic benefits for suppliers and customers alike. Her claims are indisputable. One wonders whether she is thinking clearly about the issue, however.

It is unarguably true that a supplier who holds a many-year contract from a major company like an automobile manufacturer is going to be more than willing to invest wherever necessary to improve either the cost or effectiveness of the system it is supplying. Given the security of a long-term contract, who wouldn't? But the long-term economic gains that derive from that investment are much more likely to accrue to the supplier itself—even if some of the gains are shared with the customer. The supplier in such a relationship is, after all, in the catbird seat. As long as the supplier does what is required to retain the contract—a process made simpler by the consolidation of the supply industry in the 1990s, which means there may well be only one or two firms capable of taking on the contract at all—the supplier is in a position to dictate where the savings go. That this is occurring is evidenced by the increasing margins throughout most of the 1990s of major supplier companies such as Lear (seen earlier) and Dana. (See Figure 8.4 on page 142.) compared to the lackluster margins of their major customers, the automobile companies themselves. Absolute levels aside, since these reflect more on the capital structure of the industries than on company performance, the trend in mar-

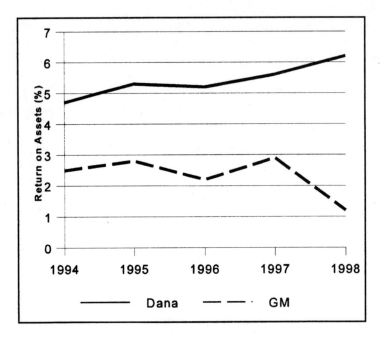

FIGURE 8.4   Trend in Dana and GM Margins

SOURCE: Dana and GM Annual Reports.

gin performance is clearly in favor of the supplier, Dana. Why wouldn't it be, given the shift in relative power in the buyer-supplier equation?

Suppliers responded aggressively to the assault by shareholder-value-driven clients because they had to. Their continued existence was at stake. Consumers, too, have borne the brunt of the shareholder value movement. But the attack on consumers was not life-threatening, only annoying. I look more closely at their reaction in the next chapter.

CHAPTER 9

Customers Vote with Their Feet, Pocketbooks, Voices . . .

In the rush to achieve ever higher levels of shareholder value, the last con-stituency companies should ignore is customers. But customers were not immune from the corporate world's attempt to squeeze every last ounce out of short-term earnings. Product lines were pruned to eliminate all but the most profitable items. Customers noticed. Major discount retail stores, the darlings of Wall Street and the buying public, employed predatory practices against smaller competitors to drive them out of business so the discount chains could raise their prices to profitable levels. Customers noticed. Big names in consumer goods cut corners by locating plants overseas in countries desperate for employment, sometimes even using child laborers at poverty wage levels to make their products for Western consumers. Customers no-ticed. Other companies skirted the edges of environmental protection laws to avoid the costs of cleaning up after their manufacturing processes. Custo-mers noticed.

It would be a gross overstatement to claim that the combined actions of shareholder-value-driven companies triggered a mass consumer protest movement in the late 1990s. The temper of the times was not one to pro-duce a mass movement for anything, except perhaps personal enrichment. Instead of uniting in an organized reaction, consumers responded more or less as the urge struck them.

Consumers everywhere became more cynical about what they were being asked to buy. Survey after survey registered the steadily declining consumer preference for brands. New discount retail outlets sprang up and took busi-ness in droves from older, better-established, and pricier stores. Then the Internet came along. On the Internet, consumers could not only buy more conveniently, but they could also check out best bargains at the click of a mouse. Although conventional retailers sought to cover all the bases by opening their own Web sites, many of them missed the point: Internet shoppers are not loyal to anyone; all they want is the best available price. As Internet use and shopping grows, as it undoubtedly will in the years ahead, most retail-oriented companies are going to find it increasingly hard to retain margins.

Along with changing their buying behavior, consumers began to band together to oppose specific corporate actions. Special interest groups formed to pursue the issue of the moment (and the companies thought to have caused the problem in the first place). Having become the focus of consumer interest (or, more accurately, disdain), companies were forced to pay attention and make adjustments in how they went about their business.

This chapter chronicles the evolution of the relationship between companies and arguably their most important stakeholders, their customers. Because consumer behavior is diffuse and subject to a lot of competing influences over time, most of the trends outlined in this chapter are nascent. All the trend lines point in the same way, however. Consumers are not happy with the way they have been treated in the rush to maximize shareholder value, and they are making their displeasure known by every means available to them.

The "Value" in Reducing Consumer Choice

An article in the winter 1997 issue of the prestigious *McKinsey Quarterly*, a journal of self-promotion, proclaims, "Brand consolidation makes a lot of sense." The authors—two consultants from McKinsey's Oslo office and two from its London office—go on to explain, "The reduction in the cost of goods sold (because the product range has been streamlined and advertising and promotion are more focused) could bring the operating margin up from between 5 and 7 percent to 16 percent—approaching a tripling effect on the bottom line." To add credibility to what appears to be a conceptual argument, they cite the experience of Procter & Gamble, which "eliminated almost a quarter of the variety of its brands between 1991 and 1994." The authors state that one of the benefits of P&G's consolidation is "to make it absolutely clear what are the best choices for the customer." They also cite the $20 million in annual cost savings achieved by P&G's rival, Colgate-Palmolive, by cutting out a quarter of its brands. The authors fail to comment on whether consumers cared that their choice in the supermarket was being reduced. Indeed, nowhere in the article do they even mention the consumer. Perhaps they assume that consumers were without interest or options.

Pricing and Managing for the Bottom Line

In an entirely different arena, the U.S. Federal Trade Commission sues the leading bricks-and-mortar toy retailer, Toys R Us, accusing them of "bullying major toy makers into deals that kept the toys from being sold at lower-priced warehouse stores, such as Sam's and Price Clubs, thereby curbing competition." Toys R Us responds that there are economies of scale associated with dealing with the big chains. The American Booksellers Association sues five publishing firms on behalf of its members, independent bookstores around the country, saying, "The ability of these bookstores to compete had been increasingly harmed by unlawfully favorable deals, prices, and promotional allowances that certain book publishers, including defendants, had given to a limited number of large chains of bookstores and discount outlets in the country." The publishers defend their position by citing the same argument as Toys R Us—economies of scale. Home Depot, another discount retailing giant, sets its prices in Atlanta (where it faces almost no real competition) almost 10 percent higher than its prices in Greensboro, North Carolina, where it is in a head-to-head battle with another chain, Lowe's. In defense of its actions, Home Depot points to differences in overhead and transportation costs to serve the two markets.

One of the big companies' tactics, the practice of using differential pricing across retail outlets, is fairly modern. It got its big boost in the 1980s, when Shell Oil Company was trying to survive a vicious price war in the UK retail gasoline market. To stem its losses, Shell hired a brilliant young consultant, Jacques César, to run price elasticity experiments across its retail network in the UK. From these experiments, Shell was able to optimize the amount of revenue it received despite the raging price war by moving prices up and down by fractions of a penny depending on the competitive situation of any particular outlet—tor example, a gas station at an intersection facing competition from rival stations on each corner would be priced aggressively, whereas prices at an isolated station on a rural back road would be set much higher. Buoyed by its success in the UK, Shell employed César to roll out the technology in many other countries and markets around the world. With Shell as an enthusiastic reference, César, ever the entrepreneur, was able to persuade a number of other retailers to adopt the practice. In fact, he seemed somewhat taken aback when Archie Norman, then the CEO of ASDA supermarkets, rejected the idea because he thought consumers would feel ripped off if they encountered unjustifiably different prices in their visits to the chain's stores. Other retailers had no such compunction, and César's practice spread around the world.

With Wal-Mart's recent acquisition of ASDA to give it a major beachhead in the UK, one wonders if Norman's scruples will become a thing of the past. Wal-Mart makes no bones about the fact that individual managers have discretion over the prices they charge in their stores. That this means stores located only miles apart have radically different prices is irrelevant, according to Wal-Mart. They are simply responding to local competitive conditions.

Any company that is large and successful and in the public eye, as is Wal-Mart, is bound to become the focus of some criticism. Wal-Mart more than most seems to be a magnet for such censure because of the sharpness of its business practices up and down the value chain. Wal-Mart seems to have been sued in virtually every aspect of its operation: In Texas and Colorado, pharmacists who worked for the chain sued because they were not being paid for overtime they were required to work. According to an attorney involved in such a suit, 25,000 cases have been filed by customers who were injured by merchandise that fell on them in the stacked-to-the-rafters, barnlike structures Wal-Mart uses for all its stores. In Missouri an employee of Wal-Mart successfully sued the chain for forcing him to work on Sunday in violation of his religious beliefs. The national Advertising Review Board, an offshoot of the Better Business Bureau, forced Wal-Mart to change its much-used slogan "Always the Low Price" because it simply wasn't true. The attorney general of Florida cited Wal-mart for selling inferior watches labeled as Seikos and telling consumers they came with Seiko guarantee.

In addition to a seemingly never-ending list of lawsuits against the firm, Wal-Mart has been widely attacked in the press on a number of counts. Its employment policies cause an outcry because most Wal-Mart "associates" are paid at minimum-wage levels and offered no or few health care benefits; the company defines a full-time employee as anyone who works twenty-eight hours a week—just few enough to avoid paying them benefits. Its "Made in America" marketing theme draws criticism because it is in fact one of the largest importers of goods from Third World countries (and often accused of allowing its suppliers to use child labor in their factories). Finally, Wal-Mart has been called to task for its relationship with its suppliers, all designed to squeeze another buck out of the deal in Wal-Mart's favor. The company routinely calls suppliers collect to complain about details on orders; charges back to suppliers for goods supposedly damaged in transit (but never proves the actual damage occurred); asks for huge numbers of free samples; asks for special discounts for new store openings; commissions cheap knockoffs of branded products; sends goods back on the excuse they didn't sell and demands immediate refunds; and pays late for goods that are delivered on time and to specification.

Wal-Mart always builds on the outskirts of town, where it can find cheap land, often special tax deals, and access to major highways connecting to other small towns in the region. The result is the devastation of Main Street, Small Town, USA. A 1995 survey in Iowa of the effects of Wal-Mart's entry into the state measured the destruction across small retailer segments:

50 percent of clothing stores had closed
42 percent of variety stores had closed
30 percent of hardware stores had closed
29 percent of shoe stores had closed
26 percent of department stores had closed
25 percent of building material stores had closed
17 percent of jewelry stores had closed

The remaining stores likely survive out of sheer obstinacy. Their economics have been undercut almost as badly as the economics of those who were forced to close. Ever helpful, Morrison Cain, a vice president of the International Mass Retailers Association, the trade association for the big players, offers a menu of things the small stores can do: find a niche, sell items not carried by the giant discounters, refocus on upscale merchandise, improve store marketing and image, price competitively, and emphasize service that discounters do not provide. He does not, however, offer any advice on how small retailers can afford to do all or any of these things.

Having wiped out many a small-town center, Wal-Mart is only too eager to close one of its stores on the outskirts of town and divert retail traffic to an even larger megastore somewhere in the region. In light of these statistics, it is little wonder that more and more small towns across America are mounting effective campaigns to keep Wal-Mart out of their territory.

And yet even as communities struggle to keep Wal-Mart out and suppliers increasingly refuse to do business with it, consumers flock to its stores. Consumers are well aware of Wal-Mart's reputation for sharp dealing. They shop at Wal-Mart because they still believe it has the best prices going. Until viable alternatives come along, their loyalty to Wal-Mart is unlikely to be tested. When it is, Wal-Mart's history will probably come back to haunt it.

Putting One Over on the Consumer

Sharp dealing is not exclusively the province of manufacturers and retailers who sell to end-use consumers, although it tends to concentrate there because individual consumers are generally thought to be too small to make much difference if they object to these practices. Similar practices can be found in other, more sophisticated (or thought to be) markets as well. For example, airlines routinely charge a bewildering range of prices for the same seat on their planes. Everyone knows this but accepts it as just another example of the fouled-up airline industry. Phone companies have bombarded U.S. consumers with solicitation calls trying to induce them to switch carriers. Pressure from consumers finally forced the Federal Trade Commission to set up strict rules governing when and how individual consumers can be switched. Most people just hang up when they recognize the next phone call offering some fantastic savings in telephone rates. The price of phone calls has indeed come down, particularly in the long-distance segment, but most consumers no longer believe the hype associated with each new offer.

Federal Express deliberately runs second deliveries during the day so there is no chance customers will confuse its run-of-the-mill next-day service with its premium "express" service, which promises delivery by 10 A.M. each morning. Because they are incurring the costs of the extra delivery trip whether it is needed or not, there is some justification for the different prices they charge. Not so in the case of IBM, however. IBM wanted to bring out a low-end version of its popular LaserPrinter Series E, which printed at a speed of ten pages a minute. To differentiate the low-end machine, IBM put an extra chip in it. The function of the chip was just to mark time, so that the low-end and otherwise identical machine could print at only five pages a minute. Similarly, Microsoft offers two versions of its Windows NT operating system, a workstation system that sells for $260 and can support only ten PCs at a time and a server system that goes for between $730 and $1,080 and can support virtually an unlimited number of users. According to an analysis by Reilly Software, the two systems are identical, a view Microsoft disputes. The problem for both IBM and Microsoft is that computer users are both smart people and inveterate tinkerers, and the companies' attempted deception of customers soon came to light and was posted for all to see on the Internet. Although these practices were cited as examples of good marketing by a couple of consultants from McKinsey, Carl Shapiro and Hal Varian, few customers would agree.

Looking back on the litany of practices carried out in the 1990s in markets that touch directly on consumers, one truly wonders what the managers were thinking. Did they somehow believe consumers wouldn't notice? Did they figure that even if consumers noticed, they really wouldn't care? Consumers noticed and they cared. But instead of mounting a mass demonstration, they did something more insidious and threatening to the future welfare of companies: They slowly began to change their purchasing habits, undermining often decades of work by those who want to sell to them. That evolution is ongoing. Where it will end is anyone's guess. But it does not augur well for the future of companies.

Consumers Turn Away

Most consumers, especially American consumers, are bombarded with information trying to induce them to buy one product or another. Each day American consumers are presented with 12 billion display ads, 3 million radio ads, and more than 300,000 television commercials. On average a U.S. consumer is the target of 1 million marketing communications every year, about 3,000 a day. American consumers are fed up with the assault on their senses and sense by these ads, many of which are misleading or at best disingenuous. There are any number of figures showing American consumers' ad fatigue:

- 83 percent of those contacted in a 1996 survey by DIRECT said there should be a law requiring an opt-in procedure before direct marketeers can put a consumer's name on their list.
- 72 percent of Internet users in a 1998 survey by Graphic, Visualization & Usability (GVU) believed there should be laws to protect privacy on the Internet.
- 53 percent of American respondents to a 1998 *Business Week* survey said laws should be enacted now to cover how personal information is captured and used on the Web.

A dislike of ads and a call for regulation to protect individual rights is threatening enough to many industries. Coupled with a gradual decrease in the level of loyalty consumers are showing in some of their purchases, this rise in consumer rancor is truly alarming, if a sign of the times.

Consumer loyalty is at best a nebulous concept. Does it mean a consumer is willing to buy something more than once or shop regularly at the same retail outlet? Or does it mean a consumer has a regular and immutable pattern of buying only one brand and not another? With the concept difficult to pin down, measuring where consumer loyalty stands at any point in time is even more problematic. Nevertheless, it is so central to the business of marketeers that repeated attempts have been made to gauge it over the years. Even conceding that each of these episodic surveys probably used a slightly different definition of the concept and slightly different means of measurement, the trend of the results is clear (and to most businesspeople should be disturbing).

Let's look at four such surveys. A 1975 survey by Needham, Harper, and Steers advertising agency reported that 80 percent of men and 72 percent of women agreed to the statement, "I try to stick with well-known brand names." When the agency repeated the survey in 1980, these figures had declined to 64 percent and 56 percent, respectively (although other students of brand loyalty have disputed the decline). In contrast to these earlier figures, a survey conducted by Kurt Salmon and Associates and reported in *Women's Wear Daily* in 1998 showed that 41 percent of female consumers said a brand name was important in purchasing apparel; this figure was down from the 46 percent reported in the 1996 survey. A survey of food-buying behavior conducted by Marketlink Strategic Marketing Services in 1997 suggested that

- fewer than one in four consumers in any food category relies on a brand
- 26 percent of consumers who do have a preferred brand buy instead what best fits their budget at the time
- 37 percent of those who think of themselves as brand loyal indicate they try other brands all the time
- 71 percent of those surveyed who did switch brands said they experienced no difference from the switch

A 1998 Yankelovich survey of traveler brand loyalty found that 65 percent of travelers professed loyalty to a brand in 1998, down from 75 percent in the same survey in 1997; however, 45 percent of the leisure travelers polled said they were more than willing to change brands, and business travelers said their brand allegiance (often purchased at great expense through airline or hotel loyalty programs) applied only when it was convenient. Finally, a 1996 research study of loyalty to 500 separate brands tested by the NPD Group using a technique they call the BrandBuilder concluded that only 12 percent of consumers were "highly loyal to any brand."

Because there is no continuity or consistency across these surveys (and the hundreds of others I could have cited), it is impossible to say with any degree of certainty what consumer loyalty is today. Looking at the dates the various surveys were conducted, however, we can draw one incontrovertible conclusion: Consumer loyalty is down to record-low levels almost everywhere. The data emerging from surveys are so compelling that Frederick Reichheld, a guru of loyalty management, started the first chapter of his breakthrough book on the subject, *The Loyalty Effect*, with the words, "Loyalty is dead, the experts proclaim, and the statistics seem to bear them out. On average, U.S. corporations lose half their customers in five years, half their employees in four, and half their investors in less than one. We seem to face a future in which the only business relationships will be opportunistic transactions between virtual strangers." Later in this important book, Reichheld attributes part of the problem to the attitude of the young and upwardly mobile MBAs in the workforce, noting that on average Harvard MBAs change jobs three to four times in the first ten years after they receive their degree.

The Move to Buying Only on Price

Cynics of the modern business scene (and there are a lot of them around) respond to the loss of consumer brand loyalty by saying, "Consumers always buy on price. What else is new?" There is certainly some truth to this story, but it doesn't go far enough. Consumers buy exclusively on price when they have been ripped off so many times by deceptive vendor practices that they no longer trust what major companies say to them about their products. Let's look at some of the evidence.

That consumers are price conscious is demonstrable. A survey conducted by Roper in 1997 found that fully 73 percent of U.S. consumers bought primarily on the basis of price. The same survey noted that 37 percent of the Americans they surveyed would fall into the marketing category of "deal makers,"—that is, people who were always looking for a good deal. A further 36 percent could be labeled "price seekers," always gravitating to the lowest-price comparable item available. As evidence that this force is real in American society (and increasing in European society as well), one need only look at the growth of discount store sales relative to sales from more conventional retail channels. Wal-Mart, founded only fifty years ago, is now the largest retailer in the world. By contrast, venerable Sears, which used to be America's favorite retailer, stumbles from crisis to crisis as it tries to reestablish a mission in life. Wal-Mart is not alone in the discount category. Large discount-oriented chains now dominate almost every segment of the U.S. retail market. CVS and Walgreen prevail in the pharmacy segment. Home Depot is the major force in the huge do-it-yourself category. Best Buy and Circuit City own the electronics segment. Office Depot and Staples are rapidly moving to the fore in the office supplies and stationery category. Toys R Us is the largest retailer of toys for children in the United States. Aldi discount food warehouses is the fastest-growing retailer in Germany and feared across Europe almost as much as Wal-Mart is in the United States.

Why are consumers so attracted to discounters? It's obvious, isn't it? Because they perceive that they get better prices when they shop in these outlets. Any new retail concept that comes along promising even lower prices (the best examples in the United States being the discount clubs such as Sam's and BJ's Wholesale Club) enjoys rapid growth and nearly immediate consumer acceptance. The discount-oriented stores are perceived to offer real value to consumers at the point of purchase. Because of their scale, they can drive incredibly hard bargains with their suppliers and offer lower prices than smaller retailers. By investing in systems, they have cut the supply chain from supplier to the store, achieving even more economies and allowing them to respond quickly to consumers' shifting preferences. Through their aggressive tactics, they have been able to drive higher-priced competitors out of the market. So consumers are flocking to the discount chains. But does this represent a real transfer of loyalty on the part of the consumer, or is it only an expedient to get the lowest price today?

There is evidence emerging in different parts of the world that consumers, however price driven they may be, are not quite as enamored with the major retailers and discounters as they once were. The rise of hypermarkets, massive discount supermarkets in France and Spain, has leveled off after near explosive growth since the mid-1980s. At a more aggregate level, the life cycle of retail "concepts"—new retail brands like the Gap and Next—is declining dramatically around the country, from a median life for a single concept of about ten years as recently as 1970 to a median life of only four years for concepts launched in the 1990s.

What is going on? Why are consumers behaving in such disloyal fashion? Consumers have lost faith in the companies that supply them, and they show it by taking their trade to whatever new opportunity catches their eye. Some call this the "postmodern pattern of consumer behavior," where all consumers are fickle and manufacturers and retailers alike have to be willing to turn on a dime to meet their changing needs. I call it common sense. Old aphorisms like "Once burned, twice shy" or "Fool me once, shame on you; fool me twice, shame on me" seem perfectly adequate to explain the behavior of modern consumers in light of what they have had to put up with during the bottom-line-driven decades of the 1980s and 1990s. For manufacturers and retailers, the worst of the consumer reaction is yet to come.

The Age of the Internet

Manufacturers and retailers may think they have seen the full impact of consumer disdain and indifference. They should think again; the Internet is coming. As respected economist Robert Kuttner says, "The Internet is a nearly perfect market because information is instantaneous and buyers can compare the offerings of sellers worldwide. The result is fierce price competition, dwindling product differentiation, and vanishing brand loyalty. Imitators, especially those with deep pockets, can steal innovations as fast as they are invented and marketed. . . . The development is good news, for it revives the often-breached ideal of consumer sovereignty."

Although estimates vary all over the lot, the growth of e-commerce is astounding. The Internet seems to have accounted for about $10 billion of retail consumer sales in 1998. Forrester Research projects total on-line sales of $108 billion by 2003. Jeff Bezos, the CEO of leading Internet retailer Amazon.com, is even more bullish. He predicts on-line sales of $450 billion by the end of the first decade of the twenty-first century. Even conservative forecasters say the Internet will account for between 10 and 20 percent of all retail sales—a total of $60–120 billion—by 2004. Take any forecast you fancy. They all add up to one conclusion: The Internet is going to be a major factor in consumer sales.

The Internet is already a significant threat to conventional retailers (and therefore the companies that supply them) right now. In mid-1999 Forrester Research looked at consumer purchase patterns over the previous six months. The percentages of consumers who purchased various items on-line were as follows:

books	35 percent
music	34 percent
computers and computer peripherals	31 percent
clothes and accessories	19 percent
consumer electronics	14 percent
health and personal care items	9 percent
food and beverages	6 percent
household appliances	5 percent

Forrester Research also probed whether these on-line buyers were likely to be loyal to the vendor or the brand. Seventy-three percent of satisfied on-line book buyers said they would be willing to purchase their next on-line book from another vendor if the offer (meaning price) were more attractive. Other observers of the Internet are even less sanguine. Some, like Kuttner (quoted above), believe that the convenience of comparison shopping on the Web will translate into an almost complete disappearance of brand loyalty. John Hagel III and Arthur G. Armstrong of McKinsey & Company argue in *Net Gain: Expanding Markets Through Virtual Communities* that the Internet fundamentally alters the economics of supply and demand in industries, as shown in Figures 9.1 and 9.2 on the next page.

The good news from Hagel and Armstrong is that the development of Internet communities will provide a real spur to demand, as members of these communities compare notes and encourage one another to purchase the same items. The very bad news for suppliers is that such interaction among members of an on-line community will involve sharing information

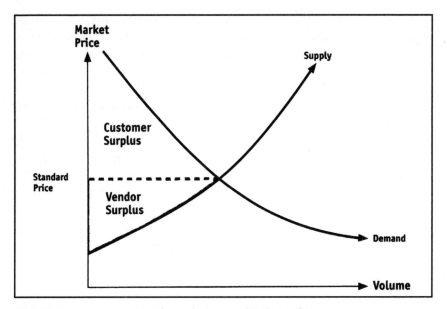

FIGURE 9.1   Economics of Supply-Demand Relationships

SOURCE: Hagel and Armstrong, *Net Gain,* p. 25.

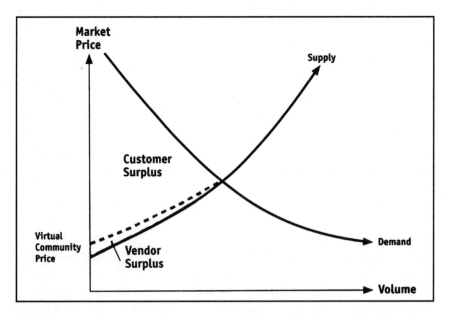

FIGURE 9.2   Economics of Internet Community Supply-Demand Relationship

SOURCE: Hagel and Armstrong, *Net Gain,* p. 25.

about price, features, and terms on offer. At a minimum, this will guide individual members of the community to the best deal available. The net effect of this information sharing, then, is that it will allow Internet-based consumers to capture most of the economic surplus available in any market for themselves at the expense of the vendors. Other Internet-savvy authors like Hagel and Marc Singer of McKinsey (*Net Worth: Shaping Markets When Customers Make the Rules*) have presented a strong case for the rise of infomediaries—firms that do the searching and product comparisons for the consumer. I am inclined to share their views. The Internet will allow all buyers to find the absolutely best deal available. The Internet is also the perfect vehicle for consumers to express their true feelings about how they have been treated by those who supply them by searching out other vendors to better fit their tastes and pocketbooks. Sellers beware.

The Rise of the Consumer Boycott

Declining loyalty and an increasing tendency to purchase what they need on the basis of price are not the only reactions consumers have had to their perceived exploitation by companies overly focused on the short-term bottom line during the 1980s and 1990s. These decades have witnessed the rise of truly effective consumer special interest groups, which have become powerful enough to alter the behavior of companies. The first of these movements to have a real impact was the movement spearheaded by Leon Sullivan to boycott companies with ties to the apartheid regime in South Africa. Backed by church groups across America and by millions of sympathetic individuals around the world, this antiapartheid movement succeeded in getting company after company to sever ties with South Africa and divest itself of anything to do with the racist regime then in power. It would be an overstatement to say that the antiapartheid movement succeeded finally in toppling the government, but it certainly deserves a prominent footnote in the history of the amazing transformation that country has undergone.

The antiapartheid movement was only one of a number of movements spawned by the social turmoil of the late 1960s (which in fact gave the word "movement" its modern meaning). The environmental, or green, movement is likely also to have a substantial long-term impact on the world of corporations. The movement started with people protesting, often vociferously, against corporate pollution of the environment. Its growth was aided by corporate disasters such as the explosion of the Union Carbide plant in Bhopal, India, where thousands of lives were lost. Along the way, however, the environmentalists moved into the mainstream because of the degree of support for their various stands from the public at large. Now the environmentalist Green Party is part of the majority government in Germany and a major factor in politics across Europe. It has had similar success, if not the same kind of visibility, in the United States, where federal legislation like the Clean Air and Clean Water Acts have become facts of life for all corporations.

While busy on the political front to effect change, activists have also been working behind the scenes to affect corporate behavior directly. Following Bhopal, individual corporations were asked to adopt a voluntary code of conduct to ensure such disasters became a thing of the past. Many did. As the success of the activists increased, their sophistication increased as well. They began demanding that companies issue regular reports to their shareholders on their compliance with environmental laws. By 1999 seventy-eight of the top 100 companies listed on the London stock exchange routinely delivered such reports to their shareholders—and the rest of the world. Now the greens have elevated their agenda once again, calling for corporations to pledge to contribute to the "sustainability" of the planet. Pressure has also been applied to the International Standards Organization (ISO) to develop standards specifically related to the environmental sustainability of corporate actions—similar to the standards it has established for quality around the world.

The environmental and antiapartheid movements are not the only ones to gain widespread support from the public. The animal rights movement continues to gain strength every year and succeeded for a time in reducing the status of fur coats from fashion statement to faux pas. More recently, an outcry over the use of child labor to manufacture goods in Third World countries for sale in Western markets has forced many prominent companies like Nike and Levi Strauss to make wholesale changes in their overseas sourcing arrangements. A recent survey by the Center for Ethical Concerns at Marymount University showed that 80 percent of U.S. consumers would be willing to pay an additional $1 on a $20 clothing item for some sort of guarantee that the item was made in a legitimate factory overseas, not in a sweatshop. Consumers may value low prices, but they also have other interests sellers must accommodate. If the corporations they deal with cannot be trusted to pay attention to these interests, consumers have shown they are more than willing to make their views known by taking their trade elsewhere.

There is no such thing as a model consumer whose views and preferences are a totally reliable guide to what the market wants. This is probably one reason major companies everywhere have been so blind to the effect their actions have had on the lifeblood of their businesses—their customers. It may be a fitting epitaph to the shareholder value movement to suggest it ended when the customer simply went home and companies with no one left to sell to had to shut down. That time is not yet here, but if current trends continue, it may not be too far in the future. Much can still be done to remedy the abuses of the shareholder value era, however, as discussed in the next and last part of the book.

PART FOUR

An Agenda for Change

If the adoption of shareholder value thinking has led existing companies to mortgage their futures in return for a higher stock price now, encouraged new entrepreneurs to float companies to a gullible investing public at insupportable prices, and triggered reactions from all other stakeholders of the corporate family that look certain to make future corporate life more difficult, who is to blame, and what should be done to get the world of corporations back on track? This part of the book tries to answer these questions.

Chapter 10 examines the role of all the major actors on the corporate stage—investors, managers, and board members—in trying to account for the shareholder value debacle. All deserve substantial portions of the blame for what went wrong. The heaviest share must fall on the shoulders of the managers, particularly CEOs of large public companies, who pursued their destructive, short-term objectives in order to cash in enormously through the inflated value of their stock options. These CEOs belong to an exclusive club, since almost two-thirds of board members of one company are current or former CEOs of another company. Within this snug little club, no favor goes unnoted. The option program voted within the confines of one boardroom is returned in kind at another board meeting. That the future of the economy should suffer while this generation of CEOs cashes in is the greatest indictment of the shareholder value era of business.

Chapter 11 focuses exclusively on the task ahead for managers who will have to build a viable future out of the shambles left by the shareholder value movement. The key will be to home in on the long-term health of the company and to change business processes and practices to ensure consistency with a farsighted vision for the company.

Chapter 12 centers on the changes needed among boards of directors if a long-term management agenda is to be pursued successfully. Drawing extensively on the work of other critics of current corporate governance practices, this chapter calls for a revolution in board composition, compensation, and focus.

A brief afterword to the book suggests that shareholder value thinking, which had some positive elements related to the increased accountability of managers for their performance, should evolve toward the creation of long-term shareholder wealth. An economic system focused on producing wealth would soon find it could do so only by taking care of the legitimate interests of all of its major stakeholders, to the greater gain for everyone.

CHAPTER 10

What Went Wrong and Who's to Blame?

The change in the mindsets of employees, governments and communities, suppliers, and customers in response to the actions of shareholder-value-driven businesses has had at least two profound consequences for the future of business everywhere. First, these revisions in perspective among stakeholders are likely to be permanent because each incrementally adds value to its own constituency. Employees who negotiate their employment contracts from a position of strength end up with better deals in the workplace. When society as a whole realizes that life goes on and in fact can be better after a job change, job mobility becomes the norm. Governments and localities that drive harder bargains with companies to protect their interests (whether these bargains relate to new jobs, an improved environment, or more restrictions on what constitutes acceptable commerce) will not now back off because of the complaints of a few business spokespersons. Suppliers who consolidate and find they can control negotiations with their clients to their own advantage are not abruptly going to fall over and accept ever more arduous terms and conditions. Customers who are satisfied using lower-cost outlets and new-brand or no-brand products will not suddenly get religion and return their loyalty to an old vendor out of nostalgia. Companies around the world are going to have to cope with the new thinking of their various stakeholders.

The second major result of the shareholder value movement is that if not all members of the major stakeholder groups have adopted the me-first ethic yet, they soon will. One feature of modern society is the speed with which information flows around the world. When one person finds out a neighbor has landed a juicy job and used the services of a third-party agent to enrich the package, how soon do you think it will be before that person gives it a go as well? When someone gets a bargain buying a no-name computer on the

Internet, how long do you think before her friends follow suit? Already suppliers are following one another's lead in securing an improved negotiating posture vis-à-vis their major customers. Even governments, which can be notoriously slow to act, are showing signs of setting examples for one another in negotiating with the business sector. Before long, what now sounds like an emerging trend will become a fact of life everywhere.

Companies will have to adapt to these altered circumstances to put right a situation that is rapidly threatening to get out of control. The adaptation will likely come piecemeal: an amended policy here, a special deal there, an accommodation somewhere else. The smart companies—one might even be so bold as to say the winners in the new economy—will make wholesale changes in what they do.

Before we look at specific suggestions for how the key actors need to adjust to the new realities of the broader marketplace, it is important that we understand just what went wrong and who is to blame. This chapter attempts to spell out both the strengths of shareholder value thinking and the corruption of that thinking that created the backlash from exploited stakeholders.

Welcome to the World of Corporations

The vast majority of business in the modern world is carried out by corporations. Corporations as a legal form are only a relatively modern phenomenon in historical terms (compared to families, partnerships, and so forth). They arose in Europe in the seventeenth and eighteenth centuries as royally chartered organizations to carry out specific tasks on behalf of the crown. The ships that carried the original settlers to America were, for the most part, chartered by such crown corporations. It was in America more than anyplace else that the corporate form thrived. In the landmark 1819 Supreme Court case *Dartmouth College v. Woodward*, Chief Justice John Marshall defined its legal standing: "The corporation is an artificial being, invisible, intangible, and existing only in the contemplation of the law." This "artificial being" has several attributes that make it ideal for the pursuit of commerce:

- limited liability for investors (up to the limit of their investment, of course)
- free transferability of investor interests (i.e., the right to buy and sell shares)
- a legal personality (i.e., attributable powers, a life span, and a purpose)
- central management

How was this useful artificial entity to be managed? Alexander Hamilton, acting as an entrepreneur, established the first such entity in America in 1791, the Society for Establishing Useful Manufactures. His prospectus for this new organization said, "The affairs of the company [are] to be under the management of thirteen directors." The interests of investors were thus to be looked out for by a board whose members would be known as directors. The conduct of the day-to-day affairs of the corporation was to be carried out by full-time employees, the most senior of whom are known in modern parlance as "management." If management did its job well and the corporation prospered, investors would be satisfied. If management failed to perform, the board of directors would intervene, often replacing management in the process, and set the company back on a viable course. If both management and the board somehow failed, investors were free to sell their interest in the company to someone else (if they could find a willing buyer). That's the way the system was intended to work. In fact, with some adjustments to current realities like the role of large institutional investors, that is how the system works to this day.

Although the incorporation papers of any corporation spell out its purpose, to allow for maximum flexibility down the road these legalistic definitions are left very broad. In essence what most of them say is, "This entity is here to make money for its investors." The real definition of purpose, as discussed in Part 1 of this book, is a product of the times in which the company operates and the people most materially involved in it.

Thousands of books have been written on the subject of how best to manage a corporation. To a greater or lesser extent, managers everywhere are expected to be familiar with best managerial practice and are held to a standard of performance based on the common public denominator of the knowledge and insights contained in the management literature. Hundreds if not thousands of books have also been written on the role of the board in overseeing corporations and their full-time managers. How well board members have carried out this responsibility has long been the subject of debate and will continue to receive critical scrutiny in the years ahead. Investors are the third major group of players on the corporate scene. Unlike managers and board members, investors have the prerogative to walk away from a company when they do not approve of what they see going on in the company. Most of the literary guidance offered to investors, not surprisingly, offers advice on when to buy and when to sell.

Investors, managers, and board members are therefore the critical actors on the corporate stage. If the shareholder value movement that started with such promise around 1980 went sour, some or all of these actors are at fault.

Since all three main actors work in concert, however, changes that affect one group of players inevitably affect the others as well.

The "Value" in Shareholder Value

The idea that discounting cash flows was a better way to predict stock price levels began as an academic discussion in the late 1970s. It caught the eye of a particular breed of investment banker and fueled the LBO craze of the 1980s. In the takeover boom of the early 1990s, all managers began to pay attention to the idea. By the end of the 1990s, it had become the very raison d'être of business.

Ten years is a remarkably short time for a sea change in thinking to occur. There seem to be two major reasons why shareholder value thinking took hold so quickly. First, the notion of shareholder value was powerful and extremely useful. Shareholder value could be easily measured. Anyone who could read the stock price tables in the newspaper could follow the value investors were placing on a company. Published stock prices, though subject to fluctuation, are not prone to the kinds of distortions that routinely make accounting calculations move around with abandon. Because shareholder value as reflected in stock prices can be measured and tracked, the adoption of the shareholder value standard almost immediately increased managers' accountability for performance. A lot of underperforming companies and management teams were suddenly exposed as a result, and companies everywhere began to pull up their socks. The increases in performance achieved became a major contributor to the long economic expansion of the 1990s.

Second, with the adoption of stock-option-based incentive pay for managers, there was a real convergence in the immediate interests of managers and investors alike. Both groups wanted higher stock prices now. Managers who might once have shied away from taking hard decisions, such as closing old plants or getting out of traditional but money-losing businesses, became enthusiastic proponents of such moves. Investors who might once have cringed at proposed management actions such as downsizings because of the negative effect they would have on society at large applauded because of the immediate rise in stock prices these actions seemed to spur. This correspondence of interests became a major force for improvement. Stock prices moved only when managers took actions and made changes. In a very real sense, the adoption of shareholder value thinking spelled the end of an era of moribund management in many companies. Who could possibly object?

If the shareholder value movement was so good, what went wrong? Why is it threatening to bring a crisis down on the heads of its most ardent exponents?

Shareholder Value Becomes Short-Termism

In an academic or technical sense, shareholder value is the sum of the values of discounted future cash flows from the operations of the company, added to whatever residual value the company has at the end of the period being assessed. Getting these calculations right involves picking the right discount rate to apply to future piles of cash. Although there is a vast literature on this subject, there is an even simpler reality in the minds of most managers: It is the stock price and the market capitalization of the company that matter. Let investors worry about what discount rate to apply to future earnings. Let investors fuss over just how high a multiple of current earnings to attach to a stock to arrive at its latest price in the market. The simple measure everyone pays attention to in the real world is the stock price. If the share price goes up, the company is worth more. If the share price comes down, the company is worth less. Managers who want to maximize the value of their companies are going to do anything within their power to get the share price to move higher.

Most managers recognize that their job is to improve the long-term value of the companies they run. But they measure value by the current movement of the stock price—even when they know this is only a crude approximation of the kind of calculation required if true shareholder value maximization is to be achieved. Unfortunately, the stock market itself is not always the most rational place in the world. As discussed below, it tends to be driven by extremely short-term thinking. Because of the competition among fund managers to attract new funds to invest, all fund managers pay close attention to every nuance of performance variation in the companies in which they invest. Therefore, nonsensical as it may seem, fund managers carefully scrutinize quarterly earnings reports for any "surprises" they had not anticipated. Fund managers often buy and sell holdings of stock because of pennies' worth of differences in reported quarterly earnings. If that is how investors are going to behave, and it surely is, then managers have to respond in kind. However silly it is to do so, managers must make sure their quarterly reports meet all the expectations of the investing public. Thus, what started as a focus on value has spiraled into a quarter-to-quarter race for results. Short-termism rules the day.

Managers who want to perform against the standards of the day need to do whatever they can to make sure the quarter comes in right. The heavy and continued emphasis on cost reduction is the most visible manifestation of this trend in corporate behavior. Cost cuts, especially cuts in staffing levels, fall directly to the bottom line in a totally predictable and manageable fashion. Any looming earnings gap can be closed by a surgically precise cut in costs—as long as no one is concerned about the long-term consequences of the cut. Since the stock market tends to respond positively to any announcement of an impending cut, why worry? Just keep on cutting. Shareholder value has become, for all intents and purposes, managing exclusively for the short term.

What started as a laudable and useful idea has devolved into a farce. Everyone involved in the system knows that. But with the compensation of managers tied directly into stock price levels through options and the compensation of fund managers directly affected by their ability to attract new funds based on superior investment results, no one wants to blow the whistle and call the whole charade to a halt. The noble goal of maximizing shareholder value has within only a few years become a matter of "What have you done for me lately?"

Nothing short of a major rewriting of the rules will cause this to change in the foreseeable future. Before looking toward solutions, however, it is both useful and informative to examine the question of who is to blame for this unfortunate turn of events in the world of business.

The Short-Term/Long-Term Investor

As Peter Drucker pointed out in his 1976 book, *The Unseen Revolution,* that institutional investors own the majority of stock in companies around the world. As recently as 1965, 84 percent of equity in the United States was held by private investors—albeit a handful of extremely wealthy people. This situation has changed: Institutions now control in excess of 60 percent of the equity in the major stock markets around the world.

The buildup of institutional ownership of equity was gradual but inexorable over the last forty years of the twentieth century, fueled by a series of events. First was the growing popularity of the mutual fund, a device for giving individual investors instant portfolio diversification as well as access to professional fund management expertise. Mutual funds alone would not have spurred the institutionalization of the stock market were it not for the postwar spread of pension funds as part of the basic compensation of workers. In recent decades changes in tax laws to allow individuals to fund their own tax-deferred pension schemes have added further fuel to the fire by putting even more funds into the hands of institutional investors.

Money managers who make investment decisions for institutions are typically paid to get it right. Getting it right, in this context, almost always involves beating one's peers in the world of investment institutions, which takes good judgment and nimble feet. So institutional money managers constantly change the holdings in their portfolios, looking for that last fraction

of investment performance. An article by John Byrne in *Business Week,*
"When Capital Gets Antsy," documented the average amount of time investors held the stocks of certain corporations:

Amazon.com	7 days
Yahoo	8 days
Dell	3.7 months
Delta Airlines	6.3 months
IBM	13.8 months
Exxon	29.6 months
General Electric	33.1 months

This is what passed for long-term investing in the late 1990s.

Such portfolio churning means that institutional investors concentrate for
the most part on the very short term—even if they are investing money for
the long-term benefit of their own customers. Given this orientation of the
largest single group of shareholders, the idea of what constitutes shareholder
value becomes a bit enigmatic. As one director is quoted as saying in the
book *Pawns or Potentates? The Reality of America's Corporate Boards,* by Jay
Lorsch and Elisabeth MacIver, "One thing that substantially muddies the
water . . . is that more and more people are coming to the realization that the
shareholders are really a bunch of 26-year-olds sitting behind their trading
desks." Another CEO quoted in the same book remarked, "The real conflict
of interest occurs between the short-term stock price interests of those who
own shares of stock on a given day and whose attitude toward value reflects
a desire to get the most value for the stock that day . . . and investors whose
personal situations cause them to be less interested in the value of a share
that day and more interested in the total value of the enterprise as a long-
term investment."

Although traders tend to take a very hands-off approach to the companies
in which they invest, not all institutional investors do. Pension funds, the
largest institutional investors of them all, with almost 30 percent of all U.S.
corporate equity, have increasingly exercised influence in the boardroom.
The people who run pension funds are trustees of the funds under their control. On average they monitor the investment of these funds for thirty years,
from the time an individual first contributes to the fund until the retiree
makes the first withdrawals. Pension fund managers are thus the longest of
the long-haul investors in the stock market. Moreover, as trustees, they are
legally liable for the efficacy of their investment decisions. A money manager
who does not perform may lose clients. A pension fund trustee who does not
perform may pay a fine, be permanently prohibited from managing pension

funds, or even, in extreme cases, go to jail. This places a heavy burden on pension fund trustees, leading them as a group to be very conservative investors who favor large capitalization stocks and index funds over more risky investments—a source of some criticism in the industry.

Pension funds in the United States are divided into two groups. One is composed of private pension funds that, for example, invest the funds put away for retirement by the people who work for corporations. The activities of trustees of private investment funds are most heavily influenced by the federal Employee Retirement Income Security Act (ERISA) of 1974, which was passed specifically to curb prior abuses in the investment of pension monies. As Ralph D. Ward puts it in his book *21st Century Corporate Board,* "ERISA responsibilities make terms like 'innovation' and 'concentrated ownership' dangerous to pension fund managers, who are encouraged to keep their heads down and follow the herd."

The other and larger half of the pension fund pie is the world of public pension funds, which invest retirement monies for government employees at all levels. Included in this group, although actually a private trust rather than a public pension fund, is the granddaddy of all pension funds, the Teachers Insurance and Annuity Association—College Retirement Equities Fund (TIAA-CREF), the largest single pool of investment money in the world. Although they generally comply with the provisions of ERISA, trustees of public pension funds are not strictly covered by its terms and have taken the lead in shareholder activism, especially in relation to issues of corporate governance.

Public pension funds first became involved in corporate governance in the early 1980s. They advocated primarily social issues—demanding firms divest themselves of operations in South Africa because of the apartheid regime then in place, requiring firms to produce special reports on their compliance with environmental and affirmative action laws, arguing against firms' involvement in the production of military equipment. To get their points of view across, they put forward resolutions to shareholders espousing their specific special interests. These resolutions virtually never gained enough support from voting shareholders to place real restrictions on management actions, but they got the attention of management and often led to changes in corporate behavior.

The nature of pension fund activism began to change in the mid- to late 1980s because of the wave of takeover-related activity that hit the corporate market. Takeovers themselves may initially have served the purpose of increasing shareholder value, since any successful takeover invariably bought stock at a price higher than the prevailing stock market levels. But it was corporate actions to escape the daring raids of the 1980s that drew the most direct response from pension funds. Companies fearful of being taken over began to enact a series of measures to make it hard for takeover firms to succeed. These included so-called poison-pill provisions that specifically made sure that stock bought by a firm intent on taking over another would receive disadvantageous treatment. Takeover defense also often involved the issuance of new classes of stock to preferred "safe hands" investors, the staggering of the terms of board members to make it difficult for a new company buying stock to remove directors, and just about anything else corporate managements could think of to fend off the unwanted suitors. All these measures in one way or another were designed to preserve the position of incumbent management teams, something pension fund (and other institutional) investors began to look increasingly askance at. In 1987 alone over thirty shareholder proposals were put forward by institutional investors, mainly pension funds, specifically aimed at stopping the use of poison pills. These resolutions drew much more backing than the earlier socially oriented proposals, garnering support from as much as 30 percent of voting shareholders. Pension fund trustees quietly began to realize how much clout they really had and became more convinced than ever of their commitment to corporate activism.

The 1990s began with a recession that shifted the impetus of shareholder activism even more to the issue of corporate performance. With the collapse of the junk bond market in 1989, the immediate threat of takeovers—or, for that matter, inappropriate defenses against them—receded. The shareholder value movement and its focus on tying senior management compensation more closely to performance through stock options raised a new issue for corporate activists to get their teeth into. Executive compensation soared in the early 1990s and became front-page news in the business press around the world. When compensation did not match demonstrable corporate performance, the pension funds could and did take action. The CEO of the California Public Employees' Retirement System (CalPERS) put it most succinctly: "How can we make corporations accountable again? We believe the answer is to focus on the board." Shortly thereafter, this same CEO announced a formal strategy of meeting directly with the board members of underperforming companies and began publishing a list of the laggards.

Pension fund activism continued on an issue-specific basis throughout the 1990s. For example, as reported in Margaret M. Blair's *Ownership and Control*, TIAA-CREF in 1993 called about twenty other large pension funds to encourage them to vote against the reelection of three directors to the troubled Eastman Kodak's board. In 1995 TIAA-CREF was instrumental in getting the board of W. R. Grace to oust its long-standing chairman, Peter Grace. TIAA-CREF also took the lead in 1997 in urging both Heinz and

Disney to increase the independence of their boards by appointing more out-side directors, which each did with little fanfare once the immediate public controversy had died down. Aside from these occasional forays against spe-cific abuses, however, even large, long-term investors like the pension funds have been willing to let corporation after corporation pursue higher stock prices today whatever the consequences for their long-term welfare. The most persuasive voice in the debate on corporate actions has been the voice pension funds exercise when they buy and sell stocks at the drop of a hat. It is this voice that managers and board members listen to most carefully and use as a guide in running their companies.

Investors, especially large, long-term institutional investors, are therefore clearly in part to blame for the short-termism so rampant in the corporate world. Do they care? Not much. Delighted by the returns gained from a booming stock market, they are content to let the circus continue.

The Insidious World of the Board

If investors seem not to care, what about boards? From the late eighteenth century to the present, the duty of boards to provide oversight has been clear. How carefully have they fulfilled the responsibilities attendant on these duties?

The operation of boards of directors has been pretty informal. Many claim that the appellation "board" originally referred to a plank spread across two tree trunks around which the board met. The "chair," needless to say, was the only one guaranteed a seat at these proceedings. Whether this is historically true or not, the practical reality for boards throughout most of the eigh-teenth and nineteenth centuries was that their proceedings were dominated by the controlling investor—either the founding entrepreneur or the fi-nancier who came along to commercialize the venture. Other members of the board were mostly along for the ride. This began to change quite notably in the early decades of the twentieth century, when outside investors were in-creasingly brought in to help finance the growth of American business. The stock market crash of 1929 brought the role of the board as the representa-tive of investors in the business even more to the fore. When the early 1930s saw a succession of legislation designed to protect the interests of small in-vestors in companies, the pressure on directors of companies to carry out their role of oversight increased because of the very real risk that they would be subject to serious legal sanctions if they were derelict in their duties.

The growth of legal interest and case law in the roles of directors and boards spurred a lot of academic and legal thinking on precisely what re-sponsibilities directors had to shareholders. Although not much has changed in substance since the days of Alexander Hamilton, the weight of legal opinion is firm in specifying the two primary duties of directors: (1) the *duty of loyalty* to the company, which essentially makes sure board members avoid direct conflicts of interest (e.g., serving on the board of one company that is making an offer to buy another company on whose board the director also serves), and (2) the *duty of care,* which is designed to ensure that any director exercises due diligence in making decisions that have an impact on the company. Case law over time has reassured directors that if they follow a reasonable process in reaching a decision, they will not incur any liability with regard to its outcome.

Any number of groups have worked to refine and specify what these two duties imply in the real world. For example, in 1990 the Business Roundtable published a list of the five primary functions of a board of directors:

1. Select, regularly evaluate, and if necessary replace the chief executive officer. Determine management compensation. Review succession planning.
2. Review and, where appropriate, approve the financial objectives, major strategies, and plans of the corporation.
3. Provide advice and counsel to top management.
4. Select and recommend to shareholders for election an appropriate slate of candidates for the board of directors; evaluate board processes and performance.
5. Review the adequacy of systems to comply with all applicable laws and regulations.

Although far more specific than previous sets of ill-defined duties, this was still pretty mushy stuff. John Harvey-Jones, once the highly successful CEO of Imperial Chemical Industries and now a much-quoted management guru, tried to make it clearer: "The job of the board is all to do with creating momentum, movement, improvement and direction. If the board is not taking the company purposely in the future, who is?"

Boards of directors of large public companies are staffed largely from a pool of highly privileged and heavily inbred people. Focusing on Fortune 1000 companies, we find that the average board in the late 1980s was composed of thirteen members, nine of whom were outsiders to the company. Fully 93.8 percent of these directors were white males. In 1987 two-thirds of them were over the age of fifty-five and 63 percent were CEOs or former CEOs of other companies. In the United States, boards are chaired by the CEO of the company almost three-quarters of the time. In the UK, outside chairmanships predominate, but board composition is still slightly in favor of insiders to the company rather than outsiders. These transatlantic differences have gradually narrowed in recent years, and in response to public criticism membership of women and minorities on boards has slowly been increasing everywhere. Yet the board remains the domain primarily of older, white, male CEOs.

Life as a board member is pretty relaxed. A typical board meets nine times a year, with an average meeting lasting three hours. Most boards have standing committees, the nominating, audit, and compensation committees being the most popular. Outside of full board meetings, directors spend about 35 percent of their board-related time in meetings of these committees. This all adds up to an onerous commitment of less than two weeks' work a year, for which the average director receives $36,000 in cash, about 20 percent of this amount in stock or options, a pension plan, and access to a variety of perks, such as the use of corporate airplanes. Since the average CEO serves on about five other boards, board membership provides a nice little outside income and a chance to get together with old friends every month or so. Serving on a board is in effect like belonging to an exclusive club.

History would certainly suggest that boards have done very little of any note. To be fair, however, the cozy little world of board life is becoming busier. Increasing shareholder activism, especially by the large public pension funds; growing numbers of lawsuits against directors;[1] and soaring executive pay at a time when corporate performance was lagging because of mismanagement or the recession of the early 1990s all converged to generate an unprecedented couple of years of board activity between late 1991 and early 1993. Thirteen CEOs of Fortune 500 companies were given the sack by their bosses, their boards. The first to go was Rod Canion, the founder of Compaq Computer. Shortly thereafter the board of General Motors demoted its CEO, Robert Stempel, and then six months later fired him outright. Soon after, the CEO of Tenneco was let go. He was followed in a few more months by Ken Olsen, the founder of Digital Equipment Corporation. In late January 1993, John Aker of IBM was dismissed after having announced the biggest single corporate loss in the history of business. The day

---

[1]The issue of director liability and the series of court cases and legal precedents in the 1970s, 1980s, and 1990s had many directors running scared. A 1995 survey by Lou Harris and Associates indicated that 42 percent of all Fortune 1000 directors had been sued in connection with their board duties. Another survey, the Wyatt D & O Liability Survey, put the cost of settling a typical suit at $4.6 million, excluding legal fees. My own view, however, is that developments on the legal front were side issues to the evolving activism of large shareholders. Others, especially lawyers heavily involved in these cases, would likely disagree.

after Aker was fired, the CEO of Westinghouse was canned. By the end of the month, the CEO of American Express, Jim Robinson, got the ax. Had boards of directors, asleep at the switch for years, suddenly woken up? Had board members all at once decided that they really were in charge and were going to begin actively managing the enterprises for which they were responsible? Or were board members just reacting to a confluence of factors that were making them more and more uncomfortable with the status quo? The answer is surely that all of these influences were at work—as well as a whole serious of specific factors unique to each of the situations. Whatever the cause of the shift in attitude and response, the relationship between boards and managers has likely changed forever.

Since this burst of activity in the early 1990s, the boards of most companies have gone back to sleep. Particularly as the United States emerged from the recession and the stock market began to soar to unprecedented levels, individual directors of major companies have been lulled into a false sense of satisfaction by the ever higher stock prices of the companies whose fates they are supposed to monitor. Senior managers of large companies, only too aware of what happened to colleagues who did not pay enough attention, have gone out of their way to make their own directors comfortable. Director compensation schemes increasingly include options or share grants so the directors themselves participate directly in the bonanza coming from an overexuberant stock market. The perks available to most directors of large companies, though now discreetly hidden from public scrutiny, are inexorably on the rise. With directors safely back in their box, managers have done everything they can think of—usually copying programs other executives have successfully put into place elsewhere—to create even more buzz about their company's prospects and provide a further prop to its stock market valuation. And since everyone gains from a higher stock price, it must be all right. But is it? Standing on the sidelines looking on, it seems fair to do as Robert Monks and Neil Minow do in their book on corporate governance and ask, "Who is watching the watchers?"

Managers in the Hot Seat

If investors don't care and board members are mostly asleep at the switch, then the obvious villains in the shareholder value puzzle must be the managers. It was managers who decided to cut staff levels by downsizing. It was managers who told their purchasing agents to get tough on suppliers. It was managers who told their underlings to cut back on product lines and concentrate on only the most profitable products (or find a job somewhere else). It was managers who whipped up the merger frenzy gripping almost every industry in the 1990s. They must have asked for and got support from their boards before they took any of these actions, but it was the managers themselves who led the charge. Surely it must be the managers, therefore, who are to blame.

Just who are these people who are so intent on sacrificing the long-term future of companies for short-term stock gains? To answer this question, some colleagues and I looked up biographical information in the library on a randomly picked list of one hundred CEOs of the 250 largest companies in the United States. These CEOs are surprisingly young—fully 51 percent of them did not reach their sixtieth birthday before 2000. The group of CEOs we examined are very well educated: 91 percent have at least an undergraduate degree, and 66 percent have earned a graduate degree, more than half of which are MBAs. Of the ninety-one CEOs with undergraduate degrees, only seventeen of them earned their degrees at Ivy League colleges. By contrast, forty-four of them got their undergraduate degree at a public college or university in their home state. This last is a telling statistic: The CEOs of large companies today were not born with silver spoons in their mouths. Most grew up in middle-class families and went to the public college nearest to them. They then used their brains, ambition, and hard work to rise to the top of the pile.

Because I spent most of my working life as a management consultant, I was privileged to meet quite a number of this new breed of CEO (roughly one-third of the CEOs of the one hundred largest companies). This portrait of the CEO therefore rings true. These people are very bright, very ambitious, and very hardworking. Something else is true about them: Because most came from relatively modest family circumstances, almost all are obsessed with the idea of making money; they are intent on cashing in on what they see as a lifetime of hard work. Since the people voting for their pay packages were more likely than not CEOs like themselves, it is no surprise that package after generous package was created despite public outcry about the excesses.

There is another characteristic these CEOs share: They are incredibly competitive. Most, if asked to describe their rise, would tell stories about the adversity they had to overcome along the way. They would tell about besting rivals for the top job and how they single-handedly saved their companies from disaster. This intense competitive streak carries over to how they run their companies and is one of the primary explanations for why the management trends of the 1990s spread with such fadlike speed across the business environment. Having reached the top, members of this new breed of CEO watch like hawks what their peers in other companies are doing. As soon as one company does something and the stock price of that company rises in response, you can be sure there are movements afoot across the corporate landscape to copy the successful move. Hence, reengineering barrels across the business landscape even though its effectiveness is being seriously questioned by those who have looked at it carefully. Similarly, the urge to consolidate industries by buying up any and all available companies is copied from one industry to another whether or not the underlying economic logic is there.

In 1980, around the time the shareholder value revolution was beginning to sweep the business scene, E. Digby Baltzell wrote a wonderful book, *Puritan Boston and Quaker Philadelphia: Two Protestant Ethics and the Spirit of Class Authority and Leadership,* which attempted to explain the origins of both leadership and nonleadership traits in successful Americans. Much of the book focused on the contrasting behaviors of Richard M. Nixon (a Quaker) and John F. Kennedy (an Irish Catholic but brought up in the Puritan ethic of Massachusetts society) in their respective tenures as president of the United States, especially Kennedy's tendency to take the ethical high road on issues and Nixon's instinct to attack those he perceived as his enemies. Baltzell's portrait of these two famous individuals is a useful analogy to the behavior of modern CEOs. There are a lot more Nixons out there in CEO land than there are Kennedys. The CEOs of today are for the most part an extremely combative lot who keep score not by what they accomplish but by what they personally gain.

Still (and it needs to be said), few of them are villains. Most are trying to do the best job they can running their companies. Unfortunately, almost none of them can even imagine what it will be like when they are no longer at the helm of the company. Fewer still even care. When I queried a friend of mine who is the CEO of a Fortune 50 company about the viability of his long-term strategy, he said "What the f—— do I care? I'll be long retired by then." If his lack of interest in the future of his company could rightly be deplored, he surely wins high marks for candor. (This CEO, who is a superb manager, did in fact take steps to shore up his company's long-term strategy, although the jury is still out whether his actions were timely or aggressive enough to solve the problem.) Hence, the short-termism that became the true face of the shareholder value ethic has found a perfect home in the hearts and minds of the CEOs of today. Success in the short-term is about the only thing they know and the only thing they care about. That will work and has worked for a while, but it does not bode well for the future. To protect that future, key players—managers and directors, shareholders and investors—will have to change their behavior radically. I turn to this issue in the two remaining chapters of the book.

CHAPTER 11

New Marching Orders
for Management

Managers, albeit with the agreement of their boards and investors, have led too many companies single-mindedly down the path of maximizing shareholder value now. In doing so, many of these managers have mortgaged their companies' futures in return for a higher stock price. Virtually all of the CEOs that adopted the shareholder value mantra achieved gains for their shareholders at the expense of other legitimate stakeholders. These stakeholders are beginning to strike back by demanding their own share of the bounty and setting themselves up in such a way that their demands will have to be met. The confluence of these two significant developments—an already mortgaged future and increasingly powerful stakeholders grabbing more—points to declining performance for the companies that pursued the shareholder value grail so religiously since the mid-1980s.

Managers got the companies into this bind; managers will need to lead these same companies back from the precipice. The journey will not be easy, because it will involve a fundamental rethinking of where the company has come from, where it is heading, and where it should be heading. The length of the journey will vary from company to company depending on a realistic assessment of how much damage has already been inflicted on long-term prospects and stakeholder relations. Once the map has been unfolded, companies will have to communicate the route to shareholders to persuade them to sign on for the ride.

Companies that refuse to face up to the reality of their situation or are unwilling to do the hard work of repositioning themselves for a viable long-term future will be assaulted from all sides. Current and prospective employees will demand a bigger and bigger share of the corporate pie and get it because of their willingness to sell themselves to the highest bidder. Suppliers will turn the tables on their customers in negotiations and threaten to put the companies out of business if they do not give in. Governments will extract onerous penalties from their corporate clients if they fail to live up to their commitments. Customers will insist on being sold again with each transaction as the only basis for continuing to give the company their business. Disappointed investors will dump their stock when historical performance trends turn down as a result of these attacks from all quarters.

This chapter lays out a comprehensive program for redirecting any company toward a sustainable future based on the creation of real wealth for all important stakeholding groups, including shareholders. In the sections that follow, I describe

> setting the right course
> taking stock of the damage to the long-term future prospects of the
>   company
> taking stock of the damage to relations with essential stakeholders
> investing to reinvigorate the corporate future
> building a real employee franchise
> rebuilding a franchise with suppliers
> building a real customer franchise
> reconnecting with important communities
> communicating with shareholders
> changing decisionmaking processes
> monitoring progress (against long-term objectives) and reporting results

Because it is my intent to offer a complete program that will work, parts of the plan will be more relevant for some companies than for others. Moreover, in striving to be specific and actionable, I acknowledge that there is more than one way to skin a cat. Individual companies will find their own ways to accomplish the array of tasks outlined in what follows. More power to those who do. Finally, as the chapter moves deeper and deeper into the set of recommendations, they become more and more specific and thus likely of less use to individual readers. Despite these drawbacks, may this chapter provide a helpful set of road marks even if it fails as an itinerary. My sincere appeal to all managers concerned about the problems outlined in this book is that you begin the journey soon, while you still have the chance.

Setting the Right Course

Let's start with the basics. Companies got themselves in trouble pursuing shareholder value maximization because they didn't think through the consequences of what they were about to do. Maximizing shareholder value may well be an appropriate objective for an owner of a business whose time horizon is very limited. If such an owner has the sole objective of buying on the cheap and unloading at a higher price as soon as reasonably possible, shareholder value is right for him. The living proof is in the considerable fortunes accumulated by the raiders and LBO specialist firms of the 1980s and 1990s. They knew what they wanted. They made enough of the right moves to be able to go after what they wanted. And they were handsomely rewarded for doing so.

Equally, shareholder value maximization in the short term is a totally inappropriate objective for managers of a large public company. If their ongoing success is to be ensured, their goal must be the maximization of long-term value—to shareholders but also to all other major constituencies they deal with. Put another way, the proper objective for a manager of a large public company is wealth creation, with all that phrase connotes about the staying power of what is achieved.

During the shareholder value era, people got hung up on two important side issues related to corporate purposes. The first was measurement. As we have seen, one reason the shareholder value movement gained such rapid and widespread acceptance was because it was easy to keep score. In the booming stock market of the 1990s, almost all major public companies began to do so publicly, proudly proclaiming in their annual reports how much value had been created for shareholders in the past year. Measurement and accountability are important. Public companies should be held publicly accountable for what they have accomplished. But there is more to be accomplished in a large public company than simply reaching a new stock price high. Creating wealth in a company includes managing technology to make sure the company retains its technological advantages into the future. It requires maintaining or even enhancing a real customer franchise in whatever markets the company competes in so that customers today will continue to be customers tomorrow. It requires having loyal and committed employees and suppliers willing to go the extra mile to help the company succeed and sustain itself. All of these elements (and in particular companies there may be others as well) can be measured and tracked, and the results of these measurements can be made publicly available. It just requires a bit more work and the mindset and clear thinking to consider these elements an important part of the puzzle.

The second element that spurred the adoption of shareholder value as the driving ethic of business was that through the expanded use of stock options, it closely aligned the interests of managers and shareholders. These interests continued to jibe until a generation of managers in the 1990s gave in to sheer greed. Once managers began to be paid with stock options, most quickly saw they could make out like bandits by inflating the current stock price. This tactic had little downside for them: If the stock market slumped, their option awards would be repriced to make sure they retained an appropriate level of incentive. The problem is and was that these incentive payment plans did not effectively match managerial interests with those of shareholders. Managers had no capital at risk. Moreover, all the incentives for a manager were pointed at making a killing now, not achieving gains for a planned but still distant retirement, as it was for most investors. This is simply a structural problem in most executive incentive plans today that urgently needs to be fixed. (In the next chapter, addressed to boards, I return to some specific suggestions for how to correct the worst of these abuses.)

Allowing a large public company to be run on the basis of greed is inappropriate and fraught with the kinds of problems and outcomes I have been talking about for most of this book. In setting a new and more fitting course, managers should make sure that it is designed to make the institution and its stakeholders prosper over the long term. If they can figure out how to make some money for themselves in the process, fine. But that must never be the primary goal.

In summary, the first task of a management team must be to define the real purpose of the business and how its achievement is to be measured and tracked. The purpose must, virtually by definition, look to the long term. (The only exception to this would be when a company is founded with the sole objective of exploiting a particular technology or niche and has every intention, and so states, of liquidating itself when the specific opportunity it is exploiting has expired. Few companies today would even consider such a course of action, although certain high flyers in specific technology niches might give the idea some thought.) Once this purpose has been defined and published, managers can get on with their real job as custodians of the welfare of the enterprise they have been chosen to manage.

Taking Stock of the Damage: Long-Term Future Prospects

Although managing is complex in detail, it is dead easy from a broader perspective. It involves picking a target, figuring out the steps required to achieve that target, motivating people to work effectively toward it, measuring progress against the goal, and making appropriate course corrections along the way to ensure the target is actually reached. That's why figuring out the right target is such an important first step, as outlined above.

For a company trying to save itself from the worst downside of excessive pursuit of short-term shareholder value, the task is a bit more complicated. Many companies in pursuit of the shareholder value objective have in effect mortgaged their long-term position to achieve higher profits now. Consider, for example, General Electric, whose progress I discussed in detail in Chapter 4. The General Electric Company is over a century old. It was founded to exploit the new and important technology of electricity. Fifty years after its founding, it was a colossus sitting firmly on top of all the key electrical technologies in the world.

Back in the 1950s, the CEO of the company, Fred Borch, recognized that many of the technologies GE was so superior in were becoming old. In response he launched three major investment programs: one into the emerging world of computers, one into the nuclear power industry, and one into the nascent field of aircraft engines. The simultaneous pursuit of three major new technologies turned out to be more than even GE could handle, and less than two decades later the company sold off its computer interests. Ten to fifteen years thereafter, the public reaction to nuclear technology effectively shut down the second of GE's great investments, leaving it only with a small operation to service nuclear power plants already built. Put that whole series of events into perspective, however. Borch had his eye on the ball: He was looking to preserve GE's position as a leader in the important technologies of the day.

Run the clock all the way forward to 1999. Jack Welch, the highly regarded CEO of GE, is approaching his twentieth year in office. His accomplishment has been to deliver an unprecedented amount of value to the shareholders of GE over that period of time. GE still sells the world's best turbines. It has a market-leading position in aircraft engines, medical systems, and plastics. Nevertheless, it has reduced the real level of its investment in R&D as a percentage of sales steadily throughout Welch's tenure. The bulk of the earnings gain achieved while he was CEO came from an expansion of its financial services activity—credit cards and various leasing businesses—and by the acquisition of an aging TV network. On a per share basis, this earnings growth has been even more impressive, since Welch's biggest single investment during his time in office has been the $30 billion he spent on buying back shares in the company from investors. It has no real position in the information technology sector so critical to the functioning of the modern economy. It is not a factor in the semiconductor industry. Although it has a fledgling presence on the Internet, few would view it as a likely dominant player going forward. Where is this company's real future to come from? A path to remaining a preeminent company into the foreseeable future is far from clear.

GE is not alone; it is just a good and prominent example of what the shareholder value movement has done to the future prospects of many companies. Therefore, the second major task for managers determined to get back on a sustainable course must be to take stock of just where they stand in terms of fundamentals to ensure them a viable and profitable future. This assessment must encompass technology, distribution, brands, and customer franchise if it is going to produce an accurate picture of what the future likely holds. My guess is most companies that undertake such an assessment will find themselves exposed on a number of fronts. Measuring the gap between where they need to be and where they will end up if current programs are allowed to continue is the crucial first step in planning a catch-up program.

Taking Stock of the Damage: Relations with Essential Stakeholders

Just as the shareholder value movement has done damage to the long-term prospects of many companies, it has done severe damage to many companies' relations with core constituencies they will need to rely on for a viable and profitable future. In order to get headed back in the right direction, companies will need to figure out where they stand vis-à-vis key stakeholders and what remedial actions might be required to get relations back on an even keel.

In the case of employees, so many companies have downsized so ruthlessly that they will have a hard time rebuilding their position against the broader workforce they will eventually need to attract to create a sustainable future. There seem to be two obvious starting points for assessing the damage, however. The first is an objective evaluation of what has happened to previous employees who were downsized out of their jobs. What do these former employees think about the company today? What might the company do to reinitiate a constructive dialogue with its former employees? This may seem like an improbable starting point since it is highly unlikely in most industries and companies that future employees will come from the ranks of the recently terminated. What most companies fail to recognize, however, is the influence these former employees have on the workforce of today and tomorrow. The children of these dispossessed workers are going to listen carefully to what their elders tell them about the company as a place to work. These children in turn will relay this folk wisdom to their friends. Especially in companies who at one time were dominant employers in a town or region, the influence of this informal network of intelligence is strong. Rebuilding ties with former employees is a key to making sure this informal network works in favor of the company.

The broader problem of measuring where the company stands as an employer in the eyes of the general population is much more difficult. Surveys regularly spell out the public perception of different employers. These surveys, however, tend to be general in content and broad in the audiences they address (for example, a lot of them are targeted at graduating college seniors). A much more useful exercise would be for a company to figure out the kinds of people, by education level and skill base, it is likely to need and then survey the pools of such potential employees to find out how the company might attract them. The company should undertake such a survey in most geographical areas where the company is likely to operate. Failure to take the action to build the kind of image that draws desirable job candidates and the kind of working reality that retains these people will leave any company at the mercy of the vicissitudes of a job market increasingly hostile to its needs.

Taking stock of how much harm has been inflicted on key suppliers is easier than gauging damage to the company's image as a workplace, but it must be done explicitly. If a supplier is critical, by implication it will have had a long-term relationship with the company. Its financial performance over a longer time frame can be checked, at least for all publicly held suppliers. If pressure from a key customer has been driving a supplier under or turning it into a marginal performer at best, then that customer must plan remedial action. Similarly, the company can analyze the history of contracts with any particular supplier and document the consequences of successive contracts on both the company's economics and the economics of the supplier. For a relationship between a company and its suppliers to flourish, there must be a fair sharing of gains across the divide.

Assessing the state of relations between a company and the governments and communities it operates in is inherently complicated and sensitive. Large, modern companies often have many different locations and ongoing relationships with many local and national political jurisdictions. Moreover, because relationships with political bodies inevitably are exposed to some degree of public scrutiny, no sensible large company is going to get on a soapbox and proclaim to the world that it has been exploiting community X, is sorry for past transgressions, and promises to do better in the future. That would be political suicide. Despite these complications, a company that wants to have a secure future must be willing to look objectively at how well it has performed relative to the different jurisdictions it operates in and plan to change its ways as need be.

The final constituency group whose position must be assessed may be the most critical: customers. Every company has one or more sets of customers who are absolutely key to its survival. A highly diversified company like GE has many, ranging from utilities who buy its power generation equipment, to oil companies and oil field service companies who buy its gas turbines, to airlines who buy its jet engines, to hospitals who buy its medical equipment, and so on. The relationship between a company and its customers is by nature adversarial because the company wants to get as much money for its products and services as it possibly can, and most customers want to pay as little as they can. That fact of life said, a company cannot exist without its customers. Any company hoping to build a sustainable future should identify explicitly the customer groups it believes it will be relying on and then formally audit exactly what these customers think about the company and its products.

Investing to Reinvigorate the Corporate Future

Figuring out the gap between where the company needs to be and where it is likely to be on key dimensions of its competitive posture, as suggested above, is the starting point for making that future happen. For most companies captured by the lure of a higher immediate stock price, closing the gap will take an investment program of a number of years. In some companies this investment may take the form of increased spending on R&D in core technology areas on which the company intends to base its future. In other companies the kind of investment required will be in brands or distribution channels to make sure customers can depend on a steady supply. In still other companies that plan to build their future around a secure customer franchise, the investment will entail building or expanding truly responsive customer service capabilities to guarantee that customers get value and satisfaction from their dealings with the company. What the investment will almost certainly not entail is another stock buyback program to enrich current shareholders and members of the management team. The critical remedial task for any company looking to position itself for long-term success is deciding what specific investments are required and making sure they happen.

Building a Real Employee Franchise

An important part of any investment program designed to create a defensible strategic franchise for the company will be an investment in people. Companies caught up in the false appeal of shareholder value have for the most part devastated their existing workforces. Valuable employees have been forced out, many into unwanted and inappropriate early retirement. Workers who remain on the job, those who survived the succession of downsizings these companies undertook, are all in varying degrees frightened for their jobs, cynical about the intentions of the company, and more than ready to move on to a new employer willing to offer them even a small premium over their current pay package. None of these workforce attitudes is conducive to getting employees to put in the effort required to make sure the company will prosper into the future. Indeed, the net effect of these employment practices for most firms has been to guarantee that they will have to pay absolutely top dollar for any new employee they want to recruit— removing from employees the potential they inherently offer to be the cornerstone of a competitive advantage. To get out of the bind they have put themselves into, companies will simply have to change how they deal with their employees.

To keep it simple from a management point of view, we must acknowledge that not all employees are of the same strategic value to a company. For a company that hopes to build its future on technology, engineers and scientists are likely the key part of the workforce. For a company that hopes to build its future around brands and a customer franchise, marketing skills most need to be nurtured. Other companies will place primary emphasis on selling or customer service skills, depending on the precise kind of sustainable competitive advantage they are trying to construct. Whatever the skill set that is key to a robust future, that is where to start in an employee investment program.

The kinds of specific employee investments to focus on will vary greatly depending on the kind of skill set a company is betting its future on. At one extreme, if the company's future is to rely on superior skills in a specific area of technology, establishing a position as the company that pays these specific technologists best and provides them a working environment that allows them to pursue technological excellence may make a great deal of sense. The money the old AT&T spent in its Bell Labs operations over the years leading up to its breakup is ample proof of the viability of such a program. But money and working environment may not be the magnets for particular skills. Investment in training may be attractive to some; investment in modern infrastructure and amenities may be the draw for others. Implicit in any investment program in people must be a commitment to sustained if not lifetime employment for the key employees.

But a company can't exploit all other workers while pampering a favored few. The most effective way of building an attractive workplace for all, and likely the most inexpensive way as well, is to revive a robust and appealing corporate culture in the company. The actions of managers obsessed with the bottom line have truly devastated the cultures of most large companies. Nevertheless, people still are people. They approach work as a place to go to earn a living. They also approach it as the community in which they spend the majority of their waking hours. Making this community inviting to all employees, putting a meaningful human dimension back into it, is key to restoring an effective culture, which is in turn a proven way to guarantee long-term success.

Rebuilding a Franchise with Suppliers

Suppliers have been pummeled by companies seeking to improve their bottom lines and enhance their current stock price level. Although much of the modern rhetoric of supplier-customer relations is focused on building partnerships, the reality is almost 100 percent the opposite. To counter the pressure from their customers, as described in Chapter 8, surviving suppliers have been taking steps to boost their own power in the supplier-customer nexus. A company that wants to ensure a robust future cannot do so if it drives all of its major suppliers out of business. Nor can it do so if it has put itself into a subservient position with its major suppliers. The rhetoric of partnership needs to be turned into a reality.

Major supply contracts are always the subject of extensive up-front analysis to ascertain what levels of cost, quality, and support are essential for the company itself to produce the goods it wants to sell at the price point and quality level demanded for success in the marketplace. The critical point is to use these analyses differently from what has tended to be the practice—using them to beat the supplier over the head for even more reductions in cost. Instead, these analyses should be a basis for determining a fair and equitable sharing of the fruits of whatever gains in cost or quality are to be realized. This is not such a revolutionary program. Some progressive companies like Motorola already have programs like this in place. Making this the norm for all supplier contracts is the goal a long-term-oriented company should be looking to achieve.

In the very long term, it makes sense to me that key customers would take meaningful equity stakes in their major suppliers so that the fates of both customer and supplier are inextricably linked. Such a suggestion raises so many issues of fundamental industrial policy—especially in light of recent Japanese experience, where such a system of links has long been in place—that I leave it be. It warrants some thought, however, and may be right for some companies in some industries even now.

Building a Real Customer Franchise

No company can exist without customers. Rhetoric to the contrary, company after company undermined its own customer franchise in the pursuit of shareholder value in the last decade of the twentieth century. Declining customer loyalty and changing consumer buying habits are only the manifestation of this sad development in the world of business. Turning this around is essential for all businesses. Without committed customers, there is no future. Even monopolists like Microsoft should remember this.

The best companies in nearly every industry are almost always those that have invested heavily to build and sustain a real franchise with their target customers. Books like Jim Collins and Jerry Porras's superb *Built to Last* and the business classic by Tom Peters and Bob Waterman, *In Search of Excellence,* provide example after example of companies that put their money where their mouths are to cultivate customer loyalty. Whether they involve expensive product recalls, as Johnson & Johnson did with Tylenol, or writing birthday greetings to customers, as Joe Girard, the world's greatest car salesman, used to do, these examples all have one common denominator: going the extra mile in some unexpected way to win a customer's lasting loyalty.

An effective program to cultivate customer loyalty does not have to break the bank. Nor does it have to involve explicit giveaways, such as selling products below cost. It really is the thought that counts, and the consistency with which the thought is communicated to the targeted customer group. The advent of Internet technology and the prospects it presents virtually any company to develop individually tailored offers to tie customers and companies together should make the launching of such loyalty programs even simpler and more cost effective in the future. What has been lacking in recent years is simply the recognition that such programs are essential for long-term success and the will to spend money on them that otherwise would have been allowed to drop to the bottom line.

Reconnecting with Important Communities

In the arena of corporate citizenship, it is practically a given that most companies should adopt a code of conduct to govern their dealings with governments around the world and make every effort to live by both its spirit and its letter. In fact, many companies already have. The unfinished work for many companies is rebuilding effective partnerships with the local communities they intend to be a part of for the foreseeable future. Having devastated a lot of towns and regions with the plant closings and layoffs of the shareholder value era, most companies have a lot of catch-up work to do to become once again true good corporate citizens in these key communities.

Opportunities for the low-cost cultivation of special relationships are everywhere. Companies have facilities, often very nice ones, in all of the communities they consider important to their future. Why not make these facilities available to appropriate local groups when they are not in full use by the company? Most companies invest in training and have training facilities associated with most of their major operations. With the crisis in education affecting most of local government in the Western world, why not use the skills of company employees and the available and underused facilities to augment local school programs? Most employees would gladly volunteer to participate in such programs. A company committed to a specific community for the long haul will be dependent in the future on employing people based in or near that community. Why not start the process early and build goodwill in the community and among the future workforce by hiring students during the summer and giving them worthwhile work to do in the hours and months when they are not tied to school, training them in what it means to hold a regular job and providing them with money to spend or save?

In an ideal world, communities would like guarantees from employers to a continuity of jobs in the community. In an ideal world, companies would not relocate facilities from one corner of the world to another to take advantage of special tax breaks or other inducements. In the real world, unfortunately, until governments stop offering such incentives to companies to relocate, companies are bound to accept such offers. If one company does not take up an attractive offer, it may suffer the consequences if one of its competitors does and thereby gains a cost or other competitive advantage. Short of refusing to look at such offers, companies can go a long way toward cultivating good community relations by honoring their commitments in their new locations for a reasonable period—probably measured in decades—and doing all within their power to create meaningful career experiences for the employees they hire at these new sites.

Communicating with Shareholders

Most of the steps outlined so far involve an investment of time and money toward securing a viable and prosperous future for the company. This investment has to come from somewhere, likely from monies that would otherwise have been allowed to flow directly to the bottom line. How can a company that undertakes such a program of long-term revitalization afford to divert such monies? Wouldn't such a company get clobbered in the stock market for not doing everything it could to maximize current earnings?

Until enough companies embark on such programs, it is only speculation to provide an answer to these questions. Nevertheless, I believe that a company that invested consciously for the long term, told its shareholders and the investing public what it was doing, and measured its progress toward achieving long-term goals on a regular and public basis would receive a warm reception in the stock market. Most investors in stock are in for the long haul. Although junior investment analysts may jockey with one another to earn a fractionally higher return on the funds they manage and thus spur their own money management careers forward, the trustees of most funds realize that their job is to make sure investors get the best return they can over an extended period. A company that communicates its long-term objectives clearly, performs against these goals, and is willing to share with the investing community both progress and problems as they arise will win a following. Wall Street hates surprises. Even though much of Wall Street seems to function as if next week were the long term, a lot of investors would be only too eager to stay with companies who seriously focused on securing a sound future in the years and decades to come. The key to making the change from a focus on this quarter's results to the long term is open communications and execution of a sensible plan.

Smart companies are already taking steps in this direction. They are seeking out institutional investors less prone to high levels of portfolio churning and more attuned to the gradual evolution of the business. They are pitching their plans to such investors and looking, over time, to build a more stable base of investors to back the company. These efforts to manage the investor base of a company do bear fruit. Any company that wants to commit itself to reconstruction should carefully consider the experiences of these leaders and try to emulate them.

Changing Decisionmaking Processes

I have already laid out most of the elements of a long-term revitalization program. Committing to such an initiative, however, is not just another management fad to be tried and ultimately discarded. The only way to make such a program work is to institutionalize it in the management processes of the company. The most important of these are the company's decisionmaking processes.

Companies go about making decisions in a variety of ways. In some companies final decisions are the prerogative of the CEO, who seeks counsel from a variety of sources before searching his own mind and conscience and reaching a decision. In other companies decisionmaking is inherently a more democratic and consensus-oriented process in which groups of relevant people come together to mull over the facts and reach a consensus on what to do. In some companies decisionmaking is formal, with set-piece analyses required before any major action is initiated. In others decisionmaking is so informal that it gives the appearance (it seldom is) of being totally seat-of-the-pants. No matter how an individual company goes about it, every company has a process to reach decisions. The key to managing for the future is to ensure the decisionmaking process is appropriately focused on the long-term consequences of any decision taken.

At a simplistic level, this can involve nothing more than asking the right questions at the right time: What are the long-term consequences of x? What are our future plans for y? What will this do to our long-term relationship with z? At a more formal level, however, specific changes in decisionmaking processes can see to it that the company examines the long-term consequences of actions. For example, instead of just looking at the savings the company will achieve over the life of a certain supply contract, the decisionmaking process can call for consideration of the effect of the contract on the health of the supplier. In actions that affect employees (decisions on promotions or staff cutbacks in response to business conditions, for instance), the process can be modified so that it takes into account the influence of the decision on the culture of the company and on its attractiveness as an employer to future generations of staff. The decisionmaking process in a sensitive area like personnel can also be required to consider explicitly alternative courses of action designed to have a greater or lesser impact on employee morale and well-being. Finally, in making decisions to launch a new product or start a new marketing campaign, specific attention can be given to how the product or campaign will influence the long-term customer franchise of the company. A company like Apple Computer under Steve Jobs seems to do a superb job of this even now, despite the heavy pressure the company has been under because of its position in the marketplace.

Of all decisionmaking processes companies have, none is as important or as central to running a business as its budgeting process. In budgeting to ensure the long term, this process must drive all others—just as budgeting for the very short term became the sine qua non of the shareholder value era. In some companies it may be as simple as requiring each manager who presents a budget to identify specifically the monies being budgeted to support the long-term position of the company and the results to be achieved from spending these monies. Other companies may prefer to follow the path pioneered by Shell: In its strategic planning, plans are always required to be measured against a series of long-term scenarios developed by the corporate planning staffs. Each company will have to find what works for it—that is, what is familiar, comfortable to use based on experience with the ideas involved, and meaningful to all participants in the process. Getting the budgeting process focused on the right objective is the single most important process change for any company attempting to refocus itself on the long term.

Monitoring Progress and Reporting Results

No one can manage without a clear goal in mind. As flagged at the beginning of this chapter, the first responsibility of a management committed to long-term success is to ensure that the goal is firmly established and communicated to all concerned. Equally, however, no one can manage what isn't measured. One of the strengths of the shareholder value movement that should not be lost in the transition to a new, more long-term-oriented mode of operation is the transparency with which progress can be monitored. Therefore, a final key to making a program of long-term revitalization work is coming up with a means to measure success, marking them over time, and regularly and fully reporting on them to the investing public.

Designing such measures is not easy. Moreover, the right measures to use and track will differ somewhat from company to company. Even the appropriate time frames will vary according to the unique characteristics of an industry: An Internet company could well be right in looking at the long term as three years down the road.

The concept behind the right kind of measurement program is outlined by Robert S. Kaplan and David P. Norton in *The Balanced Scorecard: Translating Strategy into Action*. As they point out, a proper measurement program for any company should retain conventional accounting measures of progress like return on capital employed and economic value added, the favorite of the shareholder value crowd. It should also include measures of long-term keys to success like customer satisfaction ratings and measures of the amount of value created for customers. It should gauge the capabilities, morale, turnover, and even special skill sets of employees, and these measures should be applied across different geographic and tenure cuts of the company. It should calculate the technological position of the company in more concrete terms than simply counting the number of patents issued in the company's name. Finally, it should track the company's impact on the communities it lives in and the suppliers it deals with on a regular basis. If this sounds tough, it is. But it is essential if a program of future-oriented management is to succeed. The trick is to start with the most important measures and then gradually add others as the program evolves.

Not only should companies use something like a balanced scorecard to trace their progress against long-term objectives, but they should routinely make available to the investing public the key measures they track and the main targets they attempt to achieve. (Some measures used internally, especially ones related to technological progress, may be too sensitive to be published outside the company, however.) Any senior manager ready to commit to a program of long-term management should have no trouble articulating clearly

the main pillars of the company's long-term plan for success (technology, people, products, customers, whatever)

the specific targets the company is setting out to achieve against these
   pillars over a time frame such as five to ten years (e.g., new products
   representing x percent of sales; repeat purchases accounting for y
   percent of sales; customer satisfaction ratings of z percent in the
   highest percentile)
precisely where every important part of the business stands against these
   measures at any point in time

In my view, these plans for success should be incorporated as a standard
part of the annual report of any large public company. Regulatory agencies
like the Securities and Exchange Commission (SEC) should think hard
about mandating such routine reporting for the protection of the investing
public. Until that happens, however, the companies that take the lead in
such disclosure will be the ones that move rapidly to the "acquire and hold"
lists of serious long-term investors in the stock market.

It is the responsibility of boards of directors to make sure companies run
themselves to create a viable and sustainable future. The next chapter therefore examines the changes urgently needed in the boardroom to make this
objective become a reality.

CHAPTER 12

Taking the Boredom out of
Board Work—Forever

Boards of directors are clearly and unequivocally responsible to investors for the long-term viability of the corporations on whose boards they serve. If a lot of large public companies are in serious trouble or on the verge of getting into serious trouble because of the slavish adoption of the shareholder value ethic and its implicit call for higher and higher stock prices now, then the directors of these companies should be held accountable. Managers in companies may have led the charge into extreme short-termism, but it was the directors responsible for overseeing these managers who gave them the green light.

Most observers of the corporate scene are not surprised in the slightest that boards have been remiss in carrying out their duties. As described in Chapter 10, membership on boards of large public companies is akin to membership in a club populated mainly by CEOs. Because of this heavy predominance of CEOs, current and former, boardrooms are rife with conflicts between the interests of individual board members and the interests of shareholders whom board members are supposed to represent. "I vote you a nice little stock option here, Mr. CEO. In return, you vote me a modest option for my service on your board. You also tell your other CEO colleagues who happen to serve on my board what a fine fellow I am and how they ought to increase my option plan as well." Members of boards of directors don't talk that way, at least in public, but they act that way every day of the week. As long as stock prices are soaring, making members of this little club wealthy beyond their wildest dreams and keeping shareholders in a state of ignorant bliss, who could argue with the inner workings of the club?

In point of fact, a lot of observers of the corporate scene have argued strenuously against the composition and practices of corporate boards. The people presenting these arguments are not some woolly-thinking, fringe radicals but serious and respected members of the business and academic communities. My voice is just one of many in this chorus of complaint about a system gone wrong. Perhaps as more and more come to realize how much damage has been wrought by the movement to inflate today's stock prices at the expense of all else, a long-needed consensus for change will finally emerge.

Calls for Reform

The overly cozy relationship between board members and senior managers in companies they are supposed to be overseeing has long been the subject of criticism and calls for reform. The amount of energy that has gone into the debate and the degree to which the debate has gripped the public's consciousness has tended to go down in direct response to the stock market's climb. Still, board members of large public companies have little excuse for ignoring the raft of well-intentioned proposals put in front of them. The main proposals, who offered them, and where they can be found appear in Table 12.1.

TABLE 12.1   Proposals For Board Reform

Area of Reform	Who Proposed	Where	Proposal
1. Focus on Long Term	–Lester Thurow	–Sloan Management Review	–Eliminate quarterly reporting
	–James Tobin	–Twentieth Century Fund Report	–Tax on stock trades
	–Michael Porter	–Research Report for U.S. Congress	–Tax incentives for long term stock holdings
2. Improved Information for Shareholders	–American Institute of Certified Public Accountants	–Special Report	–Expanded reporting requirements
	–Michael Porter	–Research Report for U.S. Congress	–Change rules on institutional holdings –Improve quality and quantity of information flows
	–Robert Monks	–Shareholder Proposal to Exxon Annual Meeting	–Establish "Shareholder Advisory Committee"
3. Improved Information for Directors	–Jay Lorsch	–Harvard Business Review	–Encourage freer communications –Improve format/content of information
	–Hugh Parker	–Chapter in Monks & Minow book	–Improve quality of information

Area of Reform	Who Proposed	Where	Proposal
4. Qualifications of Directors	–Amar Bhide	–Harvard Business Review	–Set higher standards
	–Jay Lorsch	–Harvard Business Review	–Increase diversity of experience
	–John Vogelstein	–Corporate Board article	–Set membership qualifications
	–Ralph Ward	–Book	–Increase number of foreign directors –Set tenure limits
5. Improve Board Process	–Amar Bhide	–Harvard Business Review	–Focus board agenda on forward issues –Require more time to be spent
	–Jay Lorsch (and many others)	–Harvard Business Review	–Increase number of outside members –Shrink board size –Appoint a "Lead" Director
	–John Vogelstein	–Corporate Board article	–Make Chairman well paid non-executive –Increase role of Audit Committee –increase independence of Compensation Committee
	–Ralph Ward	–Book	–Set up several other standing committees
6. Improved Incentives for Directors	–Amar Bhide	–Harvard Business Review	–Increase director compensation by 500%
	–John Vogelstein (and many others)	–Corporate Board article	–Increase stock component of director compensation –Eliminate annual retainers (require attendance)
7. Increased Independence for Directors	–Many	NA	–Increase number of outsiders –Provide dedicated staff –Increase time spent

The main thrust of these proposals, as shown in the table, is to

- force managers to think more long-term
- improve the flow of information to shareholders and their access to and input into corporate decisionmaking
- improve the flow of information to directors of companies so they have no excuse for not doing their jobs better
- raise the qualifications for people who serve as corporate directors
- improve the process by which boards work
- heighten the motivation and incentives for directors to perform
- increase the independence of sitting directors

If there is a single catchword that seems to encapsulate these proposals it is to "empower" directors to do the job they are surely now legally and morally responsible for doing. Most if not all of the ideas on offer for board empowerment have merit. Probably no one or few of them would suddenly revitalize boards to the point where all outside concerns would disappear. Most, however, surely deserve a more careful hearing than they have been afforded anywhere to date. Before I add my own voice to this debate, in the next two sections I profile the proposals put forward by others.

Michael Porter's Proposals

At the beginning of the 1990s, Michael Porter, a Harvard Business School professor and prolific writer on important business topics, headed a two-year research project on "capital choices" sponsored by his own business school and the Council on Competitiveness (a nonprofit think tank concerned about long-term industrial policy in the United States). One of the primary concerns of the study team was the deleterious effects of short-termism on corporate performance. The study looked at a number of options, most designed to align the incentives and interests of investors and managers toward long-term performance.

Among the many recommendations that emanated from the study were proposals for changes in capital gains tax schemes to encourage investors to hold stock positions for periods of a minimum of five years in order to take advantage of the tax breaks on offer. Similarly, the study group recommended that long-term institutional holders of a company's equity should be allowed access to a broader array of corporate performance data than they are now permitted to receive under rules designed to protect the interests of small investors. The key here was to insist that the stockholders have the stock in their portfolios for at least a year before such preferential access to information was to be granted. The team also called for restrictions on the issuance of unrestricted stock options to managers to force managerial incentive schemes to require the holding of stock or options for a long period of time before they could be exercised. On the subject of boards, Porter's project team recommended that large, long-term institutional share owners should be allowed to sit on the boards of the companies in which they had their large holdings. They also suggested that boards seriously consider adding as members "significant customers, suppliers, financial advisers, employees and community representatives" to replace the many board members they characterized as "busy, under-informed CEOs."

The Porter proposals, presented before the U.S. Congress and published in the *Harvard Business Review,* were reprinted in 1996 in a book edited by Frederick F. Reichheld, *The Quest for Loyalty: Creating Value Through Partnership.* They deserve much more attention than they received when they were initially put forward, since they are designed to address the malaise of short-termism systemically. Anticipating my suggestions for concentrating first on the fundamental purpose of business, Porter's group recommended that companies "codify long-term shareholder value rather than current stock price as the appropriate corporate goal." Amen.

Dan Bavly's Proposals

Across the river from the Harvard Business School, at the Kennedy School of Government, another author and former auditor, Dan Bavly, worked on an even more focused set of proposals to reform board practices. His reasoning and recommendations were published in late 1999 as *Corporate Governance and Accountability: What Role for the Regulator, Director, and Auditor?* Because he had almost ten more years of witnessing what a short-termism-driven economy could produce both on the upside and on the downside, it is not so surprising that Bavly's suggestions for change are even bolder than those Porter's group put forward in the early 1990s. Specifically, Bavly recommends that:

1. Independent, outside directors of companies be appointed and paid by an independent, outside body similar in structure to the stock exchange to guarantee these board members' independence.
2. Outside board members be required to spend a minimum of one-third to one-half of their working hours on a company's affairs in return for membership on the board. This would, of course, severely restrict the number of boards any one individual could serve on— which is precisely Bavly's intent—and give outside directors a much

better chance of being well informed about the companies whose boards they serve on.

3. The number of outside directors on a board be reduced substantially, and the size of most boards cut down at the same time to around five or six members, all materially involved in the affairs of the company.

4. The tenure of board members be limited to a period such as three to five years, with the possibility of continuing on the board limited to one additional term only. By forcing a regular change in the composition of the board, Bavly hopes to ensure boards retain a fresh perspective on the affairs of the company.

5. Director compensation (through an independent agency) be increased commensurate with the additional time commitment required and the extra responsibility assumed.

To most current board members, those are fighting words. It is perhaps a sign of the cumulating frustration with board performance that even mainstream individuals like Bavly are recommending such radical measures to fix an institution that clearly doesn't work well.

Where Existing Proposals Fall Short

What virtually all of these proposals miss (and their proponents are only too ready to acknowledge) is that in order for boards to take on the oversight they are tasked with on behalf of shareholders requires a change in the mindset and culture of the institution of boards. But boards are too close to the problem even to see it exists. Like elderly gentlemen in a traditional British men's club, boards occasionally rouse themselves to rail against something or other before being overtaken by their customary languor and falling back to sleep. Somehow—through shake-ups in the composition of boards, new ways to compensate board members, or revisions in the regulatory environment associated with board practices—this mindset must change. Unfortunately, it will probably take another precipitous drop in stock market averages to get people to focus on the needed reforms.

Boards today are failing the investors whose interests they are supposed to be representing and the public at large because (1) they have been lackadaisical in the execution of their duties, (2) they have allowed themselves to be co-opted by senior managers intent on feathering their own nests and eager to preserve a currently lucrative status quo, and (3) they have ignored the long-term consequences of management actions explicitly designed to serve the interests of one group of stakeholders, shareholders, at the expense of all others. My proposals for board reforms are designed to address all of these concerns. Some are uniquely my own; others I have borrowed from fellow observers of the corporate governance scene, especially Dan Bavly, because they seem most worthy of being taken seriously. There is more than enough talent on boards today, whatever their shortcomings in performance, to decide which of these proposals, mine or those of others, merit earnest attention and action.

No one of these proposals alone is likely to eliminate the problems that have arisen since the late 1980s because of corporate devotion to enhancing short-term shareholder performance. Nor are they likely to be implemented anywhere as a precise set. Indeed, any board that takes the criticism of corporate short-termism contained in this book seriously enough to consider following some or all of these suggestions will have to develop an implementation plan and process that will likely take several years to bear fruit. These proposals are intended as directional signposts for any board concerned about the problem and eager to move ahead. Taken with the raft of other proposals for reform that have been floated in recent years, they can provide a basis for designing much more effective board oversight in the future and a much more secure future for us all.

"Clear the Rascals Out"

Malaise afflicted boards of large public companies throughout the 1990s. That malaise is best described as oversatisfaction with the status quo, despite problems that have appeared on the horizon. It is a cultural phenomenon that involves the way existing board members see their role on the board and the way they relate one to another and to management. The only way to solve this problem (over time, of course) is to clear the rascals who are there now out. The specific steps I think boards should consider to this end are

- cutting most board sizes to between six and eight people
- banning all existing CEOs of large public companies from serving on the boards of other large public companies
- compensating individual board members commensurate with the increased responsibilities they will have to assume; on the assumption that the average board member will spend at least one- third of his or her working hours on any one board's matters, it might be sensible to think of tying board member compensation to a similar fraction of the CEO's compensation in the company
- limiting to no more than three the number of corporate boards people can serve on and, as Bavly suggests, enforcing strict rules for how long any one individual can serve on any one board

- removing board members from their position on a board if they fail to carry out their duties to that board with diligence (e.g., if they miss more than two board meetings in a row)
- chartering an independent body to develop tough new standards all board members must meet and make sure these standards are upheld
- mandating that all new board members adhere to these standards and go through an intensive orientation program before joining the board
- adding two or three members to the board, still keeping its total size to between six and eight, to represent the interests of major outside constituencies, suppliers, communities, customers, and/or employees—the precise constituencies to be a function of which are most important given each company's unique position

The wholesale changes recommended above in the makeup of boards will once and for all break the club system of current board membership in large public companies. There is a danger, of course, of substituting a new exclusive club for the one that exists today. In this regard, two of my specific recommendations are most important. First, banning current CEOs from outside board interests will expand the potential pool of board members enormously and protect it against the inbreeding that now affects the corporate scene. I understand that active CEOs are currently considered ideal board members because their own position on the firing line makes them especially sensitive to the kinds of pressures any senior manager likely faces. Moreover, CEOs like to take outside board positions because they learn a lot for their own CEO duties from experiencing up close the workings of another public company (as well as from the contacts they make with other CEOs and board members). This is where the rascal effect comes into play, however. Active CEOs have abused their positions of power on other boards by allowing the excesses of the current era of business to proliferate. The only way to excise this abusive behavior is to expel CEOs from the scene of the crime, as it were.

Critics of such a radical proposition will undoubtedly argue that there are simply not enough qualified candidates available to serve on boards. Excluding those with the most obvious qualifications will only shrink the pool even more. To me, this is a lot of piffle. There are thousands of potential board members active today in the academic world and in the professions. By deliberately reaching further afield in the search for board members, corporations will find that they expand the range of experiences available to them and strengthen themselves. (Giving directors real jobs to do will also make the transition easier, as discussed below.)

The second recommendation that will have a significant influence on board diversity and perspective is the proposal to add a number of representatives of important outside constituencies to boards. In Germany, where workers' councils are required by law, large companies are able to function quite effectively despite the presence of outside advocates in their innermost deliberations. The presence of such outside advocates will play a major factor in curbing some of the recklessness that seems to have overcome corporations during the 1990s. Although it may take five to ten years to complete a transition to a more diverse makeup for corporate boards, the movement in this direction will lead to nothing but positives over time.

Give Board Members Real Jobs

Getting a smaller group of more thoughtfully selected members onto the boards of large public companies will not do much to solve the boardroom crisis if the behavior of boards continues in the future the way it has in the past. First, individual board members today spend far too little time on their board duties to even know what is going on, much less influence it. Second, the way boards work today, board members are almost totally dependent on the management they oversee for information about what is going on in the company. With no independent sources of information for themselves, how can they possibly act as more than a rubber stamp to management-led initiatives? Finally, beyond certifying compliance with relevant laws and accounting practices, appointing new CEOs, and selecting new people to serve on the board, boards today have no real, specific duties to perform. As a result, it is all too easy for individual board members to pat themselves on the back for a job well done when all they did was show up at meetings and raise their hands at appropriate times. This should be changed so that board members have genuine duties to perform, duties for which they can be held individually accountable.

Following this line of reasoning, I suggest that boards

- limit the number of insiders on a board to a maximum of two people (CEO, CFO) and consider making them nonvoting members of the board; this would more clearly than anything else shift the balance of power on any board to its outside members
- require any company to provide dedicated, professional staffing for its board: This board staff should have full access to anything that goes on in the company (like an audit function already does) but should be chartered specifically to (1) maintain board-specific reporting systems designed to allow the board to keep its eye firmly on

the long-term ball (of which, see more below) and (2) conduct special investigations, as requested by individual board members. Even in the very largest companies, a board staff of carefully selected individuals numbering no more than twenty to thirty people, the size of a large but not dysfunctional consulting team, should be enough to give board members all the information they need to carry out their responsibilities.

- charge boards explicitly with responsibility for developing targets for the company—targets predicated on the company's remaining viable over the long term—and require an annual report from the board on the progress the company has made in moving toward these goals
- require a respected outside agency to conduct regular third-party audits of the effectiveness of board members and the overall functioning of the board

The essence of these proposals is to give boards their own staff (so they have no excuse for ducking their responsibilities) and give them a real job to do. Critics of the first part of this proposal, board staffing, will argue that many companies made progress in performance during the 1990s by getting rid of unnecessary and superfluous overhead functions. Although there is undoubtedly some truth in this assertion, enabling boards to function independently of the managements they are responsible for overseeing is hardly a superfluous function in any large company. Some trial and error in implementing this suggestion should quickly determine what kind and level of staffing will allow this to happen without creating an undue burden on the companies being monitored.

Critics will also attack (on at least two counts) the second recommendation, giving boards the job of spelling out and reporting on the long-term goals for the company. The first criticism will be that this is what management is already paid for and parachuting boards into this realm will needlessly interfere with the proper exercise of managerial prerogatives. I beg to differ. Ensuring the long-term sustainability of the enterprise in a large public company is precisely what boards are there to do. It is management's job to execute against this set of priorities and be held accountable if they screw up in such a way that the long-term health of the enterprise is jeopardized. Moreover, I said nothing about how a board should go about establishing such goals. In the vast majority of cases, a board would undertake this responsibility in close concert with the management team it had put in place to run the company. Only when this management team set out on a path that looked as if it would clearly prevent long-term goals from being achieved should any board act independently to right the course. That's what a board is there for in the first place.

The second criticism that will be leveled at the proposal to give the board explicit responsibility for long-term goals is that the world changes too quickly for that task to be sensible or even doable. Especially in a world with record levels of mergers and acquisitions threatening to reshape the face of business in industry after industry, how could anyone, let alone a part-time body like a board, ever hope to set meaningful long-term goals? Once again, I beg to differ with these criticisms. The world does change, and perhaps it is now changing faster than ever. Moreover, merger and restructuring proposals do come out of the woodwork, sometimes when they are least expected. So what? It is still impossible to run anything without a clear idea where that thing is headed. If circumstances change, so be it: Adapt thinking to accommodate the new circumstances. That is what happens in the real world when an unexpected takeover bid is received. Let it happen the same way in the future. An absence of absolute predictability is no justification for not having a firm idea about where you want to go in the first place. In fact, having thought through long-term goals a priori, boards may well be in a much better position to fend off unwanted and inappropriate advances when they occur.

The benefits of giving boards real jobs to do, jobs that zero in on the long-term viability of the company, are enormous. This one move would liberate boards from the near servile positions they occupy today in relationship to strong-willed managers. It would also make board work much more interesting and challenging, which would attract many more talented people to the position. In fact, because the effectiveness of what boards did with this responsibility would be subject to both public scrutiny and audit, giving boards this responsibility would help professionalize the institution of board membership. Over time, with forced rotation of board members, serving on the boards of smaller public companies could begin to become a kind of farm system for consideration for promotion to the big leagues, board membership on some of the largest companies in the world. As a result, real standards for board membership could evolve so that the overall governance of companies would improve. A new profession, board membership, may well emerge, to everyone's advantage.

Fix the Incentive Compensation Issue Now

Executive compensation ran amuck during the 1990s. Everyone knows that. CEOs of large public companies, the chief beneficiaries of the executive pay boom, know it. Board members in large public companies know it. What should be worrying for all is that the general public surely knows it, too. Politicians in all major parties are just waiting for the time to be ripe, such as the advent of a significant recession, to raise the issue on a populist banner to help them get elected to office. Moreover, the short-term, stock-price-oriented incentives associated with the executive pay boom are likely the single greatest cause of the serious impending problems I have spent much of this book documenting.

If something is so obviously wrong and so potentially damaging to all concerned, why not fix it now? The solution to the compensation issue is so simple it is a wonder it has not been addressed before. Fix the incentive compensation issue for senior managers, particularly the CEOs of large public companies, by making any stock options or grants awarded them vest only some period of time, let us say five years, after their service in office is completed. Make such a process mandatory across the whole corporate spectrum.

In terms of base pay and benefits, CEOs of large companies are already paid more than well enough to allow them to live the kind of life-style they aspire to. The incentive parts of their pay packages are designed to build their wealth—wealth most will never be able to spend in this lifetime. These incentives were also put into place to align managerial interests with the interests of shareholders, the majority of whom are investing for a long-term objective. Delaying the vesting of these incentive grants until well after managers have left their posts will harm no one and will in one stroke force managerial interests to focus on the long-term welfare of the company.

Critics will undoubtedly cite the tight job market for the qualified senior executives needed to run large companies as the one impenetrable barrier to the implementation of such a proposal. In some respects they are right. The superstar CEOs of today will undoubtedly demand their rewards now if these rewards are on offer. Sitting boards who approve these awards should think long and hard about the consequences of such thinking, however. If the CEO they have hired to run the company they are responsible for is unwilling to take the job without an incentive scheme that allows him or her to cash in quickly, just what does this say about the kind of executive they are hiring to protect the long-term interests of the company? Perhaps the company and the world would be a better place if boards refused to appoint such CEOs in the first place.

Focus Boards on a Sustainable Future

The impending crisis for boards today is that they have allowed management to push key constituencies so far into a corner that trust and cooperation are limited and each major stakeholder group is taking steps, some of them pretty effective, to redress the imbalance in the relationship. Tomorrow's burning issue for boards may well be different. For example, it may be making sure the company is doing all in its power to conduct an environmentally sustainable business. The steps outlined below are intended to address today's main problem head on but can be used to address whatever critical issues top the board's agenda in the future:

- require boards to set up a standing stakeholder committee with ongoing responsibility to monitor the effect of company actions on each important constituency group; require regular reporting of the findings of this committee (e.g., as part of the annual report)
- require companies to identify the major stakeholders they deal with in specific detail (e.g., identify the specific communities the company is committed to, name the major suppliers it is dependent on) and report regularly on how the company's actions impinge on these stakeholders
- require companies to disclose any long-term contracts they enter into with each major designated stakeholder (including special employment deals with individual employees)
- require companies and boards to make an annual statement to shareholders of what specific actions are being taken to build the long-term future of the company; force these statements to be strategic in context, that is, to spell out specifically how the company expects to compete in the future and where it expects its sustainable competitive advantage to come from

Critics of this set of proposals may shake their heads and say, "I've heard this all before. This is yet another attempt to convince me of the rightness of the stakeholder view of the corporation." It is not. For many years now, there has been a viewpoint (or theory, if you will) that the purpose of a corporation is to serve fairly the interests of its stakeholders. This theory is one of the major competitors of the shareholder value view of the world. It has a long provenance even if it has never won the day. For example, in a landmark article published as long ago as 1932, E. Merrick Dodd Jr. quoted the near legendary chairman of General Electric, Owen Young, as saying, "If you will pardon me for being personal, it makes a great deal of difference in my attitude toward my job as an executive officer of the General Electric Company whether I am a trustee of the institution or an attorney for the investor [the notion of shareholder value advocates]. . . . My conception of it is this: That there are three groups of people who have an interest in that institution . . . shareholders, employees and customers and the general public. . . . One feels the obligation to administer . . . fairly in the interests of all." In voicing these sentiments, Young was verbalizing an idea that had been around for a long time. For example, in another landmark article dated 1916, J. Maurice Clark said, "The world is familiar enough with the conception of social responsibilities [of corporations]. These do not need to be rediscovered in the year of our Lord 1916."

This old idea about the responsibilities of corporations to society at large and their stakeholders in particular has received greater notice in light of the runaway abuses of the shareholder value era. For example, in the UK, the Prince of Wales Trust recently sponsored a meeting of the Prince of Wales Business Leaders Forum devoted to the topic of "responsible business." North American readers may find this obscure, but as one who has lived in the UK for many years, I can tell you it is an event of note in the business community there. Closer to home, hundreds of articles and a score of books have been published every year for the past twenty years extolling the virtues of stakeholder management. Specialized organizations have been set up on many North American college campuses focused on related topics spun out from the stakeholder theory of the corporation, such as business ethics, corporate responsibility, corporate community relations, and corporate citizenship. Although this book may appear to be simply defending one side in the long-raging debate between two major schools of thought, I believe it is something else. One reason the shareholder value theory of the world gained such wide acceptance is that it rang true for so many people. And as far as it goes, it is true. I have argued that the shareholder value theory of the corporate world, though perfectly valid, went wrong in its exploitation of stakeholders when it forced their backs so much to the wall that each and every one of them had to respond aggressively, so that the future viability of corporations is today threatened. That is not an argument for the stakeholder view of the world. Rather, it is an argument that the market is working quite well to regulate the relationships among various stakeholders. It is working so well, in fact, that corporate managers and board members should take heed, or they will be overwhelmed by the forces set in motion against them. There is nothing wrong with the idea that people, even theoretical "people" like corporations, should do "right." It just belongs in the province of religion, not commerce.

Afterword

The shareholder value movement, though not wrong in concept, has led business into a potentially serious and threatening trap. In particular, the emphasis within the shareholder value movement to measure success in the short term and not account for the long-term consequences of actions is the villain in the piece. But once discredited, it is hard for a movement to regain momentum. What, then, should replace shareholder value thinking as the driving ethic of business in the twenty-first century?

My own belief is that shareholder value thinking should be broadened beyond the notion of value, which already connotes cashing in, toward wealth, with all it connotes in terms of permanence and legacy. My candidate for an ethic to replace the idea of maximizing shareholder value thinking would be building and sharing wealth. Why? Shareholder value thinking was always about creating wealth. The terminology got in the way, however. The very word "value" implies an immediacy that in most cases should have no place in the conduct of great business enterprises. By contrast, both "building" and "wealth" imply something lasting. If businesses were to focus their energies almost exclusively on building wealth, I believe many if not most of the abuses we have witnessed under the banner of shareholder value since the 1980s would disappear almost overnight. How many companies would spend their wealth on stock buyback programs if their objective was to create wealth? How many companies would see fit to cut R&D expenditures if their objective was to build wealth? How many companies would cavalierly shed long-term, loyal employees, their heads crammed full of information valuable to the company, if their objective was to build wealth? Not many, I think.

From its beginnings less than two centuries ago, the world of business has come to be one of the major pillars of society. Through world wars, depressions, shifting mores and practices, and life-altering technological change, business has shown its resilience by adapting and moving ever more closely toward center stage in life. This resilience is embodied in the survival and prosperity of thousands of companies—from those founded as family businesses in the nineteenth century, through those founded by technocrats eager to exploit new technology and make a better life for themselves and those around them, to the buzz associated with Internet start-ups convinced they

207

are remaking the world by harnessing this most exciting of technological wonders. As the twenty-first century begins, the long-term resilience of business is in danger of being compromised by the idea of shareholder value and the short-term excesses that have emerged as its most visible face to the world. As recently as 1997, Marvin Bower, the man who built McKinsey & Company into the institution it now is, said, "In recent years . . . the fashionable corporate purpose has been to increase shareholder wealth. I totally disagree. Increasing shareholder wealth does not do justice to business as an institution." I hate to quibble with Bower, a man I much admire, but his perspective is only approximately right. If business truly focused on building wealth, not immediately realizable value, its future would still be secure and it would not be demeaned as an institution. May the arguments I present in this book help to get it back on course.

Notes

Chapter 1

4　Background material on James Gamble, William Procter, and the early days of the Procter & Gamble Company is from Oscar Schisgall, *Eyes on Tomorrow* (J. G. Ferguson Publishing, 1981), pp. 1–14.

6　For the early history of the companies that came together to form Unilever, I relied on Charles Wilson, *The History of Unilever* (Praeger, 1968). Most of the material was drawn from chapter 1 of book 1, pp. 3–45, and chapters 2 and 16 of book 2, pp. 4–84 and 271–308.

9　The story of Gillette's invention of the safety razor comes from Gordon McKibben, *Cutting Edge* (Harvard Business School Press, 1998), pp. 5–8. McKibben found the specific quote by Gillette about the moment of invention in the archives of the *Gillette Blade,* the company's in-house magazine.

10　The background material on Sears and the quote from Julius Rosenwald (emphasis in the original) appear in James C. Worthy, *Shaping an American Institution* (University of Illinois Press, 1984), pp. 19–28.

12　The founding of the Dow Chemical Company is described in Don Whitehead, *The Dow Story* (McGraw-Hill, 1968), pp. 18–51. The specific passages quoted appear on pp. 19 and 20.

14　The background material on Alexander Graham Bell and the founding and financing of the Bell Telephone Company is taken from John Brooks, *Telephone, the First Hundred Years* (Harper & Row, 1975), pp. 35–46, 53, 55, 56, and 63.

15　The story of Henry J. Heinz and the origins of his company appears in Robert C. Alberts, *The Good Provider: H. J. Heinz and His 57 Varieties* (Houghton Mifflin, 1973), pp. 1–69.

16　Information on Will Durant's setting up, losing control of, regaining control of, and subsequent ouster from General Motors is from Sloan, *My Years with General Motors*, pp. 3–16.

Chapter 2

20   Background on the founding and early days of the Polaroid Company is from
      Peter C. Wensberg, *Land's Polaroid* (Houghton Mifflin, 1987). Specific figures
      and dates quoted appear on pp. 20, 43, 47, 55, 67, 74, and 101.

22   An account of the formation and fledgling years of the Hewlett-Packard
      Company is in David Packard, *The HP Way* (HarperBusiness, 1995).
      Particular facts and events cited occur on pp. 18, 24, 27, 29, 32, 41, 45, 46,
      56, 64, 70, and 80–81.

23   For the story of Sam Walton and the formation of the Wal-Mart retail chain,
      I relied on Bob Ortega, *In Sam We Trust* (Times Business, 1998). Specific ma-
      terial cited in the text is from pp. 16, 22, 25, 26, 29, 31, 54, and 55.

26   Ray Kroc and the launching of McDonald's are covered in John F. Love,
      McDonald's (Bantam, 1995). Specific material cited is from pp. 11, 14, 20, 24,
      31, 40, 73, 74, and 79.

29   The background material on Digital Equipment is taken from Glenn Rifkin
      and George Harrar, *The Ultimate Entrepreneur* (Contemporary Books, 1988),
      pp. 10, 14, 29, 40, and 44.

30   The story of the founding of Intel is from Tim Jackson, *Inside Intel* (Dutton,
      1997), pp. 18, 26, and 27.

Chapter 3

33   The Alfred Rappaport book that launched the shareholder value revolution
      was *Information for Decision Making* (Prentice-Hall, 1979). The book that
      subsequently became the bible for the shareholder value movement was
      Rappaport's *Creating Shareholder Value* (Free Press, 1986).

34   For an account of Microsoft and the personal computer industry, I used
      Robert X. Cringely, *Accidental Empires* (HarperBusiness, 1996). The quote
      about Gates's fear of being left behind in the personal computer revolution is
      on p. 52. Other material cited is from pp. 53, 55, 61, and 129.

35   The background material on Phil Knight and the launching of the Nike
      Corporation is from J. B. Lasser and Laurie Becklund, *Swoosh*
      (HarperBusiness, 1993,). Specific material is from pp. 13, 16, 28, 31, 34, 38,
      50, 53, 55, 56, 58, 76, and 116.

38   The quotation from Sandy Kurtzig is taken from her book *CEO* (Harvard
      Business School Press, 1991), p. 16.

38   The quotation from Michael Wolff appears in his book *Burn Rate*
      (Touchstone, 1999), p. 53.

38   The background material on Larry Ellison and the founding of Oracle is from
      Mike Wilson, *The Difference Between God and Larry Ellison (God Doesn't*

Think He's Larry Ellison) (William Morrow and Company, 1997). Specific material cited or quoted is on pp. 6, 11, 29, 44, 58, 59, 60, and 76.

41 For the story of Bill Von Meister and the founding of America Online, I relied on Kara Swisher, *Aol.com* (Times Business, 1998). Specific material referenced comes from pp. 11, 13, 14, 15, 21, 24, 41, 42, 46, 48, and 56.

44 Rappaport's ideas on shareholder value are best explored by reading his seminal book on the subject, *Creating Shareholder Value.* My own ideas on the subject are contained in chapters 2 through 5 of Terrence Deal and Allan Kennedy, *The New Corporate Cultures* (Perseus Books, 1999).

Chapter 4

50 Some material about General Electric is taken from Thomas F. O'Boyle, *At Any Cost* (Alfred A. Knopf, 1998). The aircraft engine information is covered on pp. 225 and 226; the estimated cut in R&D spending is from p. 375. All other information about GE I culled from the company's annual reports.

54 The comparative figures on R&D spending, the quotation from Joyce Hergenhan, and subsequent quotes from Jack Welch about the significance of stock buybacks are from John Holusha, "Are We Eating Our Seed Corn?" *New York Times,* May 13, 1990.

57 I calculated comparative price-earnings ratios for financial services firms from annual reports of the companies included in each group and Dow Jones stock quotes.

61 The P/E valuation formula is taken from Benjamin Graham's classic book, *The Intelligent Investor,* 4th ed. (HarperCollins, 1973), p. 158.

61 I analyzed GE's stock price overvaluation by applying Graham's formula to data taken from GE's annual reports, adjusted as indicated in the text. To evaluate the overvaluation of companies following GE's lead in pursuing shareholder value, I used the same basic methodology. Data for individual companies were taken from their most recent annual reports; stock price quotes came from Dow Jones.

65 Roger Trapp made his observation in a personal communication, December 1999.

Chapter 5

69 The early history of Amazon.com is from an article by Robert Hof, "The Torrent of Energy Behind Amazon," *Business Week,* December 14, 1998, p. 119. In addition I used Laura E. Whiteley, ed., *International Directory of Company Histories,* vol. 25 (St. James Press, 1995), p. 17.

70   Details on the business troubles Amazon is facing as it matures appear in
      Jacqueline Doherty, "Amazon.bomb," *Barron's,* May 31, 1999, pp. 25–27. For
      supplementary details, I turned to Robert D. Hof, Ellen Neuborne, and
      Heather Green, "Amazon.com: The Wild World of E-Commerce," *Business
      Week,* December 14, 1998, pp. 108–119.

74   The background material on Yahoo comes primarily from Tina N. Grant, ed.,
      International Directory of Company Histories, vol. 27 (St. James Press, 1999),
      pp. 516–519.

77   Financial details on Yahoo's growth and performance are taken from the com-
      pany's 1998 annual report, supplemented by data from Standard and Poor's
      stock report on the company, May 8, 1999.

78   The decline in Yahoo's revenue per ad page in late 1998 was cited in the
      California Internet Stock Letter, April 16, 1999.

79   Background on the early days of Cisco Systems is covered in Paula Kepos, ed.,
      International Directory of Company Histories, vol. 11 (St. James Press, 1995),
      pp. 58–60.

82   Financial data about Cisco's performance are from Standard and Poor's stock
      reports, May 8, 1999.

83   Information about the increasing glut of long-distance bandwidth in the
      United States and its implications for companies was taken from Seth
      Schiesel, "Jumping off the Bandwidth Wagon: Long-Distance Carriers
      Regroup," *New York Times,* July 11, 1999, pp. C1, C10, and C11.

84   The issue of bandwidth glut is covered as well in Kevin Maney, "The Next Big
      Bang: Communications Capacity Exploding: What Could It Mean? 1-cent
      Long-Distance, Video E-Mail," *USA Today,* October 8, 1998, p. 1B.

84   Cisco's reliance on the Internet to conduct its business was commented on in
      Steve Hamm, Andy Reinhardt, and Peter Burrows, "Builders of the New
      Economy," *Business Week,* June 21, 1999, p. 121.

86   The description of previous bubbles is from "Shares Stall in Cyberspace: The
      Booms That Went Bust," *Observer,* April 18, 1999, p. 5. The quote from
      Mark Anderson is cited in Denise Caruso, "Internet Companies Reinvent
      Math, Contending That Each Losing Transaction Succeeds as 'Volume,'" *New
      York Times,* March 29, 1999, p. C7.

Chapter 6

93   The best description of changes in the employment compact between em-
      ployees and employers can be found in Peter Cappelli, *The New Deal at Work*
      (Harvard Business School Press, 1999). The three characteristics of the new
      work compact appear on p. 22. Data on company attitudes toward job secu-
      rity are taken from Cappelli, *The New Deal,* p. 23. The original source for

these data was *HR Executive Review: Implementing the New Employment Compact* (Conference Board, 1997). Cappelli, *The New Deal,* also discusses the increasing importance placed on ambition. Cappelli is my source as well for Jack Welch's views on company loyalty, which Cappelli took from Gary D. Kissler, "The New Employment Contract," *Human Resource Management,* Fall 1994.

95   The quotation from Ed McCabe about the changing attitudes of human re-source executives is from Cappelli, *The New Deal,* p. 231.

96   The statistic on job hopping among Silicon Valley electrical engineers appears in Cappelli, *The New Deal,* p. 173; it originated in David P. Angel, "The Labor Market for Engineers in the U.S. Semiconductor Industry," *Economic Geography* 65, 2 (April 1989).

97   Details about Lou Gerstner's compensation package for joining IBM come from John A. Byrne, "In the Pay Tourney, It's Advantage Outsiders," *Business Week,* April 18, 1994. I also referred to David Whitford, "Becoming CEO? Call Him First," *Fortune,* June 8, 1998.

98   Background material on Joe Bachelder appears in Whitford, "Becoming CEO?" and from Elisabeth Lesly, "Meet the Superlawyer Who Makes CEOs Rich," *Business Week,* January 24, 1994.

99   I gathered background on the development of Robert Adelson's executive ne-gotiation practice in a conversation with Adelson in August 1999.

99   I estimated the size and growth rate of third-party agent representation on the basis of an informal telephone survey of fifty firms located in a dozen major cities across the United States.

101   I collected the material on the array of options included in typical employee contracts from a variety of sources, including interviews with professionals in the field of human resource management. Published sources I consulted in-cluded the Society for Human Resource Management, "Commitment to Work/Life Brings Competitive Advantage," *Visions* 2, 1999; Barbara Parus, "Survey Links Work/Life Programs to Employee Performance," *American Compensation Association News,* June 1999; Shelly Branch, "The 100 Best Companies to Work for in America," *Fortune,* January 11, 1999, pp. 120 and 128; Timothy D. Schellhardt and Joann S. Lublin, "All the Rage Among CEOs: Lifetime Perks," *Wall Street Journal,* July 6, 1999, pp. A1 and A24; and Fay Hansen, "Currents in Compensation and Benefits," *Compensation and Benefits Review,* September 10, 1998, p. 6.

102   The estimate of the percentage of U.S. companies that now routinely use em-ployment contracts was taken from Hansen, "Currents in Compensation and Benefits."

Chapter 7

106   The quote from Ray Vernon appears in an his article, "Sovereignty at Bay: Twenty Years After," *Millennium Journal of International Studies* 20, 2 (1991), p. 191. In the article, Vernon quotes from his own landmark book, *Sovereignty at Bay* (Basic Books, 1971).

106   Background on the history of government investment subsidies is from Dick Netzer's chapter, "An Evaluation of Interjurisdictional Competition Through Economic Development Incentives," in Daphne A. Kenyon and John Kincaid, eds., *Competition Among States and Local Governments* (Urban Institute Press, 1991), pp. 221–223.

108   The 800-page survey of existing state financial incentive programs can be found in the National Association of State Development Agencies, *Directory of Incentives for Business Investment and Development in the United States*, 3rd ed. (Urban Institute Press, 1991).

108   The classification of state and local subsidy schemes is from Netzer, "An Evaluation of Interjurisdictional Competition," p. 224. Netzer cites a paper by Daphne A. Kenyon for the U.S. Advisory Commission on Intergovernmental Relations as his source for the classification schema.

109   The examples of investment incentive deals in the United States are from Jack Lyne's article, "The Strategic Art of the Deal: SS's 1997 Top 10," *Site Selection*, April-May 1998, pp. 190–199.

109   The description of "new wave" development programs is taken from Peter Eisinger, "State Economic Development in the 1990s: Politics and Policy Learning," *Economic Development Quarterly* 9, 2 (May 1995), pp. 180–182. This article was later included in a compendium: John P. Blair and Laura A. Reese, eds., *Approaches to Economic Development* (Sage Publications, 1999). The estimates of job subsidies for the Mercedes plant in Alabama and the steel mill in Iowa appear in this article as well, p. 183.

111   Details on the types of nonfinancial incentives offered to foreign investors around the world appear in UNCTAD, *Incentives and Foreign Direct Investment* (United Nations, 1996), p. 6, table 1.3. The examples of specific investment projects and the incentives they received occur on pp. 31–36 of this report.

113   Netzer's argument that economic development subsidies are a negative-sum game is contained in "An Evaluation of Interjurisdictional Competition," pp. 225–230.

114   The history of Ireland's success in focusing on and attracting foreign investors is discussed in F. Ruane and H. Görg, "Irish FDI Policy and Investment from the EU," in Ray Burrell and Nigel Pain, *Innovation, Investment and the Diffusion of Technology in Europe* (Cambridge University Press, 1999), chapter

3, pp. 44–46. I supplemented this information with conversations with Ruane and officials of IDA Ireland.

115 I gathered background on IDA Ireland's plans to upgrade its investor-attracting activities in a series of interviews with officials of IDA Ireland. Their plans, however, are documented in many of IDA's publications, including its annual reports.

118 The information about abuses of state incentive programs in North Carolina is from Benjamin Joshua Katz's award-winning essay in the Federal Reserve Bank of Minneapolis student essay contest for 1996–1997, "The Economic War Among the States Subsidizes Inefficiency," available at: http://www.woodrow.mpls.frb.fed.us/econed/essay/1–97.html. Katz drew on stories that ran in the *Charlotte Observer*. The Amhoist situation is described in Gene Daniels, "Use of Federal Funds to Support Relocations," in Charles Craypo and Bruce Nissen, eds., *Grand Designs: The Impact of Corporate Strategies on Workers, Unions, and Communities* (ILR Press, 1993), pp. 165–184. I also used this book as my source for the background on Navistar's role in the selling and subsequent closing of Wisconsin Steel. That material is from the chapter by David C. Ranney, "The Closing of Wisconsin Steel," pp. 65–91.

119 The information about subsidized plant closings is from interviews with officials of IDA Ireland and Locate in Scotland, supplemented by library research. For example, the closing of the Mitsubishi factory in Haddington is described in an article by Raymond Duncan and Gavin Madeley, "Electronics Companies Pull Plug on 850 Jobs: Community 'Betrayed,'" *Glasgow Herald*, April 7, 1998. The Viasystems plant closing is covered in an article by Tony Armstrong, "Viasystems Pulls Plug on 210 Jobs," *Glasgow Herald*, May 12, 1998. The story of the Siemens chip plant in Tyneside appears in Wolfgang Münchau, Paul Taylor, and Chris Tighe, "Siemens to Build £1bn Microchip Plant in Britain," *Financial Times*, August 5-August 6, 1995. The new Siemens chip-making venture in Dresden is detailed in Gale Morrison, "Siemens, Motorola Marry Fortunes in 300mm Race," *Electronic News*, January 19, 1998.

120 The estimates of subsidized jobs lost to plant closures in Ireland between 1979 and 1986 is contained in William Keating and Tom Keane, "The Contractions and Expansion Patterns of Overseas Industry," in Anthony Foley and Dermot McAleese, eds., *Overseas Industry in Ireland* (Gill and Macmillan, 1991), pp. 138–151. The estimate of the indirect effect of job creation on employment in the service industries in Ireland appears in the Economic and Social Research Institute, *The Impact of the Industrial Development Agencies* (Stationery Office, Dublin, 1992), p. iv.

120   The comments by Mary O'Sullivan on the various shortcomings of the industrial development policy of Ireland are taken from "Manufacturing and Global Competition," in J. W. O'Hagan, *The Economy of Ireland* (St. Martin's Press,1995), pp. 363–396. The quotation occurs on p. 384.

121   The material about the software industry in Ireland is from Seán Ó Riain, "A Tale of Two Globalizations: The Irish Software Industry and the Global Economy" (Economic and Social Research Institute, 1998). The quote from the software CEO was taken from p. 13 of this working paper, cited with the permission of the author.

122   The description of increasingly stringent contract terms in incentive contracts is from Larry C. Ledebur and Douglas P. Woodward, "Adding a Stick to the Carrot," in John P. Blair and Laura A. Reese, eds., *Approaches to Economic Development* (Sage Publications, 1999), pp. 51–67.

122   The quote about local governments' adopting stringent investment incentive contract terms is from Arthur S. Hayes, "Companies Are Finding It Harder to Move Out of Town," *Wall Street Journal*, March 1, 1993.

123   The European Commission documents I refer to include *A Level Playing Field for Direct Investment World-Wide*, COM(95) 42 final (European Commission, 1995), *European Community Competition Policy—1997: XXVIIth Report on Competition Policy* (Office for Official Publications of the European Communities, 1998), *Towards Tax Co-ordination in the European Union: A Package to Tackle Harmful Tax Competition*, COM(97) 495 final (European Commission, 1997).

Chapter 8

128   The first two prominent books published on Japanese management techniques were William Ouchi, *Theory Z* (Addison-Wesley, 1981), and Richard Tanner Pascale and Anthony G. Athos, *The Art of Japanese Management* (Simon and Schuster, 1981). Even though both books substantially missed the point, they collectively opened the floodgates to further research and writing.

128   The two key books on the Japanese approach to quality were W. Edward Deming, *Quality, Productivity and Competitive Position* (Massachusetts Institute of Technology, Center for Advanced Engineering Study, 1982), and Joe Juran and Frank Gryna, *Quality Planning and Analysis: From Product Development Through Usage* (McGraw-Hill, 1970). Capitalizing on the trend, Philip B. Crosby's *Quality Is Free: The Art of Making Quality Certain* (McGraw-Hill, 1978) became an almost instant best-seller.

131   The quotation about GM purchasing practices under Jose Lopez is from a special supplier report, "Charging into the 21st Century," compiled by William

C. Rappleye of *Financial World* in conjunction with staff writers, *Ward's Autoworld* 33, 8 (August 1997), pp. 41–50. There is some dispute abroad as to whether Lopez was quite the villain he is often portrayed to be.

131 The data on supplier shrinkage at Chrysler are from Jeffrey H. Dyer, "How Chrysler Created an American Keiretsu," *Harvard Business Review,* July-August 1996, p. 42. The forecast of Chrysler's future supplier base is taken from "Chrysler Pushes Quality down the Supply Chain," *Purchasing* 119, 1 (July 13, 1995), p. 112. The purchasing article also contains information on Chrysler's quality criteria and other requirements for all its suppliers. The quotation about steel supply contracts is from an automotive roundtable discussion, "The Next Generation of Partnerships," *New Steel,* May 1999, p. 43. The reference to the GM demand for 20 percent cuts in the costs of materials is from Venkat Subramaniam, "Efficient Sourcing and Debt Financing in Imperfect Product Markets," *Management Science* 44, 9 (September 1998), p. 1167.

134 Rank Xerox's reduction in supplier base is discussed in Ronan McIvor, Paul Humphreys, and Eddie McAleer, "Implications of Partnership Sourcing on Buyer-Supplier Relations," *Journal of General Management* 23, 1 (Autumn 1997), p. 57. Information on the spread of cutbacks to the retail industry comes from Robert J. Bowman, "Should You Just Say No to Wal-Mart?" *Distribution* 96, 12 (November 1997), p. 53. The information on the squeeze on minority supply firms appears in Brian Milligan, "Supplier Consolidation Brings New Challenges," *Purchasing,* August 12, 1999, pp. 60–72. The quote is from p. 60.

134 The mergers and consolidations taking place in the automotive supply industry have been widely chronicled in the business press. One source for an overview of the trend is Lisa Jenkins, "Auto Suppliers: The Outlook for Credit Quality," *Standard and Poor's Global Sector Review—Automotive,* May 1999, p. 10. The information on the consolidation in the automotive supply sector can be found in the "Automotive and Auto Parts Industry Roundtable," *Wall Street Transcript,* August 10, 1998, pp. 6–8. This roundtable discussion also includes the quote about Lear (p. 6) and the preference of one of the analysts for auto supply stock (p. 8). The specific data on Johnson Control's investments to build its position in the car seat industry can be found in McIvor, Humphreys, and McAleer, "Implications of Partnership," p. 59.

136 All of the material related to Lear Corporation is from Securities and Exchange Commission filings by the company over the years.

141 The quote from Paul Mason of ASDA is from Matt Nannery, "The Peacemakers," *Chain Store Age,* August 1999, p. 72. The information on the GM award to BBK is contained in Dale Jewett, "Financial Firm Keeps GM Suppliers Going: BBK Develops Turnaround Plans for Ailing Companies,"

Detroit News, May 5, 1998, p. F4. Nortel's partnership with suppliers is described in a number of sources. Its application to environmental areas is chronicled in John Elkington, *Cannibals with Forks* (New Society Publishers, 1998), p. 241. Susan Helper's views on the emergence of face relationships between suppliers and their customers can be found in "Strategy and Irreversibility in Supplier Relations: The Case of the U.S. Automobile Industry," *Business History Review* 65, 4 (Winter 1991), p. 781ff, and in her article with Mari Sako, "Supplier Relations in Japan and the United States: Are They Converging?" *Sloan Management Review,* Spring 1995, pp. 77–84.

142 Both Dana Corporation's record earnings and planned cutbacks are reported in Daniel Howes, "Auto Suppliers Plan Employee Cuts: Slim Profit Margins, Ailing Foreign Markets Force Companies to Reassess Their Strategies," *Detroit News,* October 21, 1998, p. B1.

Chapter 9

144 The *McKinsey Quarterly* article quoted is Trond Riiber Knudsen, Lars Finskud, Richard Törnblom, and Egil Hogna, "Brand Consolidation Makes a Lot of Economic Sense," *McKinsey Quarterly* 4, 1997, pp. 189 and 190.

145 Most of the material on retail predation comes from Edward B. Shils, "Measuring the Economic and Sociological Impact of Mega-Retail Discount Chains on Small Enterprise in Urban, Suburban and Rural Communities," also known as the Shils report, available at: http://www.shilsreport.org. Shils, the George W. Taylor Emeritus Professor of Entrepreneurial Studies and the director emeritus of the Wharton Entrepreneurial Center of the Wharton School of the University of Pennsylvania, along with several colleagues reported on an extensive research project. Most of the material I cite is drawn from chapter 7 of this important study. The background on Jacques César's price experiments for Shell come from a conversation with César. Archie Norman's reaction to the idea occurred in a meeting I attended with César.

147 The litany of complaints against Wal-Mart's business practices is available from a large number of sources, including the popular press and various anti-Wal-Mart Web sites. One of the more engaging accounts of Wal-Mart practices is by an octogenarian newspaperman from Texas: Bill Quinn, *How Wal-Mart Is Destroying America* (Ten Speed Press, 1998). I used this highly entertaining book to compile the list of complaints I recorded.

148 Most of the examples of deceptive practices used against relatively sophisticated consumers are cited as examples of good marketing in Carl Shapiro and Hal R. Varian, *Information Rules: A Strategic Guide to the Network Economy* (Harvard Business School Press, 1999), pp. 56–68. This book was a minor business best-seller in 1999, showing once again what a weird world we have

come to live in. It does offer some useful ideas on how to deal with the emerging world of Internet commerce, however.

149   The statistics about levels of U.S. advertising and American consumers' reaction to them are in John Hagel III and Marc Singer, *Net Worth: Shaping Markets When Customers Make the Rules* (Harvard Business School Press, 1999), pp. 3–5.

149   The consumer loyalty data cited in the text are from several different sources. For example, I drew the historical survey data from Gordon R. Foxall, Ronald E. Goldsmith, and Stephen Brown, *Consumer Psychology for Marketing,* 2nd ed. (International Thomson Business Press, 1998), p. 17. The Roper survey results is reported in Carolyn Setlow, "Bargain Shopping Never Goes Out of Style," *Discount Store News* 36, 9 (May 5, 1997), p. 26. The Marketlink survey is described in Elizabeth Brewster, "A New Brand of Thinking (Consumer Loyalty)," *Food Processing* 58, 7 (July 1997), p. 114. The Yankelovitch travel survey is reported in Barbara A. Worcester, "Brand Loyalty Loses Luster," *Hotel and Motel Management* 214, 15 (March 15, 1999), p. 1. The Salmon survey on women's apparel is covered in Jennifer Owens, "Survey Says Loyalty to Brands Is Fleeting," *Women's Wear Daily* 176, 40 (August 26, 1998), p. 14. The BrandBuilder results appear in Allan L. Baldinger and Joel Rubinson, "Brand Loyalty: The Link Between Attitude and Behavior," *Journal of Advertising Research* 36, 6 (November-December 1996), pp. 22–25.

151   The decline in popularity of retailing concepts such as hypermarkets in Europe is described by Javier Castrillo, Ramon Forn, and Rafael Mira, "Hypermarkets May Be Losing Their Appeal for European Consumers," *McKinsey Quarterly,* Winter 1997, pp. 194 and 195. The stepped-up life cycle of retail concepts is covered in Kathryn Bye Burns, Helene Enright, Julie Falstad Hayes, Kathleen McLaughlin, and Christiana Shi, "The Art and Science of Retail Renewal," *McKinsey Quarterly,* Summer 1997, p. 102.

152   The quotation about the likely future influence of the Internet on consumer purchase behavior is from Robert Kuttner, "The Net: A Market Too Perfect for Profits," *Business Week,* May 11, 1998, p. 20.

153   Forecasts of the future size of e-commerce are taken from Tony Lisanti, "The 'Dot-Coms' Mean Business," *Discount Store News,* August 9, 1999, p. 11. The Forrester Research data on Internet buying practices are reported in Susan Reider, "Research Probes Links Between On-Line Satisfaction and Customer Loyalty," *Stores,* August 1999, p. 65.

155   Details about the environmental movement and its progress in influencing corporate behavior can be found in Malcolm Brown, "A Green Piece of the Action," *Management Today,* May 1997, p. 84ff. Statistics on green reporting come from this article.

156   The survey on consumer willingness to pay more for garments made in facto-
      ries rather than sweatshops is reported by Louisa Wah, "Treading the Sacred
      Ground," *Management Review* 87, 7 (July-August 1998), p. 18ff.

Chapter 10

162   The quotation from Chief Justice Marshall in his decision in *Dartmouth
      College v. Woodward* occurs in Jay Lorsch and Elisabeth MacIver, *Pawns or
      Potentates? The Reality of America's Corporate Boards* (Harvard Business School
      Press, 1989), p. 6.

162   The characteristics of a corporation so conducive to commerce I took with
      only a little license from Robert A. G. Monks and Neil Minow, *Watching the
      Watchers: Governance for the 21st Century* (Blackwell, 1996), p. 4; Monks and
      Minow are quoting Robert C. Clark, *Corporate Law* (Little, Brown, 1986),
      p. 2. The quotations related to Alexander Hamilton's new venture, the Society
      for Establishing Useful Manufactures, are also taken from Monks and Minow,
      Watching the Watchers, p. 169.

164   The background information on institutional investors was adapted from ma-
      terial originally published in Terrence Deal and Allan Kennedy, *New Corporate
      Cultures* (Perseus Books, 1999), pp. 52–54. Our original sources for this ma-
      terial included Peter Drucker, *The Unseen Revolution* (HarperCollins, 1976).
      The data we presented about the well-documented increase in institutional
      ownership of equities and mutual fund churn were first displayed to us in
      Michael Useem's fine book, *Investor Capitalism* (Basic Books, 1996). The in-
      formation on how long investors hold stock on average is from John Byrne,
      "When Capital Gets Antsy," *Business Week,* September 13, 1999, p. 74.

167   The quotations about shareholder interests from Lorsch and MacIver, *Pawns,*
      come from pp. 47 and 46, respectively.

168   The quotation from Ralph D. Ward's book, *21st Century Corporate Board*
      (John Wiley & Sons, 1997), occurs on p. 103. The best general discussion of
      the evolution of shareholder activism and the role of public pension funds
      therein can be found on pp. 100–120 of Ward's book. The quote from
      CalPERS CEO Dale Hansen is taken from p. 119.

169   The account of TIAA-CREF actions to influence corporate boards is taken
      from Margaret M. Blair, *Ownership and Control: Rethinking Corporate
      Governance for the Twenty-First Century* (Brookings Institute, 1995), pp. 163
      and 164. I augmented this material with information from John A. Byrne,
      "The Teddy Roosevelts of Corporate Governance," *Business Week,* May 31,
      1999, p. 77.

171 The specification of the duties of a board of directors is from the Business Roundtable, *Corporate Governance and American Competitiveness,* March 1990, p. 7.

171 Sir John Harvey-Jones is cited in Monks and Minow, *Watching the Watchers,* p. 173; Monks and Minow took the quote from John Harvey-Jones, *Making It Happen* (Collins, 1988), p. 147.

171 The data on the demographics of board membership in the late 1980s are from Lorsch and MacIver, *Pawns,* pp. 18 and 19. I also used more recent data from the Conference Board contained in a piece by Jeremy Bacon, *Corporate Boards and Corporate Governance* (Conference Board, 1993), p. 6.

172 The data on the prevalence of law suits against board directors and the costs of settling these suits are from Ward, *21st Century Corporate Board,* p. 296. The boardroom coups of the early 1990s are described in detail in the popular press. Several of the books referred to earlier in these notes—Ward's *21st Century Corporate Board* and Monks and Minow's *Watching the Watchers* in particular—also offer a summarized interpretation of these events and their significance.

174 The information on the demographics and education of CEOs of large companies is from a variety of sources, most notably *Who's Who in Finance and Industry,* 30th ed., 1998–1999 (Marquis, 1998). I selected a random sample of one hundred CEOs of the top 250 companies on the Fortune 500 list to construct the statistics used in the chapter.

175 The book on influences on leadership practices is E. Digby Baltzell, *Puritan Boston and Quaker Philadelphia: Two Protestant Ethics and the Spirit of Class Authority and Leadership* (Free Press, 1980).

Chapter 11

187 In writing this chapter, I referred to a number of books, most of which should be required reading for the CEOs of any large public companies and students of management everywhere. These include Tom Peters and Bob Waterman, *In Search of Excellence: Lessons from America's Best-Run Companies* (Harper & Row, 1982); James Collins and Jerry Porras, *Built to Last* (HarperBusiness, 1994); Terrence Deal and Allan Kennedy, *Corporate Cultures* (Addison-Wesley, 1982); Terrence Deal and Allan Kennedy, *The New Corporate Cultures* (Perseus Books, 1999); and Robert S. Kaplan and David P. Norton, *The Balanced Scorecard: Translating Strategy into Action* (Harvard Business School Press, 1996).

Chapter 12

194 The proposals for board reform documented in Table 12.1 are from a variety of sources, including, Blair, *Ownership and Control,* pp. 135–145; Amar Bhide, "Efficient Markets, Deficient Governance," *Harvard Business Review,* November-December 1994, pp. 134–137; John Pound, "The Promise of the Governed Corporation," *Harvard Business Review,* March-April 1995, pp. 94 and 95; Jay W. Lorsch, "Empowering the Board," *Harvard Business Review,* January-February 1995, pp. 112 and 113; John L. Vogelstein, "An Investor's View of Corporate Governance," *Corporate Board* 19, 110 (May-June 1998), pp. 1–4; Monks and Minow, *Watching the Watchers,* pp. 261–285, and 208; and Hugh Parker, "Re-Empowering the Board: A Proposed Agenda for Action," taken from Monks and Minow, *Watching the Watchers,* pp. 289–307.

196 The proposals Michael Porter put forward to correct the short-termism rampant in the U.S. business community are contained in his article "Capital Disadvantage: America's Failing Capital Investment System," *Harvard Business Review,* September-October 1992, pp. 65–82. The article was reprinted as the first chapter in section three of Frederick F. Reichheld, ed., *The Quest for Loyalty: Creating Value Through Partnership* (Harvard Business Review Press, 1996), pp. 75–107. The specific material quoted in the chapter comes from pp. 99–101.

197 Dan Bavly's recommendations for board reform are contained in his book *Corporate Governance and Accountability: What Role for the Regulator, Director, and Auditor?* (Quorum Books, 1999), pp. 3–6.

207 The quotation from Marvin Bower is from *The Will to Lead* (Harvard Business School Press, 1997), p. 68.

Index